AN INTRODUCTION TO
GROUP THERAPY

AN INTRODUCTION TO GROUP THERAPY

by

S. R. SLAVSON

INTERNATIONAL UNIVERSITIES PRESS, Inc.
NEW YORK   NEW YORK

Manufactured in the United States of America

FOREWORD

CHILD guidance clinicians are aware that their examinations, conducted under clinical conditions, do not yield complete cross-sections of a child's personality; and that their procedures, developed out of clinical intuition, guesswork, theory, and experience, are by no means a closed system of techniques for treating the behavior problem child. Likewise, they recognize that, if the wholeness of the individual is not to be violated, the child guidance clinic must be considered as rendering a part service which must constantly be related to other services in the community—public health, social work, education, recreation, all the organized functions of society which in the aggregate should reflect the wholeness of man.

The impact of these essential relations upon other agencies is constantly stirring up new questions and procedures in child guidance service. Particularly provocative are the diagnostic and therapeutic potentialities within group activities for children. The clinician may look with profitable curiosity upon the things that take place without design in a child when he is captured emotionally within a group of children. He may well ask: what are the elements of value in this; how can the group be used in a more designed way for revealing the personality of the problem child and for treating him; and is there here a possibility of treating larger numbers of children without great increase in cost?

The group has many meanings to the individual which bear upon him in changing his behavior. Psychiatry has considered the reaction of the individual to the group as an indication of his health, and the pressure of the group upon him as a force in molding personality. The rapid oscillations of effect and counter-effect make the group a rich resource and it is appropriately seized upon as one of the ways of understanding the individual and modifying his adjustments. This is legitimate provided it is understood that exact knowledge of the meaning and influence of the group is scant; and that theory, intuition, and guesswork are necessary preliminaries, just as they are preliminaries to the development of any child guidance procedure. The chief danger is that of being too hard and fast in the early stages of an attempt to study the individual through these group processes.

The group has already been taken seriously for its diagnostic and therapeutic values under several different concepts and patterns. Among the various experiments in group methods are, for example, one in which stutterers are brought together socially with the intention of eliminating the inferiority to the group that occurs in their everyday life; another in which the group is used as a kind of mock society so that under the guise of drama the individual may express attitudes toward others without suffering social disadvantage. In another instance children in school classes are led through discussion of stories or other presentations to deal more openly with their own experiences and problems and to understand the attitudes of other children. In somewhat the same way the group has been used in one place to set up deeper reactions approaching the psychoanalytic level. One clinic has developed a completely permissive group procedure which resembles somewhat the pattern described in this book but which goes further in allowing attacks upon the leader of the group.

Over and above all such designed procedures are the spontaneous group activities which have no other purpose than enjoyment but which probably represent the deepest form of mutual influence and possibly the most effective form for normal individuals because the process is entirely unconscious. Recreation, club work, and the like, however, have tended to effect these results by elimination of the inappropriate person rather than by adjustment to him. This is apt to injure the person already injured. The designed groups, on the other hand, give such individuals special consideration.

The particular experiment reported in this book represents the effort of the Jewish Board of Guardians of New York to develop, under the guidance of S. R. Slavson, a "group therapy" for selected cases of problem children. It differs in various respects from other experiments in group procedures. Like these others and like any advances in child guidance, it is empirical. As it is still in the experimental stage, the theory behind it has not yet been completely formulated and therefore some limitations in perspective and analysis are apparent. However, the book is the honest presentation of a method of therapy in the active stage of growth and reflects a willingness to make available what has been achieved rather than to await perfection at the expense of those who might be benefited.

The Jewish Board of Guardians has developed its services at the crossroads of social agencies and of child guidance clinics; and it is thus not surprising that its staff should seek out new and effective therapeutic procedures that fall outside the usual field of the clinician. These procedures draw heavily on social agency experience but remain to a considerable degree clinically oriented. In one respect they are a counterpart of efforts in some child guidance clinics to reduce the authoritative element of the adult in the psychiatric interview: by having the patient react to his peers rather than to his doctor, an almost complete reduction of adult authority is achieved.

Whether the pattern of work bears any special relation to one cultural group with which this agency deals predominantly, and whether the reaction of such a group to a permissive procedure has special peculiarities are questions which must be kept in mind. While the whole process is experimental, it is critically experimental and represents an honest and

intelligent effort to work out an effective therapeutic device
that is highly suggestive of progress to come.

GEORGE S. STEVENSON, M.D.
Medical Director, National
Committee for Mental Hygiene

November 1942

PREFACE

THE present volume deals with a method of psychotherapy employed at the Jewish Board of Guardians of New York since 1934 and known as Group Therapy. The Jewish Board of Guardians is a social service agency rendering a child guidance service to children presenting problems of personality. These problems may manifest themselves in the form of delinquent or neurotic behavior and may result in either individual or social maladjustment. Service is rendered to boys and girls up to the age of eighteen. The agency's child guidance services are carried on at four offices, one each in the boroughs of Manhattan and the Bronx and two in Brooklyn. In addition to the child guidance activities, the organization conducts an institution for delinquent boys and girls at Hawthorne, known as the Hawthorne–Cedar Knolls School, a home for unmarried mothers at Arrochar, Staten Island, known as Lakeview Home, a volunteer service for those children whose needs can be met by Big Brothers or Big Sisters, summer camps, and other special services in the interest of children and youths manifesting problems of behavior.

Depending on the needs of the patient and on the basis of an initial diagnostic study by staff psychiatrists and psychiatric case workers, the child may be recommended for treatment on various levels, ranging from intensive psychotherapy to the experience of having a friendly relationship with a Big Brother or Big Sister. Institutional placement is also considered as one of the treatment procedures.

Along with psychiatric, case work, and psychological services, Group Therapy is employed as one of the treatment methods, particularly where interpersonal experience is essential to children. According to their needs, Group Therapy is employed either as supplementary to individual psychother-

apy or as an exclusive treatment method, although in the
agency at the present time the latter represents a much smaller
proportion of the cases treated than the former.

An evaluation of treatment needs impressed the staff with
the fact that social (group) treatment was essential in many
cases. Referral of clients to existing recreational agencies in
their own neighborhoods revealed that the latter were not set
up to meet the individual needs of maladjusted children.
Though the majority were able to participate in the ordinary
recreational activities, many of the clients referred could not
fit into mass activities. Usually the less difficult children can
be absorbed in a group work program, but the overaggressive
and hostile whose behavior is disrupting do not fit into a
neighborhood center. Nor can the timid and withdrawn children and youths find a place in the ordinary recreational or
group work agency. To these boys and girls a large group is an
additional threat and their failure to make a satisfactory adjustment further intensifies their central difficulties.

To the extent that these boys and girls are excluded from
membership and are thrown upon their own resources, their
potentiality for delinquency and other types of maladjustment is increased. Clients who are unable to adapt themselves
to ordinary group relations or who suffer from character malformations require a special type of group. Several variations
are indicated in Chapter IX. This volume treats of one of these
types—the *activity therapy group*. The material is based upon
the records of about 750 children, between the ages of nine
and eighteen, and of fifty-five groups, each functioning for
about two years.

Detailed records were kept of the group activities and individual clients. Two group records are reproduced in Chapter
III and summarized case histories of five children form the
material of Chapter VIII. Follow-up studies of clients were
made as to their adjustment in the home, in school, in street
groups, and in organized recreational facilities in the com-

munity. These studies were made by the case workers in "cooperative cases," as well as in "exclusive cases."

Cooperative cases are those which are treated by a case worker or psychiatrist as well as through the group. In exclusive cases the treatment is carried on entirely by Group Therapy. Because the Jewish Board of Guardians is a case work agency, the intake policy is such that all clients, with but few exceptions, are assigned for exploration to a case worker and for diagnosis to a psychiatrist before they are referred for Group Therapy. In only a few cases, when in the judgment of the intake worker the client does not need individual treatment or would be inaccessible to it, is he referred directly for group treatment. The services of the Group Therapy Department are reserved for the clients of the agency, and cases that are referred directly for Group Therapy by other agencies and by hospitals are not accepted. Approximately two-thirds of the children carried at any given time by the Group Therapy Department of the agency are cooperative cases.

Group Therapy cannot be considered a substitute for other types of psychotherapy. This treatment should be offered only after a diagnostic exploration reveals a need of it. While it can be assumed that recreation and group interaction are desirable and important to everyone, Group Therapy has value for children with special needs, as described in Chapter IV.

Another fact that should be borne in mind is that Group Therapy, being a method of psychotherapy, can be carried on only in an agency or clinic where psychiatric services are available for diagnostic purposes as well as for consultation and treatment. The group therapist must be psychiatrically orientated and have a case work approach to the members of the group rather than a group work interest. This is essential and will become clear from the material in this volume.

The present volume is intended to formulate some of the basic principles of interpersonal therapy and to outline the practice of Group Therapy. It is hoped at a future date to make available record and theoretical material on Group Therapy in terms of individual problems and social dynamics with greater detail than is possible in a general discussion.

The clientele discussed in this volume is limited to the intake policy of one agency and the criteria for referral for group treatment were of necessity determined by one group of psychiatric case workers and psychiatrists with definite views on psychotherapy. Another limitation of the choice of clients was the fact that they all came from one cultural group with more or less similar backgrounds. Many of them came from families where there was definite cultural conflict between foreign parents and native children or first-generation Americans and their offspring.

A project such as this cannot be the outcome of one person's efforts. It was, from its very inception, a cooperative enterprise on the part of a large number of persons who, on a voluntary or professional basis, have contributed to its development. The group therapists particularly, the list of whom would take a prohibitive amount of space, are deserving of our sincere thanks for their earnest cooperation and unselfishness in directing therapy groups and writing records, and for their participation in supervisory discussions and in seminar sessions.

The usual "conflict" between case work and group work has been non-existent in our agency. Case workers and psychiatrists have given full cooperation to this project and have referred more than twelve hundred boys and girls for Group Therapy in the eight years since this method of treatment was initiated. Such receptivity to a new method is not common, and we wish to take this opportunity to express our thanks and admiration to this group of workers for their hospitality and vision.

The author wishes to express his indebtedness to the Board of Directors of the Jewish Board of Guardians for their financial and other support in developing this project, and particularly to Mrs. Sidney C. Borg, Chairman of the Board; to Mrs. Arthur D. Schulte, Chairman of the Group Therapy Department, whose constant and untiring help and guidance since its inception have been a source of security and inspiration; and to Dr. John Slawson, director of the Jewish Board of Guardians, whose far-sightedness in developing methods for treatment of children with behavior problems has made this work possible.

We are grateful to Dr. Nathan W. Ackerman and Maude Moss for reading the original manuscript and for making many helpful suggestions, and to Fannie Houtz and Ada Schupper Slawson for their pioneering with us during the inception of this work eight years ago.

S. R. S.

November 1942

Began in 1934

CONTENTS

CHAPTER I

PRINCIPLES OF GROUP THERAPY

AMONG the most important developments in psychiatry and psychology in recent times is the recognition that man is essentially a group animal. The destiny of man, savage or civilized, is irrevocably tied up with the group. His growth and development are conditioned by the group's values and attitudes. In the healthy personality, group associations expand to include ever wider areas and larger numbers of persons. Where this does not occur, the personality is a defective one.

As yet there is little known of the mechanisms of group life and their role in development, in education, and in therapy.[1] Until but a short time ago, the focus of interest was the effect of individuals upon one another. However, the change of attitudes and behavior in problem children when brought into a group (not to speak of normal boys and girls in free-activity day and boarding schools) emphasized the potency of group life in character formation and in psychotherapy. In institutions and hospitals where group association has been used as a part of treatment, considerable improvement has been observed in delinquents and mental patients.

The most important value to character formation of group experience is the modification or elimination of egocentricity and psychological insularity. It increases the ability to feel with other people, that is, to establish positive identifications. In the orderly development of the personality there occur ever expanding identifications. Beginning with persons in the immediate environment, such as parents, nurses, and siblings,

[1] In Chapter IV, *Character Education in a Democracy* (New York, Association Press, 1939), we have described the following group mechanisms: interstimulation, interaction, induction, neutralization, intensification, identification, assimilation, polarity, rivalry, projection, and integration.

the child extends his interest to playmates, friends, the neighborhood and, as he grows to maturity, to the larger community and the total world scene. The infant's and child's egoistic and to a great extent sadistic drives (centripetal feelings) are normally transformed into social concerns and interest in others (centrifugal feelings). As already stated, this growth first occurs through identifications with individuals; but of equal importance are identifications with groups such as family, play groups, gangs, classroom groups, and clubs. The movement from self-centeredness to responsiveness to people outside oneself represents the greatest achievement in psychological and social evolution.

The principle of the social nature of man applies to several types of therapy some of which are described in Chapter IX. Among these is Activity Group Therapy with which this volume is concerned. Group Therapy, as we employ the term, is treatment in which no discussion is initiated by the therapist; interpretation is given only in very rare instances and under specific conditions. Emotional reorientation comes from the very fact that the child experiences actual situations, lives and works with other children, comes into direct and meaningful interaction with others, and as a result modifies his feeling tones and habitual responses. We conceive a group as an aggregation of three or more persons in an informal face-to-face relation where there is direct and dynamic interaction among the individuals comprising it, and as a result the personality of each member is fundamentally modified. Applied to Group Therapy, this definition implies small numbers and age and sex homogeneity.

In Group Therapy, we work with children who are directly rejected by parents, family, school, street gang, and community center, or whose powers and personalities are indirectly rejected by pampering and coddling, as a result of which they are unable to get on with their contemporaries and with adults.[2] These children are actively hostile and destructive or reject the world by withdrawing from it. They are either excessively aggressive or excessively withdrawn; obsessed with great fears or guilt, they overcompensate for them by nonsocial or antisocial behavior. Having developed these deviant manners and methods for the sake of psychological (and often physical) survival, the child is further victimized by all the organized agencies of the community. Thus he finds himself impeded at every turn by outer stresses and inner strains. What a child needs in such circumstances is a haven of relief, a sanctuary where these distressing, threatening, and hostile pressures can be removed and relief supplied. The psychiatrist, psychiatric case worker, or a special group suited to the needs of the child can be such a haven.

That many children have found such a haven in our therapy groups is evidenced by their attendance. They miss not more than a few meetings a year, and then for illness or some such eventuality. The meetings are the most prized experiences in

---

[2] *Real rejection* includes direct and indirect rejection. *Direct rejection* occurs when a child is disliked, neglected, or deprived by his parents, siblings, and teachers. By *indirect rejection* we mean that the child is apparently loved or accepted, but the underlying motives are selfish. The best illustration of this is the pampered child who is apparently loved, but in reality his powers as a self-determining entity are rejected by the overprotecting parent who is in need of a baby. The exploited child, who is loved because the parent sees in him the realization of some ideal or striving of his own, is another example. Here the parent may want the child to become a professional, an important person, or he may use him as a threat against the other parent. Another type of indirect rejection is a poor mark in school or being "left back." Our analysis of clients indicates that overprotection, pampering, babying, and exploitation on the part of the parent are really forms of rejection. In these cases the child may be fully accepted, but his powers, independence, maturity, that is, his autonomy, are rejected.

Under *phantasied rejections* are included unintended slights which one takes to heart because of one's own oversensitiveness or paranoidal trends. The most common occasion for imaginary rejection is the advent of a younger sibling through whom the child feels that he has been displaced. Another common instance of this is the child's feeling of rivalry toward one parent for the love of the other.

their lives. One girl of fifteen said, "All week I think of nothing else but the club. I am so happy here." Another: "I should really be in school tonight, but I made arrangements with my teacher to be off Wednesdays. I can't miss the meetings." Still another: "We are moving to Long Island [some ten miles from the meeting place], but I must arrange somehow to come here to meetings." In response to which several of the girls exclaimed, "Sleep in my house Tuesday!" In one case a girl traveled to the weekly meetings for two and one half years from one borough to another, a distance of about eleven miles. When one group was closed a boy insisted on being placed in another group, six miles away, in charge of the same worker. He never missed a meeting during a period of two years. Two boys who became friends through the group walked to their meeting rooms twenty-five city blocks each way and would accept fare from the group therapist[3] only on rainy days.

The results of satisfying activity and relations are evident in the response of children as mirrored in the following abstracts from group records:

After the boys finished their milk Harold[4] took the cups down to wash. Worker suggested it would soon be time to put the materials away. Teddy said he didn't want to go home, he would like to stay all night. Worker smiled and said that he would get tired about ten or eleven o'clock. Teddy: "Well, maybe I would, but I'd like to stay anyway." Harold said he didn't want to go either, he would like to stay longer. Worker said nothing, letting them work for about ten minutes more, and then proceeded to put the materials away. Gradually the boys began to help him.

Upon arrival, Sol immediately took out the plane that he had started last week and proceeded to work on it. Presently he said he wondered what the boys would do if this club ever stopped

[3] In order to prevent the confusion between the accepted designation of "group worker" in recreational agencies and the function of the adult in Group Therapy we use the title "group therapist." The significance of the difference in functions will become clear to the reader.

[4] The names of children and group therapists are fictitious.

meeting. Worker asked him what he thought they would do, and he said he thought they would all rebel. Benjamin asked for Richard. Sol said he probably was kept after school but he'd be there, because "he'd die if he ever missed a meeting."

Alter arrived and began to explain why he had not come to the meeting last week. He had been called to the agency's office, where he expected to stay only a short while, but was kept there until eight o'clock. He said he would not meet his case worker on Thursday because he was anxious to come down to the meetings of the "club." Tonight he almost forgot about the meeting. He was skating, suddenly remembered, ran home, changed his trousers, and hurried down here. That was why he was late.

At about 5:40 George, Hal, his friend, and Simon came running in, soaking wet from the heavy rain. Simon asked, "Are we the only ones who are coming? I'll bet the rain keeps the other boys away."

Robert told worker that when he was first invited to the "club" his mother asked him if he would rather go to Sunday school or to the "club." He didn't want to go to school, but he didn't want to go to the club, either; he thought it would be rotten. He had no idea it would be so nice. Worker reminded him he wasn't at the first meeting. His brother, Joseph, had lied to him, Robert told worker; he had come back saying "we had violin and piano playing lessons." Joseph, who overheard the conversation, laughed good-naturedly and said he was kidding him.

The boys asked if they could have two or three more meetings instead of making the next meeting the last one for the season, as those who were working on baskets wanted to finish them. Worker told them that if they wanted to, they could have several more meetings this spring.

While they were eating their refreshments, Mary said that she would like to meet often, she would really like to meet every day.

(Abstract from Progress Report) Mary was referred to the Group Therapy Department by her case worker, Miss S., on November 11, 1937. Mary's attendance at the meetings has been very good. Out of a total of twenty-three meetings to date Mary has attended twenty-one.

(Abstract from Progress Report) If Ann's attendance is any indication of her interest in the group, then it is a very great interest indeed. Ann has been absent three times out of twenty-three meetings held to date. The last absence was due to a visit to a doctor for a scheduled physical examination. When the group met in the afternoons and Ann's school session permitted her to come to the meetings only after five o'clock and the group disbanded at six, Ann hurried to the meeting place every week.

In order to convince the child that the group and the group therapist do not intend to continue the persecuting and rejecting treatment to which he has been accustomed, we accept him fully with all his faults, shortcomings, destructiveness, and hostilities. We relieve him of all the censorship, disapproval, nagging, punishment that he suffered in the past, and from his own guilt feelings as well. This is *unconditional love.* He can break tools and furniture, destroy materials, and even attack his group mates physically (but not the worker).[5]

We do not approve of antisocial and destructive behavior. Rather we accept it or, shall we say, tolerate it as an expression of the child's personality and its needs at the moment. This behavior, however, goes unnoticed by the adult because it is recognized as a temporary manifestation and as a step toward growth. We have found that almost all members of our groups gave up these exaggerated acts. As their emotional pressures were reduced, their hostility and aggressiveness also became correspondingly lessened. Children who cannot make such an adjustment suffer from very deep-rooted disturbances that may require a different type of psychotherapy or even institutionalization. In some instances the child is restrained by the group therapist. In others he is found to be inaccessible to Group Therapy. The procedures in such cases are determined entirely by the treatment needs of the particular child and are discussed in Chapters IV and VI.

[5] For further discussion of unconditional acceptance by the therapist, see Chapter VI, pages 144 ff.

Basically the environment and relationships in a therapy group are free and permissive. We create for the children a *permissive environment*. This we do in order to counteract the inhibitive and restraining pressures in the child's past experiences. We also remove from the more neurotic children the overpowering fear of their impulses. In some instances the pressures of the infantile super-ego[6] must first be relaxed before the child can muster courage to discharge his suppressed antagonisms and hostilities. Many of our children are not ready to live up to the inner controls set up in them by adults; others remain so infantile that they have not developed adequate inhibitions. In both instances guilt concerning themselves and their acts only creates further anxiety, an anxiety that is resolved by deviant behavior. Thus the vicious circle perpetuates itself.

A permissive environment in effect removes the anxiety-producing super-ego and releases the child to act out his infantile impulses. It is as though we said to him, "Despite your age and size you really are an infant and you may act as you really are." At the same time we surround him with an environment that is conducive to growth. This approach is adopted on the principle that since the early super-ego is derived through fear of punishment or of being abandoned or rejected, it must be counteracted. In its stead is built a new super-ego in the group which is derived from love and positive identifications.

There is another and even more pertinent reason for giving the child unconditional love and a permissive environment. Restraint and prohibition on the part of the therapist would place the latter in the same category as all the other negative adults with whom the child has come in conflict in the past. It is of utmost importance that the child discover a person who is actually positive and accepting. The child tests the adult by

[6] For further discussion of infantile and group super-ego, see Chapter VII, pages 229 ff.

unreasonable acts which have always brought punishment or abuse in the past. In the therapy group his expectations of similar responses are not fulfilled and he is actually shocked by the therapist's neutral attitude and seeming indifference. In a real sense this is a form of shock therapy. The period of forbearance on the part of the group therapists is much shorter with pampered and infantilized children. Infantile impulses need maturing restraint, but children with behavior disorders and neurotic manifestations because of early rejections require emotional satisfaction. The first have experienced love and affection (even if they were excessive); the others have to be made to feel that there is love in the world.

The third reason why aggressiveness and uninhibited acts are allowed to run their course lies in the fact that other members of the group exert the control which in individual treatment falls to the lot of the therapist. This point becomes clear in the record material and in the discussion throughout the volume.

In Chapter VI the reader will find a detailed elaboration of the limitations of permissiveness. At this juncture it will be necessary to state only that permissiveness is a tool in treatment that has to be used with discrimination. In the first place, only children whose character structure is such that they can gain by therapy groups should be included in them. The criteria for such a choice are described in detail in Chapter IV. To allow unhampered and unrestrained action to a psychopathic child would not prove beneficial. Even the fairly well-adjusted or "average" child would be greatly harmed if his already acquired super-ego were to be given a holiday. Considerable skill and insight are necessary to distinguish those clients to whom such permissiveness would be of benefit from those to whom it might prove harmful when viewed in long-term character development. This distinction has led us to the necessity of varying our group treatment methods, and the modifications we have introduced are briefly described in Chapter IX.

In the second place, complete unrestraint is allowed in only the early periods of Group Therapy. As will be shown later in this volume, the adult in charge exerts increasing restraint, both active and passive, as the child's ability to withstand frustration is increased. Complete permissiveness is the first stage in treatment and, as already indicated, is necessary in order to give the child a new orientation toward adults and the world generally.

It is our belief that therapy can occur only through living in a world of action. The patient or client must continue his participation in the world, unless he needs a period of isolation in an institution. What we need to do in psychotherapy is to remove the patient's resistance to the world and to the people in it who may influence him in a socially desirable way. To overcome this emotional encapsulation is really the main task in therapy. The transference relation in individual treatment and the acceptance of the therapist in the group are steps in this direction. The group therapist's permissiveness and acceptance are means for breaking down resistance to the world.

The permissive attitude on the part of the group therapist in the early beginnings of our groups may result in a very disturbing atmosphere for the children and for the adult. The building in which the group is housed may also suffer. Behavior is not only boisterous, but in some cases even destructive. Pent-up hostility and aggressiveness are permitted to discharge themselves. Clay is used as a missile instead of for legitimate purposes; it is aimed at bull's-eyes on walls and ceiling and employed in other destructive and symbolic ways. Water color paints and milk are spilled on the floors. The furniture may on occasion suffer at the hands of our boys. Our clients engage in fist fights, quarrels, abuse, recriminations, and other methods of discharging hostility. Throughout, the worker remains neutral and, if others do not volunteer, sets out to clean up the mess at the end of the meeting.

In interview therapy the client is allowed to say what he pleases and expresses freely his feelings on all matters that come to his mind. These feelings are expressed in Group Therapy through actions and activities. This is termed *activity catharsis*[7] and is analogous to play therapy, except that in play therapy the child is usually alone with the adult, whereas in Group Therapy relationships are established with persons other than the adult. Active expression of hostility and aggression in the presence of other children and the therapist is one of the major dynamics in our treatment.

It cannot be expected that any group will remain constantly in a state of balance and quiescence; nor is this desirable. There must be conflict and struggle, but *a wholesome group is one in which there is a possibility of reestablishing emotional equilibrium;* a pathological group is one in which conflicts are continuous, or equilibrium is attained only infrequently and does not last. In a wholesome group, equilibrium is reestablished whenever there is conflict or imbalance. This occurs when other children *neutralize* the emotional drives of the contestants, reinforce the weaker against the stronger, or exert pressure upon the disturbing individual, when a compromise is struck, or when a common interest proves stronger than the cause of cleavage.

The records of our groups convince one of the therapeutic value of group relations and creative effort in resolving the conflicts of dissocial and otherwise disturbed children. Not only are egocentric drives modified and perception of threat reduced but, what is even more important, the child discovers the startling fact that conflict and hostility need not remain permanent, as is the case with his own family; that equilib-

---

[7] For further discussion, see Chapter VII, pages 188 ff.

rium can be restored and that hatreds are eliminated in a free group process as soon as such equilibrium is attained.

Though the adult remains indifferent and is engaged in some constructive occupation during such periods of disturbance (when he is probably also being tested by the children), the members of the group gradually calm down and become more controlled. One of the groups that had upset and littered its meeting room regularly was moved to other quarters. The members, on their own, decided to be more careful about their new room. "This is our new home," they declared. Gradually, growth in responsibility takes on more mature forms and is evidenced by the fact that the members put away materials unasked, take care of and wash the dishes, economize on the cost of trips and food. A group of thirteen-year-old boys would not let the group therapist buy them the customary refreshments because he had hired bicycles, and they felt that the cost of renting them was enough money spent for that day.

The permissive atmosphere of the group may be a strain on some children as well as on the adult. For the first time in their lives, many children find themselves in a situation without restriction or control. This confuses some of them while, as already described, a large number become anxious and fearful in very much the same way that learners experience fear when the supporting hand of the swimming teacher is removed. Many of the boys, especially the aggressive ones, ask again and again if they can really make whatever they want from the materials, as if they cannot believe it. A situation in which their aggressiveness is not controlled by an adult sets up considerable anxiety in a large number of the new members. They are now on their own, as it were, and gradually learn to bring themselves under control. They must become autonomous, self-directing personalities.

We take the following instance from the record of one of our early experimental groups that illustrates this point. Similar developments will be found in the record material in other parts of the volume.

Rosalind was a very disagreeable and power-driven girl of sixteen whose will always ran counter to that of the group. When the girls agreed to go to the park, she preferred a museum; when the preference was swimming, Rosalind wanted a bus ride. On these occasions she was very quarrelsome and threatened each time to withdraw from the "club." Nevertheless she never missed a meeting. The worker remained passive, leaving the girls to settle the matter entirely by themselves. This they did very effectively. After considerable argument and hesitation, Rosalind would submit to the group's will, though in some instances she carried her points.

The girl's extreme power drive and self-centeredness are exemplified by her behavior when the group visited the contemporarily largest transatlantic steamer, which was receiving at the time considerable publicity. Rosalind not only opposed the trip, but when they did get to the steamer, she refused to follow the guide along with the others. When the group went down to the engine room, she remained on deck and rejoined it later. When the girls went on deck, Rosalind remained in the first-class lounge luxuriating in the beauty of the surroundings and the comfort of the chairs. When the others were on the open deck, Rosalind called out to the worker, "I don't want to go up, I like it here." The worker replied calmly, "Surely, you can stay down there if you like." "No," came the imperious reply, "I want everybody down here."

However, as these excursions and trips progressed, Rosalind seemed to grow more amenable, more friendly, and less headstrong. This change was observable in other girls as well. "Our records reveal," says the worker in retrospect, "that even these few group contacts were a valuable experience in 'socialization' and have laid the foundation for further constructive work. It is interesting to consider some of the psychological changes in individual girls which occurred in spite of the brevity of the experiment."

Another illustration is the case of Marjorie, a member of the same group. We take the following from the Progress Report on this client:

Marjorie, seventeen, was struggling against the severe thwarting and domination of her parents. In the group this manifested itself in her rebellious attitude toward the worker. She refused every suggestion made to the group and insisted on carrying out her own individual program no matter how it conflicted with the interest of the others. When she realized that she was free to do as she pleased and that her actions had no apparent influence on the worker or the other girls, she soon changed her tactics and began to enjoy herself as a member of the group. This girl, so hostile to authority, learned that she could get more satisfaction by accepting limitations in a mature manner than she could by continuing to resist the group.

Both Rosalind and Marjorie, being aggressive, attempted to activate counter-aggression from the group and especially from the adult. They both had a need for being controlled and dominated. In both cases this need could be eliminated by a new type of experience. Had the reactions to frustration in the home become structuralized in character with possible neurotic manifestations, more prolonged and intensive treatment would have been required (as in the cases of Harmon and Paul, Chapter VIII, pages 273 ff.).

As would be expected, there are children who are so frightened that they are unable to face even groups of such low pressure as a therapy group. Such a child was Louise (Chapter III, page 53). But where the pattern of withdrawal does not proceed from extreme fear and the child can bear being with others, his specific manner does not stigmatize him. Because we provide materials for manual occupation, the self-effacing child is not forced upon the other members of the group. He can take refuge in work and can isolate himself both emotionally and physically through his occupation. Gradually and often imperceptibly these children gain courage to make contacts with other members. Because the total setting of the group is secure and non-threatening, they overcome their fears through an alliance with another child who is as apprehensive as they, through the recognition they receive for manual work, and frequently through being "adopted" by more outgoing children.

The sensitive and withdrawn child is the one who is most frequently left without social or community resources to aid his development and to help him with his difficulties. In gangs and clubs there is inevitably considerable aggressiveness. The fearful and shy children are threatened; they suffer from acts of hostility. In a therapy group aggressiveness is not a threat, because participation in the group or withdrawal from it is easy and inconspicuous. Shy children can be seen sitting by themselves engrossed in some work while bedlam is let loose around them. While others fight, horseplay, or plot, those who do not desire to take a hand in these enterprises remain at their self-chosen tasks. This situation is common to the setting of a therapy group and never arouses comment from the others. Spontaneous expression and the resultant flux in activity and grouping are natural here. There is complete *social mobility*. Withdrawal by a member does not arouse the derision and resentment that one commonly finds in ordinary clubs. Thus each member finds his own métier and matrix, at the same time gathering force from the others and from his work, or subduing himself, according to his need, so that his response to the situation may eventually become balanced. The following two instances from our records may illustrate these points:

Thea, fourteen, extremely shy and reticent, was making a poor adjustment at home and at school. During her early contact with the group, she was completely withdrawn and appeared disinterested. She seemed much more at ease at later meetings and after several months became an active participant in the group's activities. By the end of the season, she showed a marked change in attitude and became an enthusiastic and cooperative member of the group.

Beatrice, sixteen, with a very unhappy home life, found her satisfactions in phantasy and began by clinging to the leader and by using her as an audience. The worker was sympathetic, but did not encourage her in this. As she gained more security, Beatrice gradually began to display an ability to use social contacts instead of phantasy as a means of expression and transferred her attentions from the worker to the girls.

The value of the group in the development of a wholesome ego structure is evident. The strongest check upon pleasure drives and self-indulgence is the negative reaction of other persons. The child's (and adult's) desire to be accepted, or at least not to be excluded, is an incentive for modifying egoic trends. The desire to be accepted by the group we designate *social hunger*, which in our opinion is one of the strongest drives in human beings. It is also the major incentive for improvement in a therapy group. Just as the longing for adult affection causes the child to submit to the will and direction of the parent and to take on his characteristics, social hunger impels the individual to take on the values and mores of the group. First, the pressures of the immediate groups (microcultures)—the family, the street groups, the school groups, clubs—influence the ego structure. Later the values and importance of the larger culture (macro-culture) are absorbed into the final ego. The desire to be accepted serves the same function here as does transference in individual treatment. Just as the patient in individual therapy improves in order to please the therapist, in Group Therapy the child alters his behavior and attitudes so that he may be accepted by the group.

Among other things, maladjusted children must *experience* release through some form of activity and interaction with others so that they may establish anew, under the guidance of the therapist, patterns and feeling tones different from those that operated in their lives and which gave them and others trouble. First-hand experiences not only serve the ends of direct reeducation, but also bring forth material for the treatment interview. This can be designated as *therapy through experience.*

Little progress can be made with a patient who withdraws from life. Therapy must run parallel with living and must be based upon that living. The value of experiencing life situations as a part of psychotherapy lies in the fact that the client responds to traumatic situations in the light of his new orientation. The group serves as a testing ground for his new feelings and attitudes. If we were to remove a client from all social contacts and restrict him to association only with a therapist, there would be no improvement. Improvement comes from cooperation in the set therapy situation and the client's participation in life. This is not unlike the process in medicine. Medication, food, rest, sunshine, fresh air, and the other means employed in treating the sick are the agents through which the body is helped to effect the cure. But the cure is accomplished by the body itself. Similarly, recovery from mental disturbances is accomplished by the mind itself (emotions and intellect) as it functions in life. Psychotherapy eases, aids, and makes this process possible.

When actual situations in the life of the client are employed in therapy, we can designate treatment as *situational therapy* to differentiate it from interview therapy. Situational therapy is always coextensive with the latter, since the patient does not live in a vacuum. He constantly meets up with life, and the extent to which the therapist can set and manipulate the situation in accordance with the needs of the client determines the effectiveness of treatment. Institutionalization, for example, becomes necessary where ordinary conditions of life are either too strenuous and disturbing or too lax.

In the light of the foregoing, we can say that all psychotherapy takes place in relation to other people, in life situations. The function of the therapist is to remove the blockings to social living and to release intrapsychic tensions. The need for group experience is of particular value for those children whose early family life has been in some way inadequate, as the following abstract from a group record clearly demonstrates:

Charles (an only child, ten years old) went to the closet where supplies were kept and then turned to the worker and said, "I don't think I can open it. Maybe you'd better try." (Apparently Charles's failure to open the closet the previous week had affected his confidence.) Worker took the keys and opened the closet. Charles said to the worker, "You know, I like it when there are not so many fellows here. I think it's more fun." Worker asked Charles whether he did not enjoy playing and working with the other boys. Charles said, "Yeah, but sometimes they give me a pain in the neck." Worker laughed. Charles also laughed at this and said, "But I really have more fun when there's only a few guys around." . . . Worker asked Charles what he was going to make today. Charles looked at the closet, shrugged his shoulders, and said, "Oh, I don't know. I don't think I'll make anything today."

About this time, Danny walked in. Danny (who is one of five children) looked around the room, greeted the worker and Charles, and said, "Where are all the other guys?" Worker said that it was early and probably they would come later, or perhaps they might not come because of the school holiday. Danny said, "Oh, yeah," and added, "Some of them might have gone to the movies." Charles said, "I hope they don't come. We can have more fun just with the two of us." Danny looked up in surprise at Charles but said nothing.

Evidently Charles wished to continue to occupy the center of the stage and remain an only child. In his case the fundamental service of the group was to place him in a situation where he would have to share with other people. A large impersonal social club, without the manual activities, was not suitable for this boy. He refused to go to such a club. His attendance at this small, free-activity group of seven boys of nearly his own age was almost one hundred per cent. His social needs were satisfied here without being threatened too much. Because Danny had lived in a large family, Charles's attitude seemed strange to him.

The chief characteristic of the therapy group is its similarity to the family. Although it is based upon a number of other assumptions, chief among them is that emotional disorientation and dissocial behavior originate in family (group) relations. It is, therefore, the aim of Group Therapy to create an atmosphere and stimulate relationships among its members that will approximate, as far as possible, those of an ideal family. All the positive elements the family (group) life lacked are emphasized in a therapy group.

Manual activity in arts and crafts at the meetings is therefore incidental. Its chief purpose is to bring the members together, to stimulate contact, conversation, cooperation, mutual admiration. Such an atmosphere and such relations aid the process of identification and supply more socializing experiences than the children have had in the past. We have also found that what occurs here is more than ordinary identification. This group experience reduces the child's life-sustaining egocentricity and develops a growing capacity to fuse his life with others. The decrease in emotional isolation makes the children accessible to the influences of the world and lays the foundation for character reconstruction and desirable changes in attitudes. Such is the inevitable outcome of the intimate relations that members of groups gradually establish.

In a group where the pattern and the atmosphere are those of a *good* family, each member seeks to be accepted by the substitute-family group and modifies his behavior so as to become acceptable. That the attitude flows from the adult is quite clear from our records, but the pivot of the modifications is a face-to-face relation with others in a social setting. To accomplish this the group must be entirely informal and, in its early stages, give *complete* freedom of communication, activity, and movement. It must have no set pattern. There must be constant and free flow of feelings and thought. The members and the therapist have to be in a relation of intimacy and friendship, and the group permeated with a communal feeling and common interests—all of which can occur only in an atmosphere of informality and mutual acceptance.

The therapeutic values of a permissive environment, interpersonal relations, and group activity are set forth in greater detail throughout the book and especially in Chapter VII. We shall state here only the four cardinal needs of most clients that are met through Group Therapy.

First. Every child needs the security of unconditional love from his parents and other adults who play a significant role in his life. If this love is not forthcoming from these sources, a substitute for them must be supplied. In therapy, the psychiatrist, the case worker, and the group therapist are such substitutes. In Group Therapy the child becomes convinced of this love for the following reasons: 1) he is supplied with materials for work, which he can use in any way he wishes; 2) he can use them constructively or destructively without evoking from the adult in charge comments, suggestions, corrective or scolding remarks; 3) he is free to come and go whenever he likes; 4) his needs for crafts materials are promptly met; 5) his personality is at all times respected; 6) no restraint by the adult is employed in the early stages of the group's life; 7) he is allowed to take home anything he wants from the supply closet until the other members (not the adult) restrict, condition, or prohibit such practices; 8) the adult praises freely the child's work; 9) the child's desires for food, trips, movies, and so forth are met by the adult in charge. Some of these points will be further elaborated in later parts of this volume. Illustrations of these practices will be found in the record material.

One of our children, a boy of eleven, was habitually threatened by his mother that she would place him in an institution for "bad boys." The mother as well as the other members of the family strongly rejected him. The boy complained to his case worker that he was not loved. The latter asked him what he thought being loved meant. He promptly answered, "When people let me do what I want to do, then I know they love me." An institution for "bad boys" was to this patient "a place where people lecture to you that what you have done is wrong and always tell you to do right."

In Group Therapy we permit the child (without giving him approval) to do whatever he wants to do and we never "lecture" him. The meaning of permissiveness to the child is mirrored in the response of a member quoted by a case worker:

We found the boy very enthusiastic over his activities in the therapy group. His face beamed with joy as he talked of the freedom he has while with the group. He is happy there. They have "toys." Mr. Kraft does not shout at the children. Even when they make mistakes he is good to them. He corrects them without criticizing. The boy likes him. He goes every week. He looks forward to going.

Second. The ego and the sense of self-worth which are usually crushed in problem children must be built up. A sense of failure is one of the more common causes for personality disturbances and social disorientation in modern times. Success gives one the sense of self-worth which is essential to wholesome character formation. The need for success and achievement is not primary but rather derivative from our culture, and is determined by comparison with others in the group. When this comparison is unfavorable, feelings of inferiority and intrapsychic tensions are set up which frequently find release in dissocial behavior or neurotic symptoms or both. This is true also of adults who, by comparison with others or with the accepted values of our society, do not feel they have attained a reasonable degree of "success." They, too, tend to disintegrate socially and personally and to develop various types of neuroses and pathological substitutive gratifications.

The new psychotherapy, therefore, seeks to meet the creative and assertive needs of clients and to help them achieve an acceptable degree of success. This is particularly important because a thoroughgoing individual treatment is available only to a few of those who need it and because many clients suffer from organic and intellectual inferiorities that stigmatize them in relation to the group. Creative expression and success within the limits of one's capacities must, therefore, be incorporated in therapy. "Undoubtedly," says Dr. I. T. Broadwin, "child analysis in individual cases is the ideal procedure, but at present, practical situations interfere with such a circumscribed procedure. In the treatment of the child, the total personality and the total situation must be taken into account."[8] Thus, a job and a secure income may become the determining considerations in the therapy of adolescents and adults, and a situation in which the child can function without a feeling of inadequacy, failure, and guilt may be the center of treatment for him.

In Group Therapy the individual's need for status and success are met through 1) recognition of all constructive effort on the part of the child, praise, and encouragement; 2) the adult's acceptance of the child; 3) the group's acceptance of him; 4) the child's feeling of belonging to a group; 5) the friendships that spring up in the group; 6) the fact that the excellence in manual work often brings recognition in the home and at school; 7) the fact that destructive behavior does not evoke condemnation from the adult.

Third. Every child needs some genuine interest to occupy his leisure time. In Group Therapy we provide work in the constructional, plastic, graphic, and other arts, and in science.

---

[8] Understanding the Problem Child, *in* Sandor Lorand, ed., *Psychoanalysis Today*, New York, Covici, Friede, 1933, page 148.

There are various tools and materials at hand which the children use freely, creating or destroying in whatever medium appeals to them. Observations here confirm our experience in a "reform" school where we found the incidence of talent among problem children very high. Studies by other workers of socially maladjusted children point to the same conclusion. In an unpublished study of post-institutional careers of delinquent boys made by the Jewish Board of Guardians, we find the following significant statement: "Of boys having an interest in athletics, music, animals, reading, stamp collecting, and so on, sixty per cent adjusted as compared with twenty-five per cent of those who had no such interests." If it is true that artistic talent is greater among problem children than among "normal," then creative self-expression in a group environment looms as an important tool in prevention of delinquency.

Fourth. A major value of Group Therapy lies in the opportunity it presents for significant experiences in group relations leading to acceptance by the group. Neurotics especially are filled with an overwhelming sense of isolation and loneliness. Interestingly enough, this feeling of loneliness is present even in an atmosphere of gaiety. One girl patient expressed it thus: "People who watch me think I have a good time and that I am happy. But even at these gay parties, I feel so terribly lonely that no one would believe it."

Of primary importance is the generous praise that members of therapy groups spontaneously give one another. The members work together; they quarrel, fight, and sometimes even strike one another; they argue and haggle; but they finally come to some working understanding. Sometimes this process takes six months or more, but, once established, it becomes a permanent attitude on the part of the individuals involved. Our follow-up studies show that in all but a few cases these group adjustments are carried over to other group relations in the home, at school, and in play.

The effects of the group experience on several of our clients are given briefly in the abstracts that follow. More detailed records of the group treatment of five children are given in Chapter VIII.

Paula was a shy, withdrawn girl of twelve. Her mother died when Paula was young; her father was going blind. There were four other girls in the family, two of whom were married. None displayed any interest in our client. After her mother died, Paula was sent to live with Mrs. Wentz. She did all the housework before school and helped in Mr. Wentz's cigar store after school hours. When referred to the agency Paula was living at home again, but continued to be neglected and used as a drudge by her sisters. She did most of the heavy cleaning in her own home and continued to do the housework for Mrs. Wentz. She received no spending money from her sisters and only a very small sum from her employer. Paula had no friends and no contact with girls or boys of her own age.

At the first meetings Paula was on the defensive. When playing word games, for example, she would show off. When the other girls could not give the correct answer, she at once volunteered "I know," with an air of superiority and implied ridicule of the others in the group. She never looked the other girls in the face and appeared very sly. When the girls washed the dishes at the close of the meetings, Paula did not help.

Paula seemed very resentful of the other girls' possessions. One of the members wore a wrist watch. Paula wanted to know what she was doing in the "club." She thought it was only for poor girls! Because of her work at Mrs. Wentz's, Paula could not come regularly to the meetings. She usually came late and told the worker that she "got the devil for not coming home right after school."

After seven weeks the report on Paula reads in part as follows:

Paula seems to have lost her resentfulness and has made two friends. She insists on helping them and is always the first to offer to put away the materials. The girls are very helpful toward her too. They seem to realize that she has a hard time of it, but do not show it in any way except by being friendly toward her. She enjoys working on materials, and says she hates "to lose one minute."

At first she would not try anything unless she was sure she could do it as well as the others. Last meeting she started to paint, telling the worker that she was very poor at it.[9]

Her whole attitude seems to have changed. She is now always pleasant to everyone at the meetings and, though she herself is dressed very shabbily, admires the clothes the other girls wear and takes suggestions from them.

We may add that Paula is now, at nineteen, earning her own living, is a member of a settlement house club, has a boy friend, and is a happy, though a very limited, person.

Another member of the same group was Joan, aged thirteen, who was referred to the agency because of poor attendance at school, though her scholastic standing was good, and because she was "running wild." She masturbated in school. Her mother worked. Her father was a drug addict and always unemployed. A sister, eight years older than Joan, lived at home with her common-law husband and a son. The husband had another wife from whom he was not divorced. The sister was in the habit of discussing her marital problems in Joan's presence. The report reads in part as follows:

Joan was sophisticated, better dressed than the other girls, used a great deal of make-up, and liked to be in the public eye. From the very first, she discussed only her boy friends and the clothes she wanted for spring. During the first few meetings she worked a little on embroidery, but spent most of her time sitting around doing nothing. She would not enter into conversation, except where it pertained to her directly. She had no interest in the other girls unless they went out a lot socially. She would come in every other week or so, always late.

This attitude gradually changed and several months later we read in the report:

At the last two meetings, Joan came in promptly at 3:30 and stayed to the end. She greeted all the girls cordially and entered into conversation with them. When a discussion of modern art

9 For discussion of self-acceptance, see Chapter VII, pages 197 ff.

arose (because of a painting one of the girls had made), she listened intently and admitted that she knew nothing about it; but it sounded interesting, she said, and she would like to see some modern art. She made a very nice clay basket at the last meeting, whereas before she had scoffed at the painting and clay work the other girls were doing. At the last meeting, she asked Jean to walk home with her. Jean is the most backward girl in the group, whom the other girls ask to do odds and ends for them such as turning on the radio, getting pencils, and so on. When a trip was being discussed, Jean was the only girl who could not go on a Saturday, which seemed the best day for the others. It was Joan who suggested that they ought to go some other day, so that Jean would not miss the trip.

CHAPTER II

THE PRACTICE OF GROUP THERAPY

BEFORE a child can be assigned to a group, it is necessary to have information on his behavior toward other children; the nature of his problem; the major factors that have contributed to the formation of the problem; and his physical appearance. It is also necessary to know whether he will be aggressive toward other members or is withdrawn and sensitive. If the former is the case, other children must be considered against whom he may direct his aggression. If the latter is the case, the child must not be exposed to the rigor and strain of the excessive aggression of other members.[1] Some knowledge of the basic problem of the child is important to the understanding of the meaning of the child's behavior; it helps the group therapist anticipate attitudes and responses, and guides him as to the emotional needs of the client. Size and personal appearance help in the grouping of children in accordance with physical fitness to each other. Therefore when a child is referred for Group Therapy, a form is made out by the referring worker on which the salient features of the child's behavior and appearance are described.[2]

The emphasis in the Referral Summary is upon the social adjustment or function picture rather than upon clinical diagnosis or therapeutic goals. Clinical interpretations and analyses are made later in treatment at conferences held between case workers, group therapists, supervisors, and psychiatrists. These conferences are known as Integration Conferences.[3] The Referral Summary is intended to describe the client's

---

[1] For a more detailed discussion of grouping see Chapter V.
[2] An Outline for a Referral Summary is given in Appendix I.
[3] An Outline for Integration Conferences is given in Appendix III.

overt social behavior so that placement in a suitable group is possible.

The material submitted by the case worker, intake worker, or psychiatrist in accordance with the outline is analyzed and the child's fitness for Group Therapy determined. All doubtful matters are discussed with the referring worker or psychiatrist. When necessary, and when one is available, the full individual record is consulted. The assignment of a child depends also on whether there is a group in his neighborhood suited to his special needs. Another factor to be considered is whether he is suitable for the group (see Chapter V).

For the convenience of members, groups meet in the various localities of the city. This is necessary since the younger children cannot travel too long distances because of their own fears or the apprehension of their parents. Some of our older boys and girls traveled more than five or six miles to meetings, with perfect attendance. In some instances, where the social history warrants it, carfare is supplied by the agency. When the child is assigned to a group, he receives an invitation which states that he is invited upon the suggestion of the case worker or intake worker, and the letter is signed by the office secretary, but *not* by the group therapist. A sample letter is given below:

Dear Thomas,

Miss Berger suggested that you would like to join a club of boys in your neighborhood. This club meets at 960 Euclid Avenue on Tuesday at seven o'clock.

The boys work with all kinds of materials like wood, paints, and copper, play games, have delicious refreshments, and go on outings, picnics, and trips.

The leader of this club is George Smith and he will be expecting you.

Your friend,
ANN GOLD

Here follow instructions regarding transportation from the child's home to the meeting place.

All subsequent letters dealing with attendance and activities are signed by the group therapist. For five consecutive weeks after the first meeting the child receives a letter which reads as follows:

Dear Thomas,

Our club will meet again this Tuesday at seven o'clock in our club room, 960 Euclid Avenue. The other boys and I are looking forward to seeing you. I hope you will come.

Your friend,
GEORGE SMITH

Members of groups receive a reminder after each absence, also signed by the group therapist. The text of these varies, but their general content is something like this:

Dear Thomas,

I am sorry you were not able to come to our meeting last Tuesday. The boys and I missed you and we all hope you can come this week. We had a very nice time at our meeting.

Looking forward to seeing you,

Your friend,
GEORGE SMITH

If a trip or an outing has been planned by the group, the absentees are notified of the fact. Often it is also advisable to remind the members who were present when the plans for the trip were made. Many of them forget about it and are disappointed when they come late and the group has already departed. All information and instructions must be very specific and very simple.

Letters should be mailed so that they are received the day before the meeting or trip and not the same day. Some children have late school, others do not go directly home and do not receive mail in time. In some instances members of the family take the mail and hold it until evening, when it is too late. Receipt of notification on the day before obviates these delays. Mail should not reach children too far in advance, however, because they lay it aside and forget to come to the meetings.

Perhaps it can be said here, parenthetically, that all our children are proud and gratified to receive letters and post-cards addressed to them. They seem to feel important and grown up. Most children save these missives and show them around to their parents and schoolmates and often verbalize their satisfaction. "Gee, whiz," said a youngster to the worker, "I never got a letter before in my life. I like to see my name on an envelope!"

After the child has attended three meetings, the group therapist writes a description of him, his appearance, his initial reaction to the group situation and to individual children, his activities, and other pertinent facts. This report is known as a First Impression, and copies are filed in the master case record, in the child's individual folder within the department and, like all material pertaining to individual children, in the group record. The First Impression is checked against the description of the child in the Referral Summary, and with his subsequent behavior in the group. Quite often the initial behavior is not at all characteristic of the child and the discrepancy between this façade and his real impulses is important material for diagnostic and treatment purposes.

Every four months a Progress Report is submitted by the group therapist. This report deals with the child's social adaptation (function picture) as does the Referral Summary. It is intended to reflect any improvement or retrogression on the part of the child.

On the basis of the First Impression, Progress Reports, and other special memoranda that may be submitted by the group therapist, the child's adjustment is discussed at an Integration Conference between the group and case workers or psychiatrist in "cooperative cases" (see Preface).[4] At these conferences

---

[4] An Outline for a Progress Report is given in Appendix II, and an Outline for Integration Conferences in Appendix III.

the psychiatric implications of the client's behavior and his personality problems are evaluated and plans made for the future, both in individual treatment and in the group situation. The conferences are held at least twice during the school season and are spaced so that they are about midway in point of time between the Progress Reports. In more difficult cases conferences are held more frequently. Thus every child's progress is noted four or five times during the year and his record contains, in addition to other material on him: Referral Summary, First Impression, two Progress Reports for each school season, two Integration Conference summaries for each school season, one Camp Report for each summer, a Closing Summary at the end of treatment. In "exclusive cases" (see Preface), follow-up visits are made by a case worker to the home, school, and neighborhood center, if any, and the child is interviewed.[5]

Group therapists submit regularly reports on the group meetings. These are running accounts of what occurs in the group and are intended to reflect individual and interpersonal behavior. Two such records with brief supervision comments appear in Chapter III.

Group therapists attend weekly Supervision Conferences during the first three or four years of their service.[6] Later, supervision may be reduced to alternate weeks. Emphasis is laid upon the understanding of the mechanism of individual children, the meaning of their behavior in terms of their psychological goals, the type of response needed from the group therapist as well as changes in the group set-up to meet individual needs of clients. The emphasis throughout is on the individual child. However, in order to achieve treatment goals, it is necessary to be aware of the effect members have upon

[5] An Outline for Follow-up Study will be found in Appendix IV.

[6] All supervision, intake, and assignment to groups in this particular project were carried by the writer. He also acted as chairman of the Integration Conferences.

each other and the total atmosphere of the group. It is frequently necessary to introduce activities that will help the treatment process. Sometimes the supervisor finds that confinement in the meeting room and the resulting "nervousness" bring out more aggressiveness than is good for the treatment situation. He may then suggest either a series of trips or recreation in a gymnasium, or he may find that there is not adequate interpersonal activity in a group because of the absence of *instigators*[7] and decide to refer to the group one or two aggressive or bright children who are likely to stimulate it.

Frequently the therapist's own reactions need to be discussed. His unconscious responses, frustrations, and traumatic experiences are often activated through the behavior of some of the children. This behavior (similar to his own in childhood or to that of his siblings) may outrage his sense of justice or arouse compassion. All this must be guarded against and the adult's reactions clarified during the Supervision Conferences. Some therapists tend to block the children by asserting themselves too early in treatment. Others are unable to assert themselves, deny or use authority, because of some problem of their own. It is essential that the adult should be fully aware of his own reactions and it is the supervisor's function to clarify them for him. Of course, the most important factor in the Group Therapy situation is the proper choice of therapists and some of their qualifications are discussed in Chapter VI.

In the summaries of Supervision Conferences attached to each of the two records in Chapter III are indicated sketchily a few of the developments that arise in supervision.

On the day of the first meeting, the group therapist arrives early and sets out on a large table the materials and tools with which the children can work. Tenpins, checkers, lotto, and similar appropriate individual and group games are also

---

[7] For discussion of instigators, see Chapter V, page 119.

placed conveniently at hand. As the children come in one by one they find him busily occupied with the materials. He introduces himself by his first and last names without "Mr." They are introduced to each other by their first names. There is considerable reserve in the group at first. But by the end of the evening or afternoon (young children should meet in the afternoons and on Saturday or Sunday, while the older ones can meet in the early evening), when all gather around a table attractively set—an unusual experience for most of the children—and eat and drink in the company of a friendly adult, they regain confidence and the ice is broken.

At the second gathering some of the boys or girls no longer treat each other as strangers. Some greet one another; others cannot go quite so far, but are more responsive than at the first meeting. Most of the children undertake a project with arts and crafts materials, while some play with the games. There are always one or two who do not engage in any activity, but sit around or wander about.

The children know, or are told when they ask, that the social agency sponsors the meetings and supplies the money. They must have this security and should not feel indebted to the worker *personally* for the good times they are enjoying. It is not difficult to make the children understand this since they already have had contacts with the agency. *They do not know, however, that the group is for the purpose of therapy.* As far as they are concerned it is a "club," and such it remains in their minds throughout their membership in it.

The group therapist greets each child as he enters in a friendly and warm manner, but does not go further than this. Except in special cases, he does not start conversations, makes no remarks or suggestions. This does not mean, however, that he is stern or forbidding or even aloof. His countenance expresses gentleness and readiness to be friendly and helpful, but he does not take the initial step in conversation, nor does he suggest an activity. This is necessary for several reasons.

First, these children need to be helped to become independent of the adult. Secondly, since we cannot know in advance
what each child's real needs are, it is advisable for the group
therapist to remain inactive. Each member can take out of the
situation what he happens to need at the time.[8] However,
later in treatment, when the needs of the child are clear to the
worker, he may take some initiative in this regard.

The aim is to make the child self-reliant, but care is taken
not to arouse in the slightest degree a feeling of rejection. In
order that the child may grow up, he must make adjustments
to new and untried situations and navigate in them. The therapy group meetings are a series of such new situations, and it
is desirable that the member should adapt himself to them on
his own.

There is another reason for the adult's neutrality. If he pays
attention to any one child, he is likely to arouse jealousy in
some of the others. Almost all the children in the group are
sensitive if the therapist pays particular attention to any one
of them. They feel he is showing a preference and the pattern
of sibling rivalry is activated. If such jealousies should develop in the group, they would result in hostility toward the
therapist and toward those members he is seemingly favoring.

The abstract from an Integration Conference that follows
illustrates this point. It also conveys some of the dynamics in
the relationships of a therapy group. The boy in question had
made a constant bid for the attention of the adult and once
instigated a movement to "kick out" another member with
whom on one occasion the therapist went out to buy food (a
mistake on the part of the group therapist).

---

[8] We shall describe the function of the therapist in Chapter VI. However,
his chief function is to be a *neutral* person so that each client can utilize him
in accordance with his own particular needs. It is as though the therapist were
a screen of neutral tone like that in a movie on which different colors are
projected. Each member of the group projects on the therapist his unconscious attitudes toward adults. Neutrality on the part of the therapist makes
this possible.

It is evident from what was stated during the conference by case worker and group therapist that because of the extreme rejection by his mother and the recent loss of his father by death, Herbert is in great need of love and attention. At the present time, the group has very little significance for him, and the group therapist fears he may even prevent the group from integrating. When Herbert vies with the other members for first place with the group therapist he blocks the integrating process of the group. It is as though he set up a wall between the rest of the boys and the adult. The adult, being the center around which a group constellates, becomes emotionally inaccessible under these conditions. At the same time, Herbert's intense drive to possess the adult makes it impossible for him to reach out to the group and become accepted by the group. He isolates himself from the others. The case worker and group therapist agree therefore to watch the boy, to see whether it is possible for him to dissolve his intense fixation and dependence on the adult and to move toward a relation with the group. If he does so, it will mark a progressive step in the boy's growth. He will find it easier to attach himself to other groups later and thus function as a more mature member of society.

It was suggested that a Big Brother might be assigned to Herbert to direct his emotional drive away from the group therapist. However, the case worker (a woman) felt that this might set up a conflict in loyalties in the boy at this point, and the plan was left to be discussed again at a future Integration Conference.

This boy demonstrates the conflict that may exist between affect hunger and social hunger. At this stage his need for the affection of an adult seems to be stronger than his need for group acceptance.

The usual reaction of the children to the situation set by the group therapist is somewhat as follows. The child watches him for a few minutes and says what a nice job he is doing. Can he be of any help or can he also try something similar? To this the therapist answers that he can *make whatever he wishes*. The materials are there for anyone to use. Really, can one make whatever one likes in this place? The freedom to *make whatever one likes* seems to be the most impressive feature of the meetings. Many of our clients bring their friends to prove to them that they can make whatever they please and proudly show off this privilege. To belong to such a "club" seems a real recognition, and the friends are observably jealous and invariably want to join the group. To give the child freedom of action and choice indicates that he has been accepted by the adult, and this means a great deal to him.

Frequently the child begins to imitate the therapist's project but he gradually finds some occupation that satisfies his own interests and abilities more adequately. As other members enter the room, *interaction* and other primary group dynamics are precipitated. One member approaches another who is already at work and expresses amazement at the quality of his product. He inquires if the latter has studied art—he is so good at it—and can he work with him? Or he expresses doubt in his own ability to do anything like it. If no encouragement is forthcoming from any of the other children, the group therapist suggests casually that he might try and see, for no one in the room is expert; then again, how can he tell that he is not good at it if he has never tried? Sometimes this persuasion is effective; frequently, however, the deep-rooted insecurity is not dispersed so readily. Sometimes months go by before a child can take a chance on failing. The important contribution of the group for such children is to help them overcome their lack of self-confidence in an easy and natural way.

The materials and games are designed to suggest activities. They are simple and for the most part familiar to the children and their use requires little skill or knowledge. They are graded so as not to offer too difficult a challenge or to constitute a threat of failure. For this reason, they vary in degree of resistivity. Water is the least resistive material, then paint, clay, wire, wood, metal, and so on. A frightened and sensitive child will naturally turn to materials which can be used directly and are easily manipulated without the use of tools, such as clay and water colors. More aggressive children prefer more resistive materials, such as wood and metals. The principle employed here is one of *graded resistivity* and applies to group relations and adult restraint, as well as to materials.

Because the group therapist remains for a considerable time a passive agent, he needs to devise circumstances that will hold in check aggressiveness and hyperactivity, activate the withdrawn, and lay a basis for group interaction. Opportunities to satisfy all these needs are found in creative, manual activity, in eating together, and in trips. For this reason basic materials are provided for various types of occupations which the members can pursue in their own way. As already described, at the early meetings the group therapist places on a table the supply of materials and tools; at later periods the clients do this themselves. They prepare the room for their meetings. Here are to be found supplies suitable to engage the interest of members according to age or sex: clay, plasticine, wood-working tools and materials, electrical and magnetic toys and apparatus, paints and water colors, crayons, paper, wire for sculpture, and materials for making masks, sewing, crocheting, knitting, and leather work. Tenpins, indoor quoits, and other games of skill, chess, and a ping-pong table are also provided. Some clients make their first contacts with the other members through games, but usually it is in the later stages of treatment that games stimulate social situations and interpersonal dynamics.

In most instances activity is undertaken individually. There is little cooperation. Especially is this the case when the members are not acquainted with one another. They feel uneasy in groups, and the many blockings and fears make them inaccessible to one another. This shyness, however, soon gives way in some children to extreme boisterousness and destructiveness; other children continue to withdraw and keep to themselves.

The first response to materials and tools is usually one of investigation. Members handle and examine the various objects. Because most of the schools in large cities have shopwork and arts and crafts, and because many of these particular children have attended various "special classes," they are acquainted with the materials and the equipment. But in a large number of instances, they are afraid to touch the objects laid out for them. They just stare at them and watch the group therapist busily at work. The early reaction of children to the permissive environment of the groups is illustrated in the following abstract from a report:

At the second meeting of the group, Henry was the first to arrive. He arrived before the set time. He just sat around watching the materials being laid out on the table. No conversation was initiated between Henry and worker all the while worker was getting the room ready for the meeting. Sam arrived shortly afterward and worker left the two in the room. When he came back some time later both boys (who were total strangers to each other) were playing with a small generator, an electric bulb, and a bell. As the worker entered the room the boys stopped abruptly, evidently expecting some reprimand. When they saw that none was forthcoming, they resumed their work, timidly at first; later they cranked the generator with much vigor and played freely with other electrical materials.

After a period of acclimatization, activities are undertaken by individual members, furtively and uncertainly at first, later boldly and with assurance. The children invent and devise, experiment and try out. For very long periods, sometimes as long as a year and more, almost all activity is individual. Cooperation arises at later stages. But even during this individualistic phase, and following the example of the therapist, the members of the group are slowly and indirectly habituated to recognize each other's efforts and praise them. The therapist makes a point of praising everything a child does, no matter how mediocre, unless it is felt that he is unable to bear praise. Praise is withheld in instances of cooperation, social acts, responsibility, and the like, because it is the child's group and whatever he does for it is taken for granted.

Because of the adult's appreciative attitude, members become cognizant of each other's talents and give praise freely and with genuine feeling. Such an attitude can, of course, be engendered only in an atmosphere of mutual acceptance and emotional warmth which must emanate from the adult in charge. He praises children in the hope that they will praise other members of the group. Gradually one finds the children abandoning, in part at least, their isolation. Two or three children band together in common interests. Sometimes, though very infrequently, whole group projects emerge.

It must not be assumed that the group process is always pleasant and easy. Conflicts, fist fights, hostilities, "pet hatreds," ganging against one of the members, cursing, and vulgarities are plentiful. But the forbearance of the adult seems to wear down this pent-up hostility. His acceptance of their negativism and his recognition of their constructiveness make for mutual acceptance. Neither must it be assumed that the response to the group is always satisfactory. As in all therapy, the effectiveness of Group Therapy varies greatly. Some children completely recover; others gain only partial benefit; still others, whose problems are charged with deep intrapsychic pressure, cannot be affected very much by this type of treatment. In such cases it is employed, if at all, as supplementary to more intensive individual therapy.

As the group meetings get under way the room is pervaded with the quiet of interested children at work. Each is quietly and concentratedly occupied, paying little heed to the others. If any conversation does spring up, it is directed to the therapist. In one group the boys did not address each other for an entire year. They talked to the adult only. It was not till the second year of the group's existence that they addressed one another directly. This is a unique case, but indicates the general trend. Communication takes place after fears and tensions are lessened or disappear. Often this takes a long time. In fact, the fear of a group is so great in some children that they come to the building and leave it again without going to the meeting. Some who cannot face a group without the support of an intimate bring along friends. In some instances parents, and on occasion, though rarely, case workers, have to accompany the children to one or two meetings until the latter muster up courage to come alone.

Later in the life of the group noticeable attachments are formed and in some instances friendships are carried over into life outside the group. It must be kept in mind that the groups are made up of children who are unable to make friends, this being one of the main reasons for referring them for Group Therapy. These boys, girls, and adolescents have been rejected by the home, the school, settlement houses, neighborhood centers, and street groups. Their growing ability to acquire and hold friends must be viewed as a sign of improvement. Thus in many cases sibling-substitutes are chosen and accepted. We have here, therefore, a rather complete picture of a *family substitutive group:* the therapist is a parent-substitute, the members are sibling-substitutes, and the total group pattern a substitute family to which the children look for their satisfactions. This analogy has not been arrived at purely theoretically, nor even from the behavior and reactions of the members of the group, but, as is made clear in our records, by remarks that spontaneously escape the members. They refer to the group as "happy family," "our family," and to workers as "Mom," "Unk," "Papa."

We take the following from one of our records that illustrates our point:

Worker picked up the broom and dustpan to clean up a bit of dirt that was on the floor. Mack (ten years old—a new member) said: "Let me." Worker silently gave him the broom and pan. After sweeping up Mack looked up pleased: "Look, Morty, it's all together. Where shall I put it?" Worker told him to put it in the basket. Worker praised Mack for the good job he had done. Mack beamed and said, "Just like at home." Worker was placing napkins and cups and saucers on the table for the boys. Mack seemed impressed and most pleased. He said with suppressed feeling, "Just like a home."

(From the referral we learn that Mack grew up in an orphan asylum where he had been since early childhood and later lived in five different foster homes. Only recently did he come to live with a stepmother and his father.)

In the record of a group of girls, twelve to thirteen years old, we read the following:

Worker was serving the soup, and two girls were squabbling about their table manners. Lillian made no comment, but merely took a cracker and sat waiting until all were ready to eat. Suddenly she looked up and said, "Gee, it's just like as if you were our mother, isn't it?" Worker smiled, but did not comment. "And I like it, too," Lillian added.

Under such friendly and comforting conditions the need for committing antisocial acts no longer exists to the same degree as in the past. Constructive trends are encouraged by the adult's acceptance. The members also become more aware of materials and tools. They prevent waste, discuss costs, and check upon each other's carelessness in the use of the equipment. The room in which they meet also becomes their concern. They grow careful not to damage it, clear up the débris, and set to rights the disorder created by their activity. Members of the group plan the meal and purchase, prepare, and serve the food. They wash and put away the dishes with care. In some groups, all this is done by the entire membership with no special assignments. In others, members take turns according to a plan originated and worked out by them. The adult does not actively participate in this social development. For weeks and sometimes for months he continues to do all the work until one or two of the children volunteer to help. Gradually the entire responsibility is taken over by them.

In most of our groups the members automatically fall in with the idea of clearing up. At first offers to help come from individual members, usually from those who become most attached to the worker, feel most insecure, or have a need to ingratiate themselves. Later others, by example and through inner growth, take a hand. Soon those children who have helped the group therapist for several weeks begin to feel that the others are taking advantage of them. They demand that they, too, do their share. Quarrels and sometimes threats of physical harm are necessary to make those who will not work do their part. In one group of twelve to fourteen-year-old boys a schedule of definite duties was suggested and prepared by one of them with the approval of the other members. The schedule was then nailed to the door of the supply closet.[9] In a few groups it was necessary, after a long period, for the therapist to discuss with the members the advisability of developing some plan of housekeeping. He did not attempt this, however, until he felt quite certain of his standing with the group. Only when the group therapist is convinced that the members regard him as a *sanctioner* and not as a *prohibitor*, and do not associate him with repressive adults, does he raise the question. Such a step is always discussed first at Supervision Conferences and is taken only when it becomes clear that the group for some reason will not otherwise initiate cleaning up.

Even more important than these activities and signs of growing responsibility is the atmosphere in which all this occurs in the later stages of the group's existence. A spirit of friendship and helpfulness, not easy to describe, gradually makes itself felt. It is quite true that rifts still occur: now and then a jarring note is sounded; a curse, a challenge, or a vulgar expression bursts forth. But these do not carry the same

[9] This development is a good example of the growth of the group super-ego. See Chapter VII, pages 229 ff.

venom and hatred. They are an expression of habit more than of emotion and often are symbols of ease and friendship.

The outings, picnics, and trips, arranged according to their suitability to the particular group and to the time of the year, serve a number of purposes. They prevent monotony, supply new experiences, acquaint the members with a new environment,[10] confront the boys and girls with new types of problems and situations, offer opportunities for free groupings and interaction. A group of aggressive boys, fifteen to sixteen years old, gained more in social development in the early stages of group life through football and basketball in the park than in the more restraining environment of the meeting room. Because of the intense emotional pressure and the resultant hyperactivity, work with tools and materials was too confining (immobilizing) for these boys and the inevitable limitations of the indoors had a repressive effect. Another group of younger boys (twelve to fourteen years old), on the other hand, had the use of a well-equipped gymnasium as well as their meeting room. They chose to work in the latter, however, instead of playing in the gym. In the case of another group (twelve to thirteen years old) the gymnasium proved to be a threat because the members did not as yet feel free with each other and a number of them were too withdrawn to participate in free play.

In my book, *Creative Group Education*,[11] there is a description of a club of boys who did not want to discuss plans for an

---

[10] In a report of the club leader of the center to which Ray's group (see Chapter VIII, pages 237 ff.) was referred we find the following significant statement: "While your girls are handicapped both intellectually and economically compared with other members of the 'Y,' they seem to display an inordinate interest and understanding of music and the other arts compared to our own members." We attribute this to the fact that these girls went to many operas, concerts, and dance recitals during the two-and-one-half years of membership in a therapy group. The girls participated "quite adequately" in the house activities as well.

[11] New York, Association Press, 1937, Appendix A, page 226.

athletic program because they did not wish to take time out for it from their creative work. When the adult leader once suggested that they give more time to athletics, they quickly responded that they also wanted the "arty stuff." We found a similar response in a correctional school. Where possibilities for cultural occupations and creative work were provided, the athletic program greatly suffered in popularity. Workers and club leaders who were in a position to offer members other leisure-time occupations as well as athletics and sports have discovered (much to their surprise) that boys can as easily become interested in cultural occupations. It has also been found that the latter have a more therapeutic effect than sports and the gymnasium.

This is to be expected. Creative work and work in a group are more satisfying than athletics, which does not touch off deeper psychological processes. Athletics, while an active occupation, is really static because it is limited. It does not lead on to other more evolved activities. These conclusions are apparent in the light of our discussion of the therapeutic process in Chapter VII.

Among the most effective early social experiences in Group Therapy is the repast in which the members participate at the conclusion of each meeting. While at first these "parties" may be characterized by self-conscious shyness, this attitude is soon succeeded by aggressive horseplay, upsetting the milk and cocoa, grabbing the food, throwing it at one another, spilling the drinks, and general boisterousness. In a few instances boys punched holes in one another's paper cups, put salt in icecream, removed chairs from under one another. The most common prank (probably as a result of anxiety) is grabbing food.

We know that among the critical situations in the life of a child are eating and retiring for the night. The child at these times uses all his powers of resistance as weapons against his parents. In our groups he again reverts to his infantile pattern. In addition, in many of the economically and culturally poorer homes the gathering of the family group at mealtimes (which is the only time they are together, and does not happen very frequently at that) is the occasion for much strife, quarreling, cursing, and disorder. An unbelievable number of families do not have group meals. Each person is served individually at any hour. Numerous families do not have sufficient knives, forks, and spoons for the entire family and have to eat in relays. Thus in our group the response to the food situation is a weapon and also a habit pattern. We have, therefore, viewed diminishing food anxiety and improved table manners as indices of therapeutic success. It is also well known that young animals and children become active and boisterous after meals. The younger clients in our groups are not immune to this biological law and it is to be expected that rough play and running about should be the order of the day during and after eating.

After the initial period of general grabbing, the next step is to divide very exactly among those present the number of crackers, cakes, spoonfuls of sugar. This exactness stimulates quarrels and fights, but always a compromise is struck. Odd pieces of food are offered to the worker, matched for, or given to the younger sibling of a member, if one is present. Sometimes this food is left with a note for another "club" that may meet in the same room. When the group reaches some measure of control with respect to food, the therapist takes the opportunity to introduce a new pattern. He passes around the plate with the food, as is the custom in properly conducted homes; introduces the practice of passing the cups as they are filled, instead of letting each one grab what he wants. He tells stories, discusses current matters of interest to boys: baseball games, aeroplane flights, races, school, and so on. The conversations in girls' groups turn on topics of interest to girls. The children soon begin to tell stories themselves, ask riddles, repeat jokes, and review critically the events of the meeting. Thus they are learning the fundamentals of social living and group attitudes, As a result the mealtimes at the groups become, after varying periods, orderly, quiet, and social affairs.[12] Before many months elapse, a spirit of camaraderie prevails. In the refreshment period the group resembles a family gathering very closely.

Throughout all the initial bedlam, the worker remains quiet and continues to eat placidly. He gives the group an opportunity to discover for themselves the advantages of orderly behavior, and to evolve techniques of group control. When he finishes his food he quietly suggests that it is time to clear up as their meeting period has come to an end. Some of the children continue their hilarity in the middle of the room, while the worker clears away and sets the room in order alone or with the help of one or two "loyals." Gradually other children pitch in and soon the group as a whole takes over the responsibility of washing dishes and setting the room in order.

In this situation, as in all others, the therapist is neutral. He continues to do the work without moralizing, pressing the clients into service, or assigning tasks. This practice has been adopted on the assumption, suggested in Chapter I, that any move toward criticism or assignment of tasks on the part of the therapist in his early acquaintance with the children would increase their guilt and would at once place the therapist in the category of a compeller and prohibitor. The attitude of the children toward other adults would be transferred to him and he would then become the recipient of their spite and hostility.[13] The therapist must use every means to fix himself in the minds of his clients as a sanctioner, thereby arous-

---

[12] This is still another example of the development of a group super-ego.

[13] A girl of sixteen, a member of one of our groups, expressed this rather definitely. Having received praise for her cooperation and fine work in preparing food and clearing up, she said, "I love to cook and do kitchen work, and I always do it when my mother is not home. The only time I hate to do it is when my mother tells me to."

ing positive reactions. This is an essential part of the reeducation of attitudes.

After the room is set in order and materials are put away, the worker casually puts on his hat and coat and seats himself near the door. He reads or rather pretends to read. Usually one of the participants in the mêlée notices the worker all set to go and exclaims, "Hey, kids, George is waiting. Come on, let's scram." This has an electric effect. All rush for their coats and hats and file out. Frequently the sedate few put a stop to the disorder by some appropriate remark. In most instances, the treatment goal for these sedate boys is that they, too, should become boisterous, which would be considered an improvement in their case.

This course of events does not have to be followed very long. As some group awareness arises, the periods of havoc completely disappear, never to recur. This is easily understood: the members have matured, developed self-restraint, and have less need for infantile self-indulgence.

At the early meetings the group therapist purchases the food and brings it with him. Later the children assume responsibility for buying frankfurters, soup, cheese, bread, cake, cookies, fruit, cocoa, chocolate, milk, and sugar and such utensils as cups, saucers, spoons, and napkins. It often takes a long time before they take over this responsibility. Girls seem to reach this stage sooner than boys. It is preferable to have food and drinks prepared in the room so that the members can participate. From time to time the group eats in a restaurant for the sake of variety and for the value to be derived from an adjustment to a new situation.

The method of laissez-faire in the matter of table manners should not be used with little children who still have to learn them. We can assume, however, that older children know that their bad manners and aggressiveness are socially unacceptable and employ them because of that very knowledge. This is generally true of all restraint in education and in therapy.

Very young children require more authority than older ones because they have not as yet acquired inner sanctions for their behavior. The socially maladjusted and neurotic have acquired these inner sanctions, but counteract or reject them because of destructive drives. This point is more fully discussed in Chapter VII, pages 229 ff., in connection with the group super-ego.

The growth of order and social attitudes during the eating period is demonstrated by the following quotations taken from our records:

Worker brought the bottle of milk and placed it on the table. He then put the paper cups around at the places where the boys were to sit. He also placed crackers on a plate. As the boys began to sit down, Ike grabbed a handful of crackers. Andy came over and said, "Gee, what a pig," and pushed Ike, taking some of the crackers from him. In the scuffle between the two boys, some of the crackers were dropped and crushed, and thrown to the floor. While the boys were fighting, Louis took some of the crackers from the plate and watched the boys. The others sat down at the table quietly, and watched with interest the two boys who were fighting. Finally, Ike agreed to put some of the crackers back. Since none of the boys volunteered, worker poured the milk in all the cups.

As he finished doing this, all the boys grabbed for crackers, some putting them in their pockets. There was a free-for-all and considerable pushing. Suddenly, there was a stream of milk flowing from Kenneth's paper cup. The sly and satisfied expression on Ike's face indicated that he must have punctured it. Kenneth looked up and saw Ike's expression and said, "You louse, you did this." Kenneth threw his milk at Ike, Ike threw his at Kenneth. The bottle was upset and the milk was spilled on the table and on the floor. The others partially finished their milk, got into the spirit of the thing, and all began throwing milk and crackers around.

When the boys sat down to eat, Milton immediately grabbed for all the food. There were chocolate-covered doughnuts and Milton grabbed more than his share. Zavel grabbed the extra doughnut that Milton had taken and took it away from him and banged him on the hand at the same time. Milton with his open

hand slapped Zavel across the back of the head. Milton told him
that he would sock him once and for all if he didn't stop that, and
sat down to drink his cocoa and eat his doughnut. It was quiet
again for a while.

We find quite a different picture in a second-year group's
record:

At the table, the worker gave the bottle of milk to Saul who
poured. When the worker took the box of cookies out, Ivan (a
new member) made a move to grab the box from his hands. Paying no attention, the worker continued to open the box, which he
then set in the middle of the table. Ivan asked, "Well, aren't you
going to divvy them up?" Ivan insisted, "I still think it's better to
divvy them up." Saul and Karl disagreed with him, saying, "It's
better to take one at a time." Ivan answered, "G'wan, if we divvy
them up, then we know that everybody gets the same—nobody
gets more than the other guy." Saul said, "Suppose the next guy
doesn't want as much as you? A-a-a, that's a baby way—sharing it
up. The best way is like we had last year. We took one at a time
and nobody grabbed."

They had begun eating so that the matter was left as it was—
they took one at a time. But Ivan watched cautiously and when
he saw anybody take a cookie, he took one too. When the process
became too slow for him, he gave one each to the boys and worker
so that he could take one for himself. All put the cookies back into the box, for they were taking them one at a time; only Ivan
kept his in a pile near his cup and saucer. There was a puzzled
look on his face. He seemed to be unable to understand how boys
could give up their crackers. He had already finished his milk but
was saving up the cookies. He said, "I get hungry on the way
home." Saul asked, "Don't you have supper when you get home?"
Ivan: "Sure, but I like to eat them on the way home anyway."

After leaving the building, it is essential that the group
therapist should not travel with one or two of the members to
the exclusion of the others. This would render them "preferred
children," with disturbing effects upon the others. Neutrality
here is most essential. The group therapist must never give
any of his children a feeling of being excluded. If he is going
in the same direction as some of the members of the group, he

must find some excuse for delay or for taking another bus or subway. He can travel only with the entire group or with the majority, but not with one or a few. This is not as important in the later life of the group as it is at the beginning.

For similar reasons the group therapist must not single out any one of the group by remarking about his health, appearance, cleanliness, or other virtues or faults. Such attention not only gives the others a feeling of rejection, but also sets up many emotional repercussions in those who receive such recognition.

We found it necessary for treatment reasons to dismiss from groups, in the eight years of our work with about 750 clients, thirteen members. In each case this was done after at least a year of observation. The child's character was carefully explored and fully discussed before this step was taken. We had to be convinced that he was not accessible to treatment by our method and in three out of four instances the closing of the case was delayed a number of times before it was finally consummated. The delays were occasioned because the child gave some indication of improvement, the other members of the groups changed their treatment of the offending child, or he promised his case worker that he would modify his behavior. Some children were returned for individual treatment because the aggressive boys in the group either traumatized them further or activated their latent masochism or homosexuality. We give here the correspondence with a highly aggressive and destructive boy of fourteen:

Dear Rudolf,

Since you have not been getting along very well in the club, we think it might be best for you to discontinue coming to the meetings for the present.

We are very sorry about this. Maybe after things improve, we can make some other plan for you later on.

Yours truly,

S. R. SLAVSON

Dear Mr. Slavson,

I received your letter in which you said that you thought it might be best for me not to come to the club any more. This was very sad news for me, since my going to the club means so much to me. I realize that I have misbehaved in the past, and I regret that it happened. However, if you would be so good as to permit me to continue to go to the meetings again, I shall try my best to show my appreciation by an improvement in my behavior.

Please let me continue going to the club. If you do, I am sure my behavior won't give you reason to regret it.

Respectfully yours,

RUDOLF WARNER

In this case we stuck to our decision for it was clear to us that this particular boy could not alter his behavior. A year later he came to a meeting of the group with another former member whose case had been closed because of good adjustment. He again expressed his regret at his failure to appreciate the advantages of the "club," and asked to be reinstated. The group therapist referred him to the "office," but Rudolf did not communicate with us. This adamantine stand was taken because it became clear that the freedom of the group aggravated the boy's problem.

Cramped quarters for group meetings induces "mutual invasion," increases irritability and explosiveness, and gives rise to considerable personal aggression and hostility. This magnifies the problems of both the aggressive and the withdrawn. Aggression is activated in some members and the withdrawn children are driven even further into their shell. On the other hand, a very large room activates the running and pursuit impulses. It has the same effect as a playground or a field. The tumult that results heightens the emotional intensity of the children and reinforces their infantile and uninhibited behavior. Once young children, especially those under emotional tension, get into a state of rowdyism, there is little likelihood that they will bring themselves under control. The pitch is rather on the upswing and may reach the proportion of group hysteria requiring interference by the adult.

It is best here, as in all other aspects of Group Therapy, to create a situation that will inherently exert control. The size of the room chosen for meetings should therefore fall between these extremes, and we follow the empirical formula that the room should be five times the area of the furniture necessary for work. It must be well, but not glaringly, lighted and there should be enough windows but not a whole wall or a large area of wall entirely of glass. No glass doors are permitted and, whenever possible, all furniture should be of rough, unfinished wood. No pictures are placed on walls except those that the children hang up themselves. All these conditions are aimed at giving the children freedom of movement and reducing the possibility of personal injury.

We have had a few instances of what seemed like group hysteria. In such cases the therapist peremptorily announced that the meeting was at an end, put away the supplies and tools, asked the children to leave, and locked the door. The members usually ask for "refreshments." The first time the worker takes them out for refreshments, but at subsequent occurrences of such outbreaks he replies that there will be no refreshments that day. Our observations lead to the conclusion that these excesses are a result of faulty combining of children so that the group cannot establish an equilibrium. The function of the therapist as an inhibitor in this and other situations is discussed in Chapter VI.

CHAPTER III

TWO RECORDS OF GROUP MEETINGS

In this chapter we are reproducing records of two meetings. One deals with a girls' group, ages thirteen to fourteen years, the other with a boys' group, ages twelve to fourteen years. No notes are kept by the group therapist during meetings as the children do not know the purpose of the groups and are entirely unaware of the therapeutic intent. They do not know that they are being observed or their doings recorded. This frees the members from the restraint and self-consciousness they might feel if they knew they were being watched.

Girls' Group

The girls at their eighth meeting are seen in a state of unintegrated group life. We meet here Mary, an oral aggressive,[1] who proved so disorganizing to the group that after a year's trial it was necessary to close her case in Group Therapy. She was later placed in an institution.

[1] We designate as *oral aggressive* the individual whose pattern of relationship with other people consists of verbal attack, screaming, cursing, loudness, criticism, quarreling, ordering others about, fault-finding, and other means of making his presence felt through speech in a hostile and aggressive manner. This mechanism is a mild form of oral sadism and seems to stem from frustrations during early infancy and the resultant fixation on an oral level. It can be conceived as the lowest primitivism of behavior save for encopresis, and because of this primitivism is probably untreatable; at least, we have found it so in Group Therapy. Oral aggression is found among boys, but, never to the same degree as among girls, since boys' aggressiveness has the culturally approved outlets through games, fights, and other forms of physical activity. We found it among girls in its extreme and troublesome form. These girls were usually plump, with good complexions, and voracious eaters. In all cases these "loud-mouthed trouble-makers" had to be eliminated because the dynamics necessary for therapy could not be set up by the permissive atmosphere in our groups. For an example of oral aggression, see Chapter V, page 127.

Gladys, severely rejected by her mother who also hated her husband, was constantly compared with the mother's favorite, a younger sister. Gladys was fighting for status in the group, but was frustrated by the indomitable Mary. When a bath sponge she made in the group was used by her father, Gladys talked about it for weeks.

We are also introduced here to Jean, who came to us through a city hospital with conversional abdominal pains and whose lack of assertiveness was so great that she was almost seduced by her father who was jailed for the attempt. Group Therapy released her and at first made her over-rebellious and self-reliant. It was difficult to prevent her from leaving home. After three years of treatment, she became, within the limitations of her own personality, family, and social pathology, adjusted, happy, and constructive.

Louise, a frightened and withdrawn child, was so paralyzed by a group situation that she could not find her tongue. The case worker brought her to the first meeting. (This is an unusual procedure in Group Therapy.) Later Louise came a few times with her cousin on alternate weeks. When the cousin could not come with her, she dropped out.

Ann, a hostile girl, whose aggressiveness was a form of misdirected leadership, greatly improved in her social adjustment. In this record we see how leadership and responsibility make their appearance.

Mamie's overscrupulous, compulsive, and neurotic stepmother made life miserable for her and in this group she found release and a haven. Mamie took care of children after school hours and week-ends to earn a little money for her own needs, but she traveled more than an hour each way to the meetings, they meant so much to her.

Rose, a hypochondriacal, lonesome, friendless girl, daughter of equally hypochondriacal parents, was referred by a local hospital for psychotherapy since no physical basis for her complaints could be found. The family was impoverished.

She was referred to Group Therapy for "socialization" and to develop interests and friends that would diminish her preoccupation with her health which, in addition to other problems, kept her from attending school.

Agnes was the child of a broken home. The father was an infantile, irresponsible person and the mother a helpless woman who suffered from a complication of illnesses. The girl stole money from her mother, but the chief complaint was that she associated with older and, according to the mother, undesirable companions. She was in severe rebellion against her mother and a domineering older brother. The family lived on charity.

We see illustrated in this record some of the satisfactions that come from successful achievement, from friendly interactions with other people, and from communication. We also see the beginnings of a sense of responsibility toward the group's property in relation to setting table, cleaning up, and washing dishes.

Date. January 5, 1938 *Meeting.* Eighth
Weather. Fair and cold

Group. Girls' Group II
Worker. Elinor Schultz
Present. Gladys   Ann
          Mary   Jean
          Rose   Mamie
          Louise   Agnes
Absent. None

When worker arrived shortly before four o'clock, Ann was standing outside waiting for her. The girl greeted worker and said that none of the other girls had come yet. Worker said that perhaps it was a little early and asked Ann if she would like to walk over with her to the store to buy some cookies and milk for the meeting (A). Ann said she would love to and immediately attached herself to the worker's arm. Worker suggested that they go to a different store this time, and Ann pointed to one of two groceries across the street and said that that one looked cleaner (B). She helped worker select the cookies and insisted on carrying the package. She told worker very enthusiastically that she had had some x-rays taken and volunteered the information that the door to the meeting room was open.

When they got back to the building Ann suggested that she should take the package upstairs and wait there for the worker. Worker, having got the keys to the cabinet, went up to the room and found that Gladys and Jean had already arrived. As worker entered the room and greeted the girls, Ann rushed at her saying, "Please, may I have the keys? I want to open up all the cabinet doors" (C).

Worker gave the keys to Ann and asked the other girls how they had got home last week. [They had traveled unaccompanied as a group from a theater to their homes.] Gladys said with extreme disgust, "I'll never go anywhere with that girl again. Honestly, she is the limit. She drives us all crazy. Mary, I mean. She insisted that we get off way before it was time to, and she tried to tell the girls when they were to get off, and she was wrong all the time, and she made such a fuss about it— it was terrible. Honestly, I'll never go anywhere with her again" (D).

Worker told Jean that she was terribly sorry she had forgotten to bring her gloves along; she had thought of them each day, but just that morning she had forgotten to take them with her. She explained that Jean had left them in the back seat of worker's car, and she had not wanted to leave them there all week for fear they would get lost (E). Jean said, "Oh, that's all right, Miss Schultz. It wasn't very cold this week anyway. I didn't need them." A few minutes later Jean walked over to worker and took a nickel out of her pocket and handed it to her quietly, saying, "This is what I borrowed last week." Worker thanked her and took the nickel.

Mary came into the room breathlessly, saying hello to everyone. She walked over to the table where the worker was putting some materials down and faced Gladys, who was sitting at the other side of the table, saying to her, "Well, here's something that will make you feel good. I was sick almost all week. I was sick for three days after" (F). Worker said she was awfully sorry to hear that (G), and Gladys said, "For me, why is that such good news for me?" Her tone was hostile, and she turned very pointedly to the worker and said, "How is your car, Miss Schultz? What did you do with it?" [When the girls had traveled the previous week in the worker's car, Mary vomited twice and soiled the car rather badly both inside and out.] Worker said lightly that the car had needed a good bath anyway (H). The girls laughed in good spirits and began looking for the leather and other materials they had been working with at the last meeting.

Gladys mumbled something accusingly to Mary about getting them all mixed up and making such a fuss on the way home last week and then repeated, "I'll never go anywhere with her again."

Ann said anxiously to worker, "Will you help me cut out the rest of my doll this week?" Worker said she would. Mary and Jean came over to where worker was picking out snaps to put on the leather key holder. Jean asked worker if she would put snaps in her holder, too. Mary said that she wanted her to do the same for her.

Mamie came into the room followed by Agnes and greeted the girls happily. Worker said they had missed her on the trip to the theater last week. Mamie said she was sorry she could not go. Worker greeted Agnes and told her she was very glad to see her again, and Mamie laughingly said, "I had an awful time getting her here." Worker asked Agnes if she had received her letters asking her to come again this year. Agnes said she had and she would have liked to come, but she had been so busy she didn't have any time. She said she was sorry she didn't even have time to answer worker's letters. Worker introduced her to the other girls, and Agnes said, "I came to the meetings last year"; then to worker, "Do you remember my brother? He used to come to the meetings right after me." Worker said she remembered him and asked how he was. Agnes said, "Oh, he's terrible. He's so wild. We just can't do anything with him" (I).

Mamie looked at the other girls' work and then decided she would make something out of leather, too. Agnes took a chair next to the worker. She did not attempt to do anything with the materials, but entered into a conversation with some of the girls about camp, saying that she liked certain counselors and that one of them, whom she referred to as "Jimmy," was an awful "pain in the neck"; that she used to get food and eat it in their tent and though they were all starving, she didn't give them any.

Gladys said to Mamie that lots of things had happened that she didn't know about (J). She asked Mamie to go with her into the hallway, returning a little later. When they came back, worker was standing near the cabinet looking for some material. Gladys made a remark which worker could not hear. Mary responded vigorously, "What's the matter? Have you got a guilty conscience?" Gladys said, "Me? Why should I have a guilty conscience? Someone else should have!" Ann said facetiously, "Oh, how they love each other!" (K). Gladys said, "Oh, yes, I certainly love her!" Her tone was full of bitter sarcasm. "We're such good friends." Jean said smilingly, "Just friendly enemies." Someone knocked at the door and one of the girls answered it.

Case worker, Miss Brown, entered with Louise. Jean, seeing her, said, "Oh, hello, Miss Brown." Group therapist introduced herself, and Miss Brown presented Louise. Therapist told the girl she was glad she was able to come and introduced her to the other girls. Louise's response to the introduction was simply a frightened smile at each of the girls. Miss Brown said, "As long as Louise hadn't come before, I thought I'd come along with her this time." She asked worker if there were some other room where she could do some work. Worker said she would find one for her, but Miss Brown said that the room across the hall was empty and she would go in there.

Louise stood motionless until worker asked her if she would like to take off her hat and coat and told her she could leave them on one of the chairs in the corner of the room. As she did so, Ann came over and brought up another chair to the table for Louise (L). Worker explained to the girl that they just worked or played with any of the material they wanted to, that she might use any of it she liked. Ann offered her some spongex and asked her if she had ever worked with that. Louise shook her head. Ann handed her a piece, which she took. She sat there holding it, and worker looked around for shears which she gave to the girl. Ann said, "Now, you can just cut it in any shape you want." Louise merely looked at her. The same frightened smile seemed to be frozen on her face. She picked up the scissors and automatically began cutting into the piece of spongex. It was obvious that she had nothing in mind, but was simply cutting at random.

Meanwhile Gladys and Mary seemed to be picking away at each other over nothing at all. Just then Rose came in. All the girls greeted her enthusiastically. Worker asked her if she had got home without any difficulty last week. She said she had, and worker introduced her to Louise and Agnes. Rose sat down at the table and picked up some leather. Mary yelled out some measurements at her and said, "That's the size if you are going to cut a key holder." Gladys said, "It doesn't have to be." "Oh, shut up," responded Mary.

Ann had decided there wasn't a large enough piece of spongex for her to make the body of a doll, so she decided to work on some leather. Mary said to Jean, "As soon as you get through putting the snaps in yours, put them in mine first, won't you?" Jean said hers was almost ready (M).

Mary kept yelling "shut up" at every girl who spoke to her,

even if it was only to ask her to pass something. Her tone was loud and bold, though not vicious. Every few minutes she and Gladys would yell at each other. Gladys would shout, "Oh, you're a dope," "Oh, you give me a pain," and Mary would respond vigorously, "Oh, shut up."

Gladys asked what time it was. Worker said it was a little past half past five, and she thought they ought to get ready to have their refreshments. Just then Miss Brown came in and asked if she could sit in the room until Louise was ready to go. As worker got up from the table to put the materials away, Louise turned to her and said quickly, "I think I have to go now" (N). Worker said, "Can you stay and have some refreshments with us?" Louise walked over to Miss Brown and apparently asked her if they were to stay or not. Then she came back and sat down on her chair again.

In the meantime Jean had already given her leather case to worker to put the snaps in and worker had finished it. Mary said, "Whose case did you put the snaps in?" Worker said, "Jean was finished with hers and gave it to me to fit." One of the girls said, "How did you put those in?" Worker showed them a piece of wood that she had made with a small hole in it, into which to fit the protruding part of the snap while she pounded the other part on. Jean said, "Gee, Miss Schultz can do everything." Worker laughed and said, "Well, not everything." Mary said, "She can't give us each a million dollars." Ann answered in defense, "Well, nobody can" (O).

Some of the girls had got up from the table and were moving about the room. Gladys said, indicating Mamie. "We're going out for a few minutes to the washroom." Mary said, "I'm going, too." The three of them were out for a few minutes (P). As they were coming back through the hall toward the meeting room they were talking very loudly, though the conversation was not distinguishable. Suddenly Mary yelled in a temper, "I did not! I did not! I did not!" Her voice sounded very angry, though immediately she began to laugh as did the other girls in the hall and the remaining girls in the room. Ann said, "What are they yelling about?" They came into the room laughing, and Gladys said, looking at Mary, "Boy, has she got a temper!" Mary answered, "Oh, shut up."

A few moments later Gladys announced that she had to go to the rest room again and asked who wanted to come along. All the girls except Louise got up to go or volunteered that they would go along. Gladys said, "No, not all of you at once," and she took some of the girls with her, leaving behind Jean, Agnes, and Rose. Jean said meekly, "Oh, well, we'll go when they come back" (Q).

Worker was putting away some of the materials and the girls continued at their work, standing up around the table. The others came back into the room very shortly.

For no apparent reason Gladys and Mary started wrestling. Mary got a hold on Gladys, her hand pressed hard over Gladys' eyes, forcing her head back. Gladys' face was flushed with excitement and she seemed angered by the power Mary was exerting over her, but as soon as she loosened herself from the grasp she began laughing again. They chased each other around the room, knocking over some of the chairs and pushing part of the materials off the table. Soon the other girls entered into the game, Rose chasing Mamie around the table, then Jean (R). All the girls participated in the horseplay except Louise who was still sitting in her chair, self-consciously watching with a wide-eyed expression. The room was filled with noise, excitement, and confusion. Worker went on putting away the materials without paying attention to the girls.

As she began to set the table the girls quieted down somewhat. Worker picked up the cups and saucers she had placed on the table near Louise and asked the girl if she would like to come downstairs with her to the kitchen and help rinse them out (S). Louise responded with a quick smile and nodded that she would. She followed the worker downstairs, saying nothing. She dried the cups and saucers for worker and helped her carry them back upstairs. Then she resumed her seat again.

Ann and Jean helped set around the cups and put the cookies on the plate. Ann asked worker how many places they would need and if Miss Brown would eat with them. Worker said that she would ask her, and Miss Brown said "Yes," drawing her chair up to the table. [This is a rather unusual procedure, as visitors are not allowed at these meetings.] The other girls had seated themselves, and worker took the seat next to Louise. The girls began eating immediately and yelling at each other with their mouths full. Worker passed some cup cakes to Louise, who shook her head. Worker said, "Are you sure you wouldn't like one? We all get pretty hungry about this time of the evening." Louise said, "No, I had some milk and cookies before I met Miss Brown this afternoon." Worker passed the thin wafers to her and said perhaps she'd rather have these. She took one and said, "Thank you."

The girls went on laughing and making so much noise that the room rang with their hilarity. When the girls had finished practically all the milk in their cups, they started throwing the remaining drops at each other. Gladys picked up a cup of milk that had not been touched and threatened to pour it on Jean. Jean threw the remaining drops of milk in her cup at Gladys (T). Ann said, "Don't you dare throw that milk, Gladys. Maybe somebody wants to drink it." They offered it around the room, but nobody seemed to want it. Meanwhile Mary had thrown her cup, which was empty, at Gladys and hit her in the face with it. The girls reached around the table and pushed and shoved each other. [There is very little doubt in our mind that such excessive misbehavior even for this group was due to the presence of Miss Brown, who had two of the girls under treatment. The case worker should not have stayed for refreshments as her presence caused considerable tension.]

Worker got up and began to clean the table. She took the cups and saucers downstairs herself and washed them. When she came back, the girls had started to put on their hats and coats. Some wraps and books were on a chair. Worker asked to whom they belonged (U). Gladys said, "Oh, those are Mary's. She went downstairs. Let's leave them here." Worker said, "We'll probably meet her on the way down; so perhaps we'd better take them with us." Worker picked up the hat and coat. Gladys grabbed the pile of books, ran out of the room, and set them down in the middle of the hallway (V).

Worker's arms were full carrying a bag of waste paper, Mary's coat, and two milk bottles. Louise was standing near worker. She said, "I'll carry one for you." Worker said, "Oh, that would be fine. I have quite a load here." She handed a bottle to her. Just then Gladys walked back into the room, grabbed one bottle from Louise, the other from the worker, and said, "I'll take them back to the store." Worker suggested that they each take one. Gladys, holding on to the bottles, said, "No, I want to take them both" (W).

Just then Ann came into the room, noticed Gladys with the bottles, and took hold of one, saying, "I'll carry one back." Gladys said, "No, I'm taking them both." Ann did not relinquish her hold on the bottle, but tugged a little harder and said, "No, I want to take one. Why shouldn't I take one?" Meanwhile Louise simply stood and watched with the same wide-eyed expression. Ann was insistent, and Gladys finally released her hold on one bottle. Ann said, "Come on. We'll take them back together" (X). She and Gladys left the room, and Louise followed.

Worker was last, and as she closed the door she noticed Mary's books scattered in the hall. Worker began to pick them up (Y). As she did so Gladys giggled. Jean and Ann helped pick up the books. Jean said she would carry them down.

When they got to the floor below worker asked if any of the girls knew where Mary was. Gladys said, "Oh, I think she is in the washroom. She always goes in there and stays for an hour." When they reached the ground floor, Mary came running down the stairs and thanked worker profusely for bringing her things down. Worker then handed her a leather key case that the girl had finished and had said she wanted to take home with her. Mary said, "Oh, thank you very much. It was so nice of you to remember to bring this down, too."

Worker said good-bye to Miss Brown and Louise and asked if the latter would come back next week. Miss Brown said, "Well, she is going to come every other week. Perhaps next time she can come alone" (Z). Louise said she thought her aunt would bring her. Worker said she would expect to see her, then, in two weeks from that day. Worker asked the rest of the girls if they could remember the meeting if she didn't write to them that week. They all said, "Oh, certainly we could, you don't have to write" (YY).

We read the following in the report of the twenty-fourth meeting three months later: Gladys returned to say to the worker, "Mary would like to borrow a nickel from you." Gladys and Mary were walking together, Gladys with her arm around Mary's shoulder, holding her close (YZ).

SUMMARY OF SUPERVISORY DISCUSSION

(A) The group therapist is placed in a difficult situation as she comes up to the building and finds Ann waiting for her. She asks Ann to go to the store with her which is not desirable. This singles out Ann when upon their return the worker and Ann find the other girls in the room. Ann becomes a preferred child. The group therapist should have bought the food before she came. Failing that, she should have gone up to the room with the girl and either sent out or gone out for the food during the meeting.

(B) We notice that the group therapist encourages Ann to make a decision and accepts Ann's suggestion. This is in line with the general policy of Group Therapy to build up independence and the status of the clients with the adult and wean them away from the domination of adults.

(C) Having received special status by virtue of the fact that she went to the store with the therapist and being somewhat aggressive anyway, Ann pursues her advantage by asking for the keys to open the doors of the closets. We see in this her wanting to be the preferred child and to stand out from the rest of the group.

(D) Gladys at once reveals sibling rivalry with Mary when she attacks her even before Mary arrives. To Gladys a group situation suggests rivalry and strife; something that this group must seek to counteract.

(E and Q) Jean reveals her basic compliance mechanism and submissive character which, however, is compensated for when she gets recognition because of outstanding ability in manual work (M).

(F) Mary's oral aggression makes its appearance as soon as she enters the room. She tells Gladys that she will be glad to hear that Mary has been ill. Her oral aggression is also revealed by the symptom of vomiting when she travels in any automobile, except, significantly enough, in her brother-in-law's car. This may have some meaning in terms of Mary's relation to her sister. The vomiting may be a symptom of a reaction to a rivalry in the family, particularly with her married sister.

(G) Although the group therapist seems sympathetic toward Mary, actually it was a mistake for her to enter into this conversation. The remarks were not addressed to her and she should have stayed out of it.

(H) The group therapist uses humor to reduce the tension created by the girls. In this role she is a neutralizer.[2]

(I) When Agnes mentions her brother as she comes in, the worker makes the mistake of asking how he is. This gives Agnes an opening to express her hostility to him. The group therapist, not being able to take a position in this tirade, unin-

[2] For discussion of neutralizer, see Chapter V, page 119, and for the discussion of the use of humor, see Chapter VI, pages 169 ff.

tentionally seems to agree with Agnes by her silence. It is against good practice in Group Therapy to make inquiries concerning the health or the mental state of the children or members of their families. It would have been better if the therapist had asked, "Is he still a member of the club?" or some such neutral question.

(J) Here the struggle between Mary and Gladys reappears, Gladys now attempting to bring another girl, Mamie, into the complex on her side.

(K and O). Ann attempts to act as a neutralizer in the conflicts between the girls.

(L) When Ann welcomes Louise and helps to ease her way into the group, we note her readiness to assume leadership and her basic friendliness toward others. Usually such socialized behavior in an individual sets a pattern for the other members of the group.

(N) Louise's fearfulness of the group is so great that she attempts to escape through Miss Brown, her case worker. It is evident from reading the record that Louise was brought to the group prematurely. She was not ready for a group experience and it may prove a traumatic situation for her. The question of preparation for groups through individual therapy is now under analysis in one of our studies.

(P) Group morale makes its appearance because of the hostility toward Mary. Mary, having antagonized all the girls, brings them together in that particular feeling. Frequently such antagonism forms a basis for group unity.

(R) Jean participates in the horseplay and (T) throws milk at Gladys. In Jean's case this can be taken as a sign of growth.

(S) The group therapist apparently repeats the mistake of singling out a girl for attention. She asks Louise to go down with her to wash the dishes. It is understandable why she did this. Louise's bewilderment and fear were so great that to have left her alone with a hilarious group would have been very bad. The group therapist was placed in a difficult position and under the circumstances asking the girl to go with her may have been the best way out.

(U) The group therapist again makes an error when she asks whose books were being left behind, instead of either picking them up or ignoring them. She should have known that the girl to whom the books belonged would return to the room to get them.

(V and W). When she asked this question she activated Gladys' antagonism and precipitated her own defeat by the girl.[3] It was a mistake to oppose Gladys in her desire to leave the books in the room to spite her substitute sibling, Mary. The group therapist's insistence on taking the books to Mary placed her in the position of the mother, who always takes the part of another sibling. Hence Gladys defeats the mother (therapist) by scattering Mary's belongings on the floor of the hall. Gladys is now angry and becomes aggressive. This mood was expressed when she grabbed the bottles from Louise and the therapist.

(X) Gladys' anger is mounting and Ann steps in and again acts as a neutralizer. When she says, "Come on, we'll take them back together," she placates Gladys, at the same time creating a situation for the latter girl in which she could relate herself to another person and do something with her.

(Y) The group therapist goes into the hall and sees Mary's belongings strewn on the floor. She says nothing—an excellent move. Had she taken verbal cognizance of the incident, she would have confirmed her defeat in Gladys' eyes and probably would have activated Gladys' further aggressiveness toward the adult. By having ignored it, the group therapist escaped what might have been an unpleasant situation. As it is, Gladys defeats her by giggling.

(Z) The case worker seems to be forcing Louise into the group, which undoubtedly frightens the girl very much. It is

---

[3] For discussion of the defeat of the group therapist, see Chapter VI, pages 147 ff.

felt that Louise had not been adequately prepared for this experience. More individual therapy will be required before this girl can overcome her fear of a group. The group therapist makes a mistake in asking Louise if she will come again.

(YY) The group therapist, by announcing that no reminders would be sent the girls about the meetings, puts them in a position of responsibility and self-dependence.

The antagonism between Gladys and Mary is a real one. With Gladys it is a reliving of a sibling rivalry which is exceedingly intense in her family. Mary's aggressiveness, however, while having its origin in the home, has become diffused. This her case history reveals and we also see it at this meeting when she tells everybody to "shut up" no matter what they say. However, there is little doubt that the situation has been aggravated by the presence of another adult in the room. This is confirmed by experiences in other groups. When an adult other than the group therapist is present (during the early period of a group's existence), we get increased aggressiveness and hilarity or increased withdrawal.

The group therapist must be careful in dealing with the conflict between Gladys and Mary. There is no doubt that the two girls will attempt to draw her into their fight, each one striving to win her over to her own side. It is of extreme importance that she remain completely neutral. Any effort on the part of the girls to bring her into this conflict should be prevented. She can either pretend that she does not hear what goes on or not answer when addressed. The hostility between Mary and Gladys is a socializing situation for the group as a whole. It stimulates the group into emotional activity. If Mary had not been present, the conflict probably would have been between Gladys and Ann and would have been less violent and less vulgar. Conflict is usually necessary for therapeutic purposes, provided it holds the promise of running itself out and bringing about a better relationship.[4] Such was

[4] For discussion of establishment of equilibrium, see Chapter I, page 10.

not the case in this particular situation. Mary's effect upon the group was negative throughout. The disturbances increased. Her mannerisms and attitudes were structuralized in her character and were inaccessible to treatment either by group or by individual psychotherapy. The total environment had to be changed so that it would exert restraining pressure and she was therefore institutionalized.

(YZ) The temporary truce between the two girls was an outcome of the fact that Gladys and not Mary was elected president of the "club." This was a distinct and visible shock to Mary. Being the chief instigator of the idea and quite infantile in her self-regard, it did not occur to her that someone else might be chosen as leader. Her defeat seemed to bring her to her senses, and in order not to lose her position in the group she attenuated the situation by diminishing her attacks on Gladys and actually becoming friendly. This adaptation would be considered therapeutic for some children. Mary's, however, was a character disorder, and it is doubtful if such personality problems are affected by temporary adjustments.

It is noteworthy, however, that social rejection sets up anxiety even in a child of Mary's character and that her social hunger or the need for social survival was strong enough to produce a reaction even in her.

Boys' Group

We have chosen the report given below because it illustrates a situation quite different from the preceding record, namely, a trip. Only four boys are involved, so that the record is easier to follow.

The majority of the boys in this group were seriously disturbed. Perhaps those who were absent were in many respects more difficult than were the members whose acquaintance we make. One of the absentees was Jake. He was the fourth of six children in a poverty-stricken home. The father, a highly disturbed, sensitive, and intellectual man, who imagined himself a poet, did not earn a living for his family and was described as having a schizoid personality. The mother was a disturbed and self-pitying woman. Jake suffered from the domination of two older twin brothers who were bright and active but disoriented, and were also being treated by us in group and individual therapy. He felt extremely hostile to a younger sister who, he thought, caused his mother to neglect him, his hostility being so intense as to cause withdrawal to allay anxiety. Individual psychotherapy was impossible because he would sit for hours and look at the floor without making a sound. The group brought out his hostility. At one stage he grew so aggressive that he attempted to push boys off the sidewalk and threatened them with hammers, but he eventually became much more constructive in the group and made an acceptable adjustment. Two years later he retrogressed and his case was closed as untreatable. Psychiatric diagnosis was probable progressive schizophrenia.

Concerning Joel, another absentee, the case history states, "He has never had a positive influence or relationship in his entire life." The group was the first such experience, and he made rapid strides. Because of his low intelligence and general personality limitations, no other type of treatment was possible for the boy.

Phineas, another boy not present at the meeting, was tried out in three therapy groups before he was able to get to first base. Finally he struck his level with boys four years younger than he. He never missed a meeting. He was very happy at being accepted and being one of a group, and was beginning to show real progress. Two years later he was making an excellent adjustment in a settlement house.

Isadore's father committed suicide and his mother was a nagging woman. He lived in a pathological home environment and was described as having serious personality problems, as being unable to relate himself to the case worker, and as doing poorly at school, though his I.Q. was 117. He was in-

fantile, provocative, aggressive in a childish way, and dependent upon the group therapist to whom he related quite well.
He frequently played with fire at group meetings.

William is one of the boys whose acquaintance we make in
the record. This boy used his intellect as a bid for attention
and a compensation for his other inadequacies. He understood his own problem, as he revealed in his conversation, but
he needed the actual experience in reality which the group
provided to redirect his energies and change his attitudes. He
was still a new boy when the record was written. He is quite
different now. He is "one of the boys," has friends, and does
not have to use "such big words."

Dennis, an overprotected, effeminate boy, had never known
his father, was the son of a "highly neurotic, untreatable"
mother, and was much disturbed by the fact that he could not
make friends. He was maladjusted in school, personally offensive, disobedient, and infantile. He considered all boys "too
tough." He was found untreatable in case work. Because of his
dexterity in arts and crafts and his resourcefulness he soon became a leader in the group, and some of his co-members even
visited him at home. His activities revealed a suicidal trend in
that he destroyed everything he made. On trips he poised
himself on parapets, bridges, and the railings of ferries in most
precarious positions. He went through playfully the motions
of being hanged. Later this trend changed to homicidal
symptoms. He reported to the group that he burned a pigeon
and "it looked like a squab." He also exploded a large empty
oil can. His preoccupation with death was quite inordinate.
This is made clear by the record. Whenever he heard church
bells, he thought of someone dying. He had an excessive interest in fire, and we provided him with facilities to express it in
harmless ways. This interest no longer exists.

Until William joined the group, and despite his difficulties,
Dennis was the most constructive force in it. At the time the
record was written, William had become more a part of the

group and Dennis again was taking his place as leader. He was on the whole much happier, dressed better, and behaved more maturely. He had been a member of the group for about a year. We do not feel that treatment had reached this boy's real problems, however.

Don was a rejected child who was beaten by his father and mother when he was "bad" and particularly when he quarreled with a younger brother with whom he was in severe rivalry. He was referred to us because the case worker felt that "the individual treatment situation cannot reach his fundamental difficulties which he has to work out in real situations where he can learn to compete with boys of his own age." He overcompensated for his inferiorities by self-maximation, such as pretending to know everything and to have seen everything, finding money, and the like. He had a rich phantasy life and imagined himself in positions of great power. At first he was very annoying to the group, but largely because of his strong attachment for the group therapist, he brought himself under control. He, too, played with fire extensively. He made "surprising progress" and became a part of the group. Though he had no friends when he came to us and could not get on with boys, his adjustment in this respect is now normal.

Roland was a product of an unfeeling mother who disciplined him harshly. He reacted to her rejection by being spitefully annoying and overactive and very hostile and aggressive in the home. He always stayed at home, having no friends or outside interests, and made the place unlivable for his four siblings and his mother. On the other hand, outside the home, he was extremely withdrawn and shy. After a period of eleven months in a group and six weeks in camp, we read the following from the case worker's report: "Roland, who used to be a miserable, withdrawn child, has matured extremely well. The boy told the worker that he 'loved the club.' He enjoys going on the different trips and outings. He is generally enthusiastic about the group. The worker feels that because of the client's

innate limitations the center of his treatment was the group."
The group therapist reports: "Roland is greatly interested in
the group. His maturity is exemplified by the fact that now
(aged twelve and a half years) he earns money by selling shop-
ping bags in the market and makes many copper and leather
objects in the group which he sells to friends and relatives."
A follow-up study of the boy revealed him as a normal, constructive, well-adjusted boy at home, in school, and in all
other social relations.

Date. December 25, 1938 *Meeting*. Thirty-eighth
Weather. Cold *Group*. Boys' Group VIII
Trip to Museum *Worker*. Harry Wagner
  of Natural History *Present*. Dennis *Absent*. Jake
  William Joel
  Don Phineas
  Roland Isadore

When worker arrived he saw Dennis being chased on the
street by a member of another therapy group. Upon seeing
worker Dennis returned. The boy who had chased him told
worker that when he had hurt his head on a stone, Dennis vin-
dictively said, "Good for you!"

Don also came early. He was dressed up in his new suit,
coat, and felt hat, of which he was very proud and careful. He
asked, "Are you going on a trip?" Worker said he did not know
what the club would decide (A). Don followed worker into the
building when worker went in to find out about the new cabinet. When they returned Dennis began to tease and provoke
Don. This went on for some time with Don paying little attention. Suddenly he lashed into Dennis, hitting him viciously
around the body (B). Dennis dropped to the steps of the building, wailing that he was "dying." Don said, "That'll teach you
a lesson." Dennis said, "You took me by surprise." By that time
William and Roland had arrived. Don and Roland remarked
on how nice William looked (C).

William looked very neat, his hair was combed, his face ruddy, and he was wearing a colorful wool mackinaw. He took the compliments with the indifferent air of a man of the world who is surprised that anyone should think his neatness unusual. William had seen another group of boys gathered around worker and said, "I know why you take charge of a club. You want to learn about children. I know a teacher who does the same thing for experience." Worker said that he did it only because he liked to be with boys. William said, "I'm different. I like to be alone in soliloquy [meaning solitude] surrounded by books, just like a hermit." He then spoke of Bellamy's *Looking Backward,* and said, "Bellamy made quite an impression on me. The story takes place in the twenty-first century." William quoted a whole passage from the book dealing with Bellamy's statements on the part aristocracy played in causing the wretched conditions of the poor.

The question of what the group ought to do then came up. Roland who had a piece of leather in his hand said, "I promised to make something for my sister. I hope we are going to work inside today." He stood near worker until the group started to argue about what they were going to do: stay inside and work or go on a trip.

Roland and William wanted to stay indoors and work. Dennis and Don wanted to go on a trip (D). Dennis said that since it was rarely nice and it was Sunday, it would be good to take advantage of the nice weather and go on a trip. Don suggested going to the Museum of Science and Industry, but Dennis said there was not enough money and proposed visiting the Museum of the City of New York. William said that was not right, the name was the New York Historical Society. Dennis said, "You don't know what you're talking about." William said he was sure he was right.

The matter was dropped, and Don asked for worker's opinion whether they should take a trip or work indoors. Worker said that he couldn't decide; it was up to the boys (E). William said he thought that the museum closed early because of the holiday. Dennis said it wasn't so. The vote stood three to one for working indoors. Finally Don said, "I change my vote. I'm going to work inside." Dennis followed the group into the meeting room (F).

There were some people working in the room on an exhibit for a bazaar. They said that Mr. Powers, the superintendent of the settlement house, had given them permission to use the room. Worker said that he used the room every Sunday at the same time, and that Mr. Powers had just given him the key. The man in charge said the room would be free in a few minutes. Dennis said to William, "Now are you satisfied?" The latter did not reply. Dennis, William, and Don began to wrestle. After a while, Dennis tied a string to the closet door, went in, and closed it after himself (G).

Roland asked worker to open the supply closet and said he would work in a corner of the room. Worker suggested he should wait till the people had left, as they said they would be through in a few minutes. Roland agreed (H). A man entered and asked if anyone had a drill which would make a quarter-of-an-inch hole in a piece of wood. Roland asked worker to let the man use our drill. He volunteered (I) to drill a hole, but in doing so split the wood. He then drilled another hole in one of the pieces and, supervised by the stranger, successfully completed his work. He stood by and watched a strange boy pull nails out of a piece of wood and volunteered to help. The other members of the group were still wrestling at the other end of the room. When it looked as if the people who were occupying the room would not be finished for a long time, worker suggested leaving. All agreed (J), Roland saying, "My sister will be disappointed."

Once outside, the group decided to go to the New York Historical Society. On the way to the station, Don held on to worker's arm, but said nothing because William was doing all the talking. William walked near worker. He asked worker,

"Are you married?" Worker said he wasn't. William said, "Good. I know a young man who married a girl, and now they are starving." William told worker how the *Adeste Fideles* came to be written. He then said, "I would like to be like Mendelssohn and compose beautiful music." He said he had just read the life of this composer and was very much impressed by it.

By this time, the group had reached the station. William stood by worker on the elevated but said nothing. When the change was made to the subway train, William sat next to worker. Roland said nothing either on the way to the elevated or in the train. Suddenly he said, "I have to be home by five." William answered, "What, we just started!" Roland, intimidated, said, "Half past five will be all right." William saw a man reading the paper and said, "Look at that headline. [It said that the United States was drifting into war with Germany and Japan.] Two senators make a statement, and a cheap paper makes it sound differently. My teacher told us that *The Times* is the only impartial paper." By that time the train had arrived at the destination.

William said, after looking into the street, "Where are we? I don't recognize the place." Worker asked a policeman how to get to the museum. The policeman directed worker, and referred to the elevated as a railroad. William laughed at this. He said, "There's a certain policeman who comes into our place [a store in which he worked] and quotes Shakespeare while he takes food. I used to think all policemen were stupid." Dennis said, "You would."

William spoke about books and philosophy until the group reached the building. When he saw the inscription on the building, "The New York Historical Society," he said to Dennis, "See, what did I tell you?" The building was closed, and Dennis said, "I make a motion that the club go without food and visit the Hayden Planetarium" (K). William and Don said that it cost too much. Roland said it would take too much time and he would get home too late. Then Dennis suggested visiting the Museum of Natural History. The other boys all agreed. On the way William whistled the *Internationale*.

While entering the Museum, William grabbed Don's hat and said, "Let me have it. I look nicer with a hat in my hand." He kept the hat despite the latter's protest and said, "It adds to my social prestige." However, Don grabbed it out of his hand. William stayed close to worker, remarking on every exhibit. One of the exhibits was an Indian group. He said that his uncle had known an Indian who was the last of the warlike Indians. Roland asked, "Is the Indian still alive?" William said, "No, I think he died around 1912," and informed worker that "those Indians were very belligerent. 'Belligerent' comes from the Latin, 'bellos,' meaning war" (L). About four o'clock William said, "Let's go home. We can come back another time and visit another floor."

Roland did not enter into conversation in the museum, following the group from exhibit to exhibit. He exclaimed from time to time, "Look at this! Look at this!" He stopped in front of the Indian wigwams. He also saw an exhibit in which a mummied head of an Indian was enclosed in glass. He asked worker, "Is that real?" Worker read the inscription and said it was. Roland said, "Gee!" A little later, Dennis, who was behind, called the group over to look at two Indian mummies. Roland shuddered (M). Dennis said, "What are you afraid of? They are dead" (N).

In the subway, Dennis sat alone, opposite the group. He got up a few times, walked around, then sat down again. On the way to the museum, Dennis walked alone, behind the group, looking into store windows. He caught up to the group near the New York Historical Society. One of the first exhibits at the Museum of Natural History showed a man and a woman from Tibet. Dennis said, "I have an uncle that visited Tibet." The others laughed. Dennis wandered off alone during this part of the trip as he usually did.

Don followed the boys from exhibit to exhibit, but said nothing. The same thing was true on the way to the automat. He held on to worker's hand, but as William dominated the conversation he could say nothing.

When the group left the museum, William walked with worker and said, "You ought to decide more questions for the boys" (O). Worker replied, "You boys are intelligent enough to decide for yourselves." William countered this by saying, "Well, anyway, you ought to suggest more." Worker agreed to do this. After a while William said, "I know, you want to make this club like a democracy. My teacher said that sometimes a dictatorship is better than a democracy, if they have a good dictator. In Russia they have a good dictator, Lenin—I mean Stalin. I read about Russia and found that they have the best educational system in the world."

By this time the rest of the group, which was behind, caught up. William said, in the course of the endless flow of conversation, "I'm a neurotic. I have a—what do you call it—a neurosis." He asked if worker knew what a neurotic was. Worker said he didn't, and asked William how he knew he was a neurotic. "I find it hard to make friends, I can't find anyone who thinks like I do. I have no one to confide in, not even my mother" (P). Dennis, who was walking next to him, said, "I'm sorry for you." William and Dennis discussed friendship. Soon it developed into a wild quarrel. Dennis said he couldn't be friends with William because the latter laughed at his own jokes. William retaliated by saying, "Do you think you have a nice personality? You're loud and boisterous."

After this discussion subsided, William turned to worker and asked him what his goal in life was. Worker said his goal was helping others and developing his own personality. Dennis responded by saying that his goal was death (Q). William exclaimed in surprise at this and Dennis explained that most people were afraid of death, but he was not. William said, "I'm afraid to die. I hope I die a natural death." He asked if worker believed in reincarnation, and worker said he had no views on the subject.[5] William said, "Boy, I like philosophical subjects!" Roland chimed in at this point, "You certainly use big words." By this time the group had arrived at the automat. William said, "Boy, I'm going to eat!"

Worker went upstairs to save chairs after giving each boy money to buy his food. Don was the first one to get his food. He came up to the balcony and barely made the table. He poured his coffee into a glass. It was very hot and he spilled part of it. As worker was coming up with his tray, he met Don going down for some utensils. He had two quarters in his hand and said, "Look at what I found." Worker said, "That's swell; where did you find it?" (R). Don said he found it on the table next to the one on which the group was eating. He said this with a mischievous twinkle in his eye, and both he and worker laughed. Don then said, "I didn't really find it. It's mine." He soon returned and ate his food quietly.

Dennis finished before William, who had brought his food up last. He had shopped very carefully, it seemed, for he had bought coffee and two kinds of cake, each kind two for a nickel. He cut the cake with a knife, and when Dennis laughed at that, William said, "I eat daintily." Dennis asked him for some of his cake. William wouldn't give him any. Dennis

[5] In this connection, it may be of interest to note Dr. Paul Schilder's formulation of the significance of the attitude toward death in treatment. He says: " . . . every individual carries with him a private philosophy of death. It is very often of great importance for later actions. Sometimes it is difficult to find out which parts of an ideology are efficient and which are not. Pious Catholics may believe theoretically in heaven and hell but may forget about it completely when they start with their suicidal attempts. It is very often a difficult task to find out which parts of an ideology are efficient and which are merely accepted without inner belief and without consequence for further action. In a case of Bromberg and myself, an elaborate ideology existed that God is torturing in hell and the patient was in constant fear of death and eternal torture. To bring these ideas into a clear intellectual discussion helps the obsession neurotic patient considerably. I do not think that any psychotherapy is complete in which the death ideology of a patient is not more or less completely revealed." The Analysis of Ideologies as a Psychotherapeutic Method, Especially in Group Treatment, *American Journal of Psychiatry*, 93: 601–617, November 1936.

waited until William lifted a piece of cake to his mouth, pushed it against his face, and said, "Choke." William did not say anything. Dennis wanted to put mustard in the ketchup and mix up all the spices. Roland didn't let him. Dennis then took worker's empty plate and made believe he was a chef preparing food. He poured out a little ketchup, then added mustard, saying, "Now a little mustard," and added salt, pepper, and so forth (S).

William had finished eating and said, "Now that I'm finished, let's continue our talk about death." Dennis said, "Death doesn't bother me. I could eat a whole pumpkin pie, and watch a doctor operate on a man, and take all his guts out" (T). William seemed quite flabbergasted at such nonchalance and was unable to find words to answer. The other boys did not take part in this conversation.

After the conversation about death, worker got up, put on his coat, and walked to the exit. On the way out, Roland walked with worker and asked when the group was to meet the following week. Worker said he would send him a card. Roland and worker waited outside for the others, and Roland said concernedly, "Where are they?" Soon the three boys burst out by another exit and laughed happily at their stunt.

William asked worker which train he was taking. Worker said the Eighth Avenue. The boy said, "I'll go with you" (U). The other boys took an I.R.T. train together. Walking down to the station, William asked worker what he was studying for. Worker thought best to say at this point that he was studying to be a teacher. William asked, "Why do you have to go to school so long? You graduated from college." Worker said that he was specializing in a subject. William said, "You know, most people have the wrong attitude toward school. This attitude is a result of the educational system." Worker and William arrived at the station, and after the latter asked worker how to get home, the two parted. William had stuttered a little again that afternoon (V).

(A) At the very outset Don asks the group therapist if they are going on a trip. The therapist counteracts this effort at dependence by stating that it is up to the boys themselves to decide what they want to do.

(B) Dennis' aggressiveness makes its appearance soon after he leaves the struggle with a boy from another group. He turns upon Don who in a fairly mature manner attempts to ward off Dennis' sadistic efforts at teasing him. However, frustration tolerance in Don is not very high and he lashes out at Dennis who reveals his preoccupation with death by announcing that he is dying.

(C) The boys note William's nice clothing, showing that their awareness of one another has greatly increased. (This is the thirty-eighth meeting as compared with the eighth meeting of the girls' group.)

(D, E, F) A social situation develops. When the boys plan where they should go, there is real group unity and the boys show capacity to discuss their problems with the intent of solving them. There is no haggling or quarreling.

(G) Dennis' interest in death and dying reveals itself in an interesting symbolic form. He goes into a totally dark, airless closet and shuts himself in it.

(H, I, J) There is considerable social reaction on the part of all the boys. They are willing to wait until the other people go out of the room without any expression of resentment or disappointment, and change their plans to meet a reality situation without demurring. Roland shows increased ability to withstand frustration.

(K) A sense of reality appears when Dennis suggests that they go without food in order to visit the Hayden Planetarium. In the past, they would have demanded both the food and the trip.

(L) William's verbal obsession reaches a high point when he traces the Latin derivation of "belligerent."

(M) Roland's basic fearfulness, which he had overcome considerably since his membership in the group, is apparent when he sees the mummies.

(N) Dennis' preoccupation with death reappears when he questions Roland, "What are you afraid of? They're dead"; and again (Q) when he states that his goal is death, and later (T) when he says that he could eat a pumpkin pie and watch a doctor take the guts out of a man. Even William is flabbergasted at this.

(O) William evidently feels very insecure with other boys. He "talks big," and uses complicated words to compensate for his feeling of social inadequacy, even though he is intellectually superior to the others in the group. He seeks to dominate the group by this method and because he wishes to dominate, he suggests that the worker ought to dominate more than he does. We must note in this connection also that William is new and has not yet accepted a permissive and tolerant relationship among the members of the group and between the members and the worker.

(P) William reveals insight into his problem when he says that he is neurotic and cannot make friends. However, one feels that his comment shows only a superficial kind of attempt and is indicative rather of a resistance and exhibitionism than of a genuine desire to correct his behavior. The group therapist does well in the situation when he pretends that he doesn't understand what the word neurosis means. This prevents William from continuing his discussion along these lines and perhaps gives the boy more security with the group therapist than he would otherwise have.

(R) The group therapist displays tact when he does not deny Don's claim that he found money. If the therapist had expressed doubt, Don probably would have insisted that he did find the money, thereby defeating the adult.

(S) Dennis displayed his infantile patterns on a number of occasions, especially when he mixed condiments.

(U) The group therapist is in difficulty when William attaches himself to him and the two go off by themselves to the subway. Fortunately in this group, this is not of serious consequence, because the other three boys who had been in groups for two years feel secure enough with the adult not to resent it. Otherwise it might have produced a difficult situation. William goes with the group therapist because he is afraid to be left alone with the boys, having had no experience with a group before. It is quite noticeable that this boy was anxious throughout the trip as revealed by constant talking, by demanding attention, by such extravagant behavior as grabbing the hat out of another boy's hand, by speaking loudly about the exhibits, and by running around in the museum.

(V) Perhaps the most significant symptom of his anxiety is the fact that his stuttering returned at this meeting.

William and Dennis are instigators in this group, each in his own way: one intellectually, the other physically. Both have their value from the point of view of psychotherapy in activating the group.

CHAPTER IV

THE CHOICE OF CLIENTELE

WE have already pointed out in connection with Referral Summaries that, in choosing clientele for therapy groups, the symptom picture is initially relied upon and not clinical or diagnostic categories. Where the psychiatric diagnosis is not definite, the behavior pattern of the prospective client is the chief consideration in accepting or rejecting a child for treatment. The accepted psychiatric classifications, such as psychosis, neurosis, psychopathy, behavior disorder, habit or conduct disorder, character disorder, are not always reliable as criteria for placement in a therapy group. A specific pattern of behavior may be caused by any of these conditions or by a combination of them. We found comparatively few clients who presented a clear diagnostic picture. Usually the symptoms are mixed and it is frequently necessary to supplement the diagnostic statement with such modifying phrases as "mixed neurosis," "with neurotic traits," or "behavior disorder of habit and conduct types with compulsive qualities."

We are prepared to say with some degree of certainty that clients with unmistakable psychoses or psychopathy and severe behavior disorders do not respond to free group pressure and are therefore a poor treatment risk in Group Therapy. However, one cannot be completely certain that a child is, for example, truly psychopathic. It is therefore advisable to test the client, whenever possible, in an actual group situation for a prolonged period of time to see how he responds. It is well known that the same symptoms may be produced by different causes and sometimes it takes a long period of observation to determine just what are the mechanisms behind a child's behavior. In some instances, the child's difficulty cannot be removed by Group Therapy; in others, through free activity in a permissive culture, the child finds an adequate psychic equilibrium, as his individuality receives recognition and acceptance and he has the opportunity to function according to his own inner needs; in still others, the new environment and the new attitudes of the adult and of the group suffice to correct personality maladjustments and dissocial behavior.

In a study of Group Therapy at the Jewish Board of Guardians, Gertrude Goller found that the combination of four conditions is necessary for complete success in Group Therapy: 1) the child must be under thirteen years of age; 2) he must have had inadequate social contacts; 3) he must be neurotic or have neurotic traits; and 4) he must have been unable to get along with children or have a need to express aggression. These four "have to be combined for completely successful use of Group Therapy. At least three . . . have to exist for partially successful use of Group Therapy."[1] These conclusions were arrived at through a statistical analysis.

The important point must be kept in mind that in Group Therapy (as in all psychotherapy) the client must take his own course. The therapeutic situation is one in which he is permitted and helped to do so. Psychological determinants for what appear to be the same maladjustments may be quite different, and because of that they require different situations. Since a therapy group supplies a *neutral environment*, each member can take from it whatever his needs may be. The overaggressive child finds relief from his anxiety in such a group, while the shy and withdrawn overcomes his fears.

The basic criterion for a child's suitability for a therapy group is his desire to be accepted, to be with a group and a

[1] From a dissertation, entitled Criteria for Referral to Group Therapy in a Child Guidance Clinic, submitted to the Smith College School for Social Work in partial fulfillment of the requirements for degree of Master of Social Science, 1942, pages 39–40.

part of it. The reader will recall that we described this longing as social hunger. The presence of this hunger makes group treatment prognosis a hopeful one. The child (or adult) who is genuinely desirous of making a place for himself in a group of his peers will give up egoic mechanisms and will curb offending behavior. Social hunger, combined with the other needs met by a therapy group, disposes the child to adapt himself to a social situation and adopt values, attitudes, and behavior approved by the group—a process that inevitably leads to social recovery, even though the basic character structure may not be altered. We feel, however, that when the therapeutic group experience occurs early enough in the life of the child and in the early stages of the problem, character, too, is affected.

Rules or criteria for choosing clientele are as yet not clearly defined. To a considerable extent one must rely here upon judgment. We know, however, that the children who respond with eagerness to the prospect of joining a club when the case worker or intake worker suggests it, are among those who have made the best recoveries. This seems to be true even though there were among them a small number of boys and girls who used the group for their own selfish and power drives and had to be "closed out."

Another general assumption that can be made as a result of our observation as to the fitness of children for groups is their attitude toward siblings. Children with very intense hostility to brothers and sisters cannot accept a relation with other children. They carry over their destructive feelings into the new situation. They attack fellow group members, vie with them for attention, and monopolize the adult. Destructive criticism, interference, and physical attack instigated or carried out by them render the therapeutic process and relations in the group ineffective. Clients with very strong hostile feelings toward siblings have to have them resolved through individual treatment first, before they become fit to participate in groups. However, where the sibling rivalry is not very extreme, the child can be treated through Group Therapy exclusively. Although group relations are very helpful in treatment here, there must be a minimal facility in the child to make use of relations. When this facility is altogether absent, as in extreme behavior (conduct) disorders, group treatment has to be postponed until the client can work out a preliminary relation with an individual. These and similar considerations determine the timing of the referral to a group, that is, the stage in treatment at which the child can accept a group and gain most from it.

In the following pages of this chapter are given some criteria for discerning suitable clients for Group Therapy. They were derived from our own observation and experience and are to a large extent tentative. The list is therefore of necessity incomplete as other data will undoubtedly emerge through further observation.

We have for convenience grouped them in three categories: Social Maladjustment Problems, Typological Criteria, and Treatment Needs.

SOCIAL MALADJUSTMENT PROBLEMS

The most obvious reason for referring children to Group Therapy is "social maladjustment." Concluding a statistical study of the use made of Group Therapy by the Psychiatric Case Work Division of the Jewish Board of Guardians, the committee of case workers who made the study states:

. . . the outstanding fact noted is that . . . the category "social relationships" predominates, both as an area of problems and as a means of treatment. . . . Among the problems presented by the clients, "difficulties in social relationships" represent 31% of all problems, and is closely followed by the category "overt character manifestations" which accounts for 27% of the problems. . . . With regard to the purposes for which the referral was made, "social experience" represents 67% of all the statements made on this point in the referral summaries, and there is no other single category which has any appreciable percentage. This would seem to indicate that the case workers want their clients to have a social experience, regardless of the type of problem which the client presented.

. . . in response to the question: "For what purpose have you used the Group Therapy Department?" 38% of the replies were to the effect that Group Therapy was used to provide the clients with a "social experience" . . . ; in response to the question: "In what ways do you feel the Group Therapy Department has been helpful?" 38% of the replies were to the effect that Group Therapy has been most helpful in providing social experience.

This consistent emphasis on "social experience" should not be surprising or unexpected in view of the nature of Group Therapy, as indicated by the name. However, this emphasis should not obscure the many other uses which have been made of Group Therapy.[2]

Children who are unable for various reasons to utilize group situations constructively, whether in the home, at school, or at play, are evidently suffering from a character malformation, behavior disorder, or neurotic conflict which makes acceptable adaptation to a group difficult or impossible. These children need correction of their early traumatic experiences. They need to change their perceptions of people and their feelings toward them and toward themselves. The numerous psychic tensions that grow out of depriving, frustrating, rejecting, or debasing family relations, inadequate mental or physical equipment, or bad habit formations can be counteracted in specific cases through love, confidence, acceptance, and a positive relation with the therapist and other members of a group.

Social maladjustment proceeds from many causes. There is no one cause that blocks or vitiates the ability to get along with people. In evaluating the services of a group to a given

[2] See pages 100 ff.

child, it is necessary to ascertain, whenever possible, exact reasons for his maladjustment.

Paul (see Chapter VIII, pages 288 ff.) could not integrate with a group of boys because the mother's preference for his younger sister and her rejection of him made him desirous of being a girl and a baby. Other boys threatened this unconscious craving. Ivor Brown (Chapter VIII, pages 259 ff.) played with little girls because he was convinced he was a girl. Ray Rosen (Chapter VIII, pages 237 ff.) was so completely rejected by her three sisters and mother that her expectation of rejection became structuralized into a state that may be described as *man-shock*. John Sloan's antisocial behavior (Chapter VIII, pages 248 ff.) was conditioned by his feelings of inferiority due to size, rejection, and social stigmatization. Some children withdraw because of an overwhelming fear of being hurt, because of unconscious homosexuality, or because of guilt in connection with masturbation. There are those who fear their all-pervading aggressiveness and withdraw rather than reveal it. In others, insecurity or frustration causes their energies to be converted into self-sustaining, aggressive, antisocial acts. It is therefore clear that the concept of "socialization" has to be analyzed in relation to specific intrapsychic and socio-pathological factors.

Aggression in children is one of the common reasons for referral to a therapy group. A detailed discussion of aggression, its etiology and its significance as a mechanism of adjustment, would fall outside the intention and scope of the present volume. It will be necessary, however, for our purpose here to describe briefly its manifestations in Group Therapy clients.

Aggression is a normal mechanism of nature, for it aids survival. In human beings aggression becomes undesirable and even dangerous when it becomes so intense and diffuse as to interfere with the essential adjustments in a society or when it becomes a threat to other people. Aggression is found in children with prolonged infancy, but in these cases it is usually devoid of intent to hurt or injure. There is little, if any, hostility involved. Such children are disturbing, but they can be brought under control both through pressure of the group and through the limitations imposed by the group therapist.

Aggression that proceeds from an *extreme* behavior disorder with underlying, though not manifest, anxiety does not yield as easily to group pressure. We found these children able to throw off easily any threat that the group might offer them. Even direct restraint and prohibition on the part of therapists did not check such children and it was necessary in several instances to remove them from the group. Some gave up the symptomatic behavior in the group, but the characterological conditions that provoked it remained and were acted out in other relations through aggression and destruction. It will be readily seen that the aggression of a psychopath cannot be curbed by any mild group pressure such as a therapy group offers. We, therefore, do not accept them into our groups when the diagnosis can be definitely established in advance. The neurotic child whose aggressiveness proceeds from intense anxiety and is more or less compulsive, gains considerable release from acting out his difficulties in a free, unrestraining environment and most of these children give up their aggressive pattern.

Submissiveness as a symptom of social adjustment yields to Group Therapy. Clients with this characteristic have become progressively more self-assertive and independent. Cases in point that are mentioned in this volume are Jean (Chapter III, pages 53 ff.) and Ray Rosen and Ivor Brown (Chapter VIII, pages 237 and 259). Overcoming submissiveness and compliance not only has a corrective effect upon character formation; it is also important as a *social prophylactic*. Girls who have to gain status and acceptance through ingratiation or compliance are likely to become sex delinquents. They readily submit to sex demands because such demands represent acceptance of them as persons and as women. For the same motive boys may participate in homosexuality in a passive role or join gangs in committing crimes because in doing so they feel accepted by the gang, as in the case of John Sloan (Chapter VIII, pages 248 ff.).

Suggestibility leads to similar behavior. Having been deprived of personal autonomy as a result of early, repressive home relations, boys and girls readily take on patterns of behavior and attitudes from others in their environment. When the environment is destructive, they adopt a dissocial way of life. The difference between this response and *compliance* lies in the fact that whereas compliance is used in order to become accepted and part of a group, suggestibility does not necessarily have such a motivation. It is rather a symptom of dependence and lack of self-reliance. A therapy which counteracts submissiveness, compliance, and suggestibility has definite value in preventing delinquency.

Withdrawal is characteristic of a large number of our clients. They are self-effacing and unassertive, lack the desire to participate in the ordinary doings of a group, and seem detached from activities and people. A therapy group supplies such children with transitional experiences that overcome self-absorption and fear of people.[3]

Habit malformations that interfere with social adjustment are found among many children under treatment in social agencies and clinics. It is necessary in social treatment to help such children to overcome them. In cases where the home has failed to establish appropriate habits of cleanliness, dress, and manners, it is essential that these should be corrected in treatment. Many boys and girls are unable to act or dress in an acceptable manner and as a consequence are rejected, ostracized, or persecuted by their peers. If allowed to continue in social isolation because of this, they find many antisocial or asocial channels of gratification. In an attenuated social ma-

[3] See also discussion of schizoid reactions, pages 95 ff.

trix, the child can gradually grow, through imitation and identification, from his primitivism to social awareness.[4]

TYPOLOGICAL CRITERIA

Other criteria for clients may be described as typological.[5] A number of these will be discussed briefly at this juncture: the hyperkinetic, motor, originative, phantasy-laden, autistic, egoic, and schizoid; and the emasculated boy.

The hyperkinetic or overactive child is always on the go and is constantly in trouble with others because his overactivity disturbs everyone around him, especially adults. The home suffers because such intense activity creates a constant emotional flux and physical disorder and keeps the family and other groups in a state of imbalance. The cause of such behavior can be 1) an organic condition, such as hyperthyroidism; 2) physical or psychological compensation for organic or physical inferiority; or 3) purely psychological determinants, such as anxiety, sex conflicts, feelings of inferiority, excessive power drives. Group Therapy will be of some, though little, value to clients in the first of these three categories until the organic imbalances are rectified. The group can be of considerable value to children in the second category. Those in the third category, however, are readily reached through Group Therapy.

The motor-type child is one whose major interest is in doing things. There is a tendency on the part of modern educators

---

[4] See the case of Deby, Chapter VII, pages 214 and 218.

[5] The writer is quite aware that in making such classifications he lays himself open to the criticism that he is invoking the old, outmoded "faculty psychology" or "type psychology." While he is aware of the inadequacy of these psychologies *as systems*, it does become necessary to use some of these concepts to convey meanings. While the old "typological classification" is no longer employed by the most authoritative psychologists—each person being a blending of several or many "types"—observation of individual behavior forces the conclusion that some individuals have predominant characteristics that seem to approach these categories.

and psychologists to deny or minimize the existence of the visual, aural, and motor types of personalities. Observation of children in free-activity schools indicates, however, that if there are no such "types," some children quite definitely behave as though they had a preference for one or another of these methods of learning and expression. Results of tests of delinquents and problem children seem to point to the conclusion that a predominant number fall into the motor-preference group. This would indicate that schools which impose abstract (visual and oral) learning create problems for such pupils. For there is very little doubt "that emotional responses are set up when there is no adequate response that can be made to a situation, and that inability to make adequate response is more often the cause of emotions than are emotions the cause of peculiar behavior."[6] The child of the motor-preference type is often driven by his school into unsuitable occupations or responds to inactive education and recreation in what appears to be a neurotic manner. Such children can be said to be *allergic to school* and the activity provided in a therapy group gives expression to the motor drives of the individual with beneficial effects.

The originative child is one who derives pleasure from inventing, experimenting, investigating, and doing new things. The originative person as a type has been recognized by psychologists as differentiated from the reformer or adapter. The drive to origination, when frustrated, may become very disturbing, and as all frustration induces either aggression or regression, many such children become "problems." The artist, the inventor, the philosopher, the scientist, and the social visionary are usually originative persons. In children this tendency seeks expression in manual work (art, scientific experiments, work with tools) and in phantasy. Such children are

[6] Harriet Babcock, The Mental Functioning of Exceptional Children, *Proceedings of the Second Institute on the Exceptional Child of the Child Research Clinic of the Woods School*, Langhorne, Pa., 1935, page 13.

unable or find it difficult to adjust to routines and to inhibiting or frustrating regulations. In free-activity progressive schools pupils of this type make remarkable progress in personality development and in health. A therapy group, as our records show, is eminently suitable for children of this nature, for they find release and satisfaction through creative work and from the recognition that comes to them through it. They have here a field for concretizing their imagination and bringing their phantasy to fruition. Concrete work holds them down to reality and prevents and corrects schizoid trends.

The phantasy-laden child whose inner stress is converted into phantasy and daydreaming is brought closer to reality (actuality) through expression in some concrete form, such as the arts and crafts and other types of manual work. Our records as well as those of other therapists show that when a painting, a piece of sculpture, a marionette play, or a story expresses the latent content of the patient's problem, it has a therapeutic effect. One of the fifteen-year-old girls drew a picture of a woman. The worker commented on the fine work. The girl quickly replied, "I don't like it. She is too fat." Worker: "Don't you like fat women?" "No," came the instantaneous reply, "my mother is fat."

Because the client can find expression for unconscious strivings and phantasy through creative activity, it should be employed in treatment. This is especially true of children. A sixteen-year-old boy is described by a case worker as "sensitive, soulful, imaginative, retiring, and very unhappy." He displayed real talent in sculpture. While working with clay he once remarked, "I love to work with clay. It is so friendly. You can trust it." In this instance the boy was experiencing probably for the first time in his life a feeling of security—through materials. This feeling, if fostered, permeates other relations.

The tendency to escape into phantasy is corrected not only through creative effort but even more by the total situation and contacts within the therapy group. The need for adjusting to the group aids in awakening dormant centrifugal interests. Thus living and functioning in a group (under favorable and comforting conditions) tend to counteract and dissolve the phantasy content and the need for escaping into phantasy. Our experience has been that children with excessive phantasy trends have gained greatly from the group and the occupations it provides.

We take the following abstract from a Rohrschach examination of a boy thirteen years old to illustrate the possible services of Group Therapy to a child of this type:

The heavy weighting on the movement side would indicate that behavior is almost completely on an introverted level. The client lives in a world by himself and has little contact with reality. This picture is so much on the movement side that the only reason we can say he is not withdrawn from reality is the good form, the popular responses, and the good movement. Also, when he does see color he uses it well. There is a basis for rapport, though this will probably be gradual. The patient has possibility for outer contact and is therefore a good treatment risk.

The Rohrschach points to a very rich phantasy life. There is also evidence of good creative ability. He is, however, so wrapped up in his phantasy that he cannot create. He should be urged to do something creative, such as writing or art work, for an outlet. He is capable of doing more than mechanical work and probably would not want to settle down to anything practical. He is not impulsive but shows anxiety.

From the Rohrschach we get the impression that he is probably brighter than an intelligence examination would indicate. He has good abstract ability. He is not ambitious. This is seen in the fact that he accepts wholes where he finds them and doesn't bother to construct them where he cannot see them. It is easy for him to give good responses but he does not do so.

In view of the fact that he has little contact with the outer world yet is capable of good rapport, *he seems to be the type of boy who would benefit a good deal from Group Therapy.* He will need some preparation before he comes in contact with it. On the Rohrschach he did not seem quite as disturbed as the social history would give us reason to believe. The Rohrschach examination was given at the end of the test period, when he had adjusted to the examiner, but it is possible that he was still restricted and did not produce.

The autistic child[7] is one who withdraws into himself and away from the world as though he feared the pain and frustration it might bring. Autismus is a form of man-shock brought on in some cases by continuous painful relations with people. The condition naturally first originates in the family as a reaction to relations with parents and siblings and is carried over into contacts with other persons. Autistic individuals build a fence around themselves and painstakingly keep everyone outside the enclosure. They seem egocentric, may or may not feel little need for others, are usually distrustful and sparing of words, and do not confide in others. Autismus may be accompanied by delinquent or criminal behavior since there is no need for relating oneself to the world. Autismus may also be caused by very deep-rooted anxiety and fear of one's own impulses as well as of other people. The neurotic with delinquent impulses, but whose super-ego is at the same time tyrannical and whose fear of consequences is therefore intense, withdraws from social participation. It is as if he were escaping the temptation to commit a crime.

It is evident how beneficial a permissive environment and free group relations are to autistic individuals, for they find it little short of impossible to relate themselves to a therapist in individual treatment. To clients in this category, Group Therapy offers, in addition to other values, a preparation for individual therapy.

The schizoid child yields readily to group treatment. We have no evidence as to the effectiveness of Group Therapy in cases of schizophrenia since the intake policy of the agency bars patients with definite psychoses or near-psychoses. They are referred to city hospitals. We do have evidence that Group

---

[7] Autismus should not be confounded with introversion. The former is a neurotic symptom; introversion is a normal pattern.

Therapy is effective in counteracting excessive withdrawal and in correcting schizoid trends. A considerable number of our clientele fell within this diagnostic category and our studies indicate that progress is more rapid and improvement more thorough with them than with aggressive children.

Except in extreme cases, overaggressiveness naturally tends to correct itself under social pressure. But children who withdraw and are frightened require attenuated group pressure and social mobility. The setting of Group Therapy is therefore of great therapeutic value for schizoid children. It makes it possible for them to break through their encapsulation. The occupations, interests, and necessities of group life help them to relate themselves to the ever expanding world of reality.

During the early stages of treatment, for example, many of the children in our groups absented themselves from trips because of a fear to venture out beyond the familiar confines of their neighborhoods. In one instance a boy would get a severe stomach-ache as he neared the subway station and would have to return home. He repeated this pattern on a number of occasions, but a year later he was able to participate in trips with pleasure. Other children cannot take part in gymnasium games and sports for a considerable time until they overcome their fears and can leave the security of the "club room."

Such members remain at their task for long periods before they can break through their fears when the others in the group play some social or group game. Some children cannot eat with the group and leave before the mealtime; others eat their food apart from the rest or on the outskirts of the group at the table. In some instances the group therapist tactfully encourages them to eat with the others and to join in the games; but this is not done until we are certain that the child will not be shocked. When he is encouraged to take part before he is ready, he may not return to the meetings for long periods. In some cases children did not come back at all, for any approach to them represented an invasion of their personalities and sometimes even an attack upon them. Before groups or individual members are transferred to a neighborhood center,[8] exploratory trips to it are arranged. The response is a measure of the child's capacity to adjust to the larger social environment and there are always a few children who react with panic or near-panic, which is an indication of further need for a protected group.

The egoic child is one whose glandular, structural, or psychological state causes him to respond to the world and interpret it in terms of *himself, his* feelings, *his* needs. The "I" of such people is inextricably intertwined with all situations and thoughts. They may be communicative or withdrawn. They usually do not like people and when they are with others the only or chief motive is to use them for some end of their own. Such persons are self-centered, are conscious of their own reactions only, and do not make or hold friends easily. Ordinarily, they crave social approval, but do not know how to earn it. In extreme cases the egoic person does not even desire recognition or admiration from others. It is our impression that in many such people egoicity proceeds from organic or constitutional sources.

We recognize here difficult, if not impossible, patients for individual therapy. Being strongly egoic they are unable to establish a relation with a therapist. In the group such individuals are less difficult and the prognosis is better. If the client is found to be egoic as a result of parental rejection or persistent infantile egocentricity, considerable improvement can be expected. The acceptance which he receives from the group therapist and from the group itself counteracts to some extent his self-protective rigidity and he becomes more receptive of others. If the preoccupation with himself is not due to constitutional factors and has not become too deeply structuralized as a neurosis, the individual can, under favorable conditions, acquire the ability to identify with others. The

[8] For discussion of transitional groups, see Chapter IX, pages 326 ff.

warm relations that exist in a therapy group "soften" the feeling tones of the egoic person so that he begins to respond to others and accept them.

In such cases, as in others we have mentioned, Group Therapy must precede individual treatment. For through group experience the client is prepared to establish a transference to the psychotherapist which he is otherwise unable to do. Even in cases of constitutional egoicity, satisfying group relations take the edge off the client's feelings of isolation and hostility.

The emasculated boy. Another character malformation that responds to group treatment is emasculation. In a home where there is no father or he is weak and an inadequate male symbol, or where the child is an only boy in a family of many sisters, or where the mother is either rigid and domineering or overprotective and pampering, a boy is likely to develop pathological characteristics and attitudes. As a result he grows up fearful, submissive, suggestible, and generally unable to fulfill his biological destiny. In extreme cases such boys develop hypochondriacal symptoms and become homosexual. In less extreme cases they are unable to take their place with other boys, cannot participate in normal games, are stamped as "sissies," become socially stigmatized, and isolated. As a result they are socially maladjusted and are likely to develop serious personality problems.

Individual therapy by a case worker is frequently dangerous here. Transference to a male worker may activate the boy's latent homosexuality. At the same time such boys ought not to submit to the restrictions of a woman worker. What the boy needs, at least in the early stages of treatment, is an environment that will call forth the masculine components of his character without arousing fear and anxiety. He needs experiences and activities in the company of boys and identifications with males (without strong libidinal components) that will not constitute a threat and a danger. A therapy group, where the boy can integrate and identify with others at his own rate, is therefore the most effective treatment in such cases. The group supplies the attenuated masculine environment he needs. Being with boys, participating in their activities, having the interest of an adult male without becoming too deeply involved with him, and being accepted by boys are processes of singular value in the correction or at least amelioration of the emasculated character. In a group the member has the opportunity to break through the fear of his masculinity, to acquire patterns of appropriate behavior, and to establish more wholesome identifications.[9] However, to be fully successful, Group Therapy in such cases is indicated before the age of twelve or thirteen years.

We take the following from an Integration Conference on a boy of twelve, I.Q. 132:

When Albrecht came to the case worker, he was convinced that he would become insane and was very concerned about this fact. He told the case worker that he always played with younger children, that they compared penises and took part in other forms of sex play.

Albrecht was seen by the psychiatrist who diagnosed him as polymorphous perverse, infantile on all levels, and as having a preoccupation with anal activity. The psychiatrist said that Albrecht had been psychologically castrated by both parents and that the case worker could give Albrecht a different concept of the father person. He felt, however, that the case worker could not help Albrecht to elaborate his hostility for if he encouraged aggression, Albrecht would be frightened. The psychiatrist felt that a group would give the boy an opportunity to work with other children and to learn to express himself. This, together with case work treatment, will give the boy the help he needs. The boy was referred to a Boy Scout Troop, but failed to adjust.

Albrecht told the case worker that he enjoyed the therapy group very much and has described the role of the group worker as follows: "Mitch [group therapist] is like the court of arbitration. He doesn't say yes or no, he lets you practice your experience and you learn from that."

[9] See the cases of Ivor Brown and Paul Schwartz, Chapter VIII.

The group therapist stated that when Albrecht first came to the group, he was completely passive, somewhat ingratiating, and very polite. He would address the worker as "Mitchie dear." On one occasion when the boys took some soda while the worker was out of the room, Albrecht manifested a lot of guilt about this, although the other boys did not seem to care. In the last few weeks, Albrecht has started to throw clay at the wall and at other boys. He has fought with Gerald, a very aggressive boy, in spite of the fact that he seemed scared.

(Note: The following year considerable improvement in the boy's adjustment and general reactions was noted. He is still under treatment.)

TREATMENT NEEDS

Group Therapy is employed in a large number of cases either as exclusive treatment or as supplementary to individual treatment. The need for group treatment frequently arises because a child is inaccessible to individual treatment, or because the family is resistant for one reason or another. In a number of cases the nature of the problem is such that it requires the supplementation of a group, without which therapy is either at a standstill or impossible. When a regular club is acceptable to the client and serves the ends of the treatment aim, he is referred to such a club. In cases where an attenuated or protected group is needed, a therapy group is indicated. There are a large number of children whose treatment needs are met entirely by the group.

In the study of Group Therapy cited on page 86, the following purposes for which clients were referred to the Group Therapy Department by case workers are listed:

Social experience
    a) to gain social experience
    b) to gain security in relation to children
    c) to gain security in relation to adults
    d) to develop personal security: status,
        acceptance, self-confidence

Observation
  a) differential diagnosis
  b) testing progress of individual treatment
Development of group relations outside the family
Utilization of personality traits in constructive fashion
  a) aggressive personality
  b) withdrawn personality
Providing opportunity for self-expression
Parents being treated
Tapering off treatment
Supplementing case work treatment

Miss Goller,[10] using "the major symptom in each case . . . as the category for that child," found the following reasons for referral to Group Therapy.

Habit disorders—nail biting, enuresis, sleep disturbances; *conduct disorders*—disobedience, fighting, truancy, misbehavior in school and at home; *aggressive behavior*—stubbornness, refusal to accept orders, defiance, inability to accept limitations; *withdrawn behavior*—shy and gentlemanly manner, lack of interest, inability to make friends; *other neurotic traits and symptoms*—stealing, food fads, fears, anxieties, masturbation, restlessness, crying, excess phantasy.

GROUP THERAPY AS EXCLUSIVE TREATMENT

The conditions under which exclusive group treatment is indicated are briefly outlined below.

Inaccessible children. Clients are inaccessible to individual treatment for reasons already enumerated in preceding pages or because other intrapsychic states make them incapable of developing confidence in an adult or transference to him. They are as a result unable to participate in the therapeutic process. A group does not require the same affect attachment and children who are thus blocked can relate themselves more easily to a group and to the group therapist.

There are a large number of clients on the intake lists of

[10] *Op. cit.*, pages 14–15.

every agency and clinic who refuse treatment. Their resistivity derives from a number of sources. Frequently they refuse to accept individual treatment because of the insistence of parents or the school. Their hostility to either or both may be so strong that they reject the clinic to spite parents or teachers. When these children desire to belong to a group, they will accept a "club," provided it does not suggest therapy, but rather a social experience. In nearly all such cases the children, once placed in a group, were attracted to its activities and atmosphere and their adjustment improved as a result. In some instances they were willing to see a case worker after this preliminary group contact.

Uncommunicative children. Inaccessibility to individual psychotherapy may be caused by a client's uncommunicativeness. He refuses to impart to the case worker or the psychiatrist his thoughts and feelings, even when he comes for interviews, because he is strongly suspicious of adults and does not trust them. Since referrals are made by an authoritarian or repressive agent such as parent, teacher, or court, it is to be expected that some children will view the therapist as another enemy. When their suspicion and antagonism cannot be broken down, and it often cannot, methods other than the interview are used. Among these types of treatment are the relational, the supportive, the educational, and the tutorial. Group Therapy is especially suitable for such children, for with very few exceptions, even when they are destructive and negative toward an adult, they have a desire to be with other children as part of a group.

Another reason for a child's uncommunicativeness is a psychological blocking of expression as in the autistic and schizoid types and sometimes in the egoic as well. Case workers find it quite impossible to penetrate the protective mantle that such children assume. They need to experience actual situations and make the necessary adaptations to them. A group that is acceptable to these children is here indicated.

Uncommunicativeness may also be caused by the absence of language facility which is prevalent among children of some cultural backgrounds. There are also non-verbal children whose language capacity is constitutionally limited. They make contact with persons and the world through other means than language and are unable to participate in interviews or impart their problems to anyone. We must also keep in mind the child with low intelligence, who is able neither to formulate his thinking nor to understand interpretations given him by the case worker. Uncommunicative children are more accessible to group treatment than to interview or individual play therapy.

Infantilized children. The client who falls within this category and whose personality problems are not complicated by deeper neurotic conflicts is suitable for exclusive group treatment. The process of growing up cannot take place in an interviewing room. The child must face the realistic needs of making adaptations and assuming responsibilities that will carry him toward maturity. The corrective experiences here are the external controls and restraints that a group can supply. Placed in a non-threatening group situation, he is likely to make an effort to adjust to its needs and to the mores of his contemporaries. Attendance rate in the group is high among children whose infancy has been prolonged.[11]

Children in rivalry with siblings. Our experience with children in therapy groups indicates that sibling rivalry is greatly reduced and sometimes eliminated through group treatment. The fact that each of the siblings is accepted in a substitute family group and works out satisfactory relations with other children (substitute siblings) greatly reduces the child's need to compete at home. The many satisfactions derived from creative work, praise for achievement, and a friendly atmosphere give him the status and security that make rivalry in the home less necessary. This process is aided even more when the

[11] For further discussion of this topic, see Chapter VII, pages 222 ff.

siblings involved can all achieve the same recognition in groups. The reader will find a number of instances of the ways in which our members gain acceptance. Making useful objects and trinkets for their brothers and sisters is the most common. Other quotations from our records reveal our clients' pleasure at the recognition their work receives from parents and other members of their families. Such acceptance and recognition inevitably reduce the rivalry for love and status in which most of our clients are engaged. The following quotation from a group record illustrates the reduction of sibling rivalry between two sisters, one three years older than the other:

The older of the sisters dominated and cowed the younger. The rivalry between the girls was the center of the problem. Because of this rivalry it would have been inadvisable to admit one to group membership without extending the same privilege to the other and we had no group available for the younger girl. Besides, the rivalry was so intense that where one went, the other was sure to go. In view of the nature of this relation and the age discrepancy, we felt that the difficulty between the sisters would be allayed through the simple mechanism of substitution. As expected, after several months each girl developed friendships of her own in the group and the tie between the two sisters became less strong and the harmony between them greater. The intervening months proved trying, however. The girls carried over their relation in the home to the group in every detail, going so far as to stage fist fights. The neutral environment of the group, the friendly attitude of the worker, and the presence of other children offered conditions under which the intolerable relation could be mitigated. The improvement in this relation was carried over to the home.

Sibling symbiosis. As opposed to hostile rivalry in the home, there are siblings whose attachment to one another is overstrong and retards their individual development. This situation is frequently found in families where the mother is a rigid, unloving person and the children have to draw upon each other for affection and love.[12] Symbiotic relations of this na-

[12] See the case of Ivor Brown, Chapter VIII, pages 259 ff.

ture are found also in families where one sibling is held up as an ideal for the others and hostility in the others is repressed and turned into "admiration" and a form of dependence. It is also found among twins, especially identical twins, who often function as one person.

In all these cases group treatment is effective. In some instances it can be used exclusively. In others, where the emotional involvements are intense and deeply rooted, individual psychotherapy is also required. We have been particularly successful in dissolving strong ties between twins. Despite the fact that at first there was resistance to separation, they have finally submitted to it with salutary effect upon their personalities and character. We are now studying the dynamics in the relation of twins and the processes involved in their separation.

Emotionally exploited children. Where the parent, usually the mother, uses the child for her own emotional needs, ties him down to her, and blocks his normal growth toward autonomy, separation of the two becomes necessary. Physical separation is in almost all these cases impossible or inadvisable. What is needed here is emotional weaning rather than physical cleavage. Interests and libido-binding occupations[18] help greatly in dissolving such parasitic ties. When the character distortions are not too serious and the child can make a satisfactory adjustment, he should be referred to a group work agency or a neighborhood center. However, where he is unable to get on with others in ordinary relations, which is usually the case in exploited children, a therapy group or some other form of protected group is an essential part of treatment.

Case work treatment in this situation has to center upon the mother, since she is the focus of the problem. In order that her emotional ties to the child may be lessened, the mother must be guided toward interests that remove her from the home and give her substitute satisfactions. She, too, needs to belong

[18] See Chapter VII, pages 190 ff.

to a group. Depending upon the intensity of the problem and her personality structure, the group may be a social club, a neighborhood mothers' league, or a treatment group.[14]

Tapering-off treatment. In individual treatment we often reach a plateau; the treatment is petering out or is gradually approaching a satisfactory conclusion. While individual treatment may be no longer necessary or possible, there may still be a need for further therapy to solidify the gains made or to continue the client under observation. Sometimes a camp may top off individual treatment; a supportive relation with a Big Brother or a Big Sister may be advisable; vocational guidance is helpful in some instances. As a means of tapering off individual treatment, therapy groups have been found effective with clients who have resolved their immediate problems and are no longer productive in interviews, but who are in need of social adjustment.

Diagnostic service. Therapy groups are also employed for diagnostic purposes either exclusively or in connection with individual treatment. Frequently the description of the child's behavior by an adult—parent, sibling, or teacher—is distorted. The problem content is either overdrawn or underestimated. Not infrequently the preliminary case history, as obtained by the intake worker, case worker, or psychiatrist, is dotted with inconsistencies and incongruities. Essential facts are withheld by the referring person. Especially is this the case with relatives and teachers who desire to cover up their failures in dealing with the child. The client is also secretive. He does not fully reveal himself and adopts "party manners," skirts around his difficulties, and very often becomes defiant when his problems are brought out in an interview.

We found that in some instances the Referral Summaries contained incorrect characterizations of clients. This discovery was made by a number of our group therapists independently and can be explained by the fact that the behavior of the

[14] See Chapter IX, pages 329 ff.

children (and often the interview material they produce) in individual therapy is quite different from what it is in a group. In a group situation the child sooner or later reveals his real character. His aggressiveness and destructiveness, timidity or quarrelsomeness, fear or recklessness, his inner and outer conflicts soon emerge. For some children this happens almost at once; for others after a number of meetings. In some instances the child hides his true self for weeks.

A too-well-behaved boy, rigidly trained by his mother "to act like a gentleman," found escape in painting and drawing at the group meetings. By these means he held himself in check. Several months later he released his pent-up energies, became rowdy, and for a period even destructive. The permissive atmosphere of the group and the example of the other boys released the torrent of sub-surface pressure which in the past found expression in dissocial behavior. As a result there has been improvement in the boy's general adjustment.

As a further illustration of diagnostic possibilities in the group, the following case is cited. In reading records of the meetings of one of the groups, we observed that the behavior of one of the boys in it indicated that he had homicidal trends. We discussed this with the group therapist, who stated that he had seen no indication of it. The boy, on the contrary, was very reserved, quiet, and at times even frightened. We were convinced, however, that this apparent reserve had a deeper meaning; it seemed as though the boy was afraid of himself and what he might do. Upon further investigation and conferences with the former case worker (who withdrew from the case, as he made no headway with the boy), our original judgment of the boy's homicidal impulse (as a result of a deep-seated incestuous drive toward his mother) was confirmed. But it seemed to us, also, that the boy's trend was to introject this drive and thus turn it into a suicidal impulse. This conclusion was drawn from the fact that he always destroyed everything he made at the meetings. He would crush the objects he made in clay, tear his paintings, and break up his wood work. A year or so later a conference was held on this boy in which four workers and a psychiatrist participated. From the case history the psychiatrist, though no mention was made of the boy's destructiveness, concluded that the boy might have a suicidal trend. It was then that we offered as confirmatory evidence our observation of the symptom that had impressed us.

Physical, intellectual, aesthetic, emotional, and social activity supplies a reliable source for diagnosis. The use of colors, the shapes one draws, the objects one models, the rapidity and slowness with which one works are significant. The type of interests—physical, artistic, or intellectual—and the avidity with which the client gives himself to them are keys to his inner life. Does he seek to escape painful, external reality by preoccupation, or does he attempt to evade facing inner realities? His handiwork and his attitude toward it may disclose masturbatory activity or tendency. Occupations may indicate homicidal and suicidal compulsions. We found in our work that case histories were sometimes unnecessary to uncover the essential problems and mechanisms of children. Their behavior was revealing enough, and it was possible to reconstruct the home and the child's life by merely observing the nature of his behavior and the content of his activities. Activity reveals unconscious material that case histories do not contain. Some children present a different façade to an adult whom they aim to please than to their peers under the stimulation of a group.

GROUP THERAPY AS SUPPLEMENTARY TO INDIVIDUAL
TREATMENT[15]

Group Therapy is employed as supplementary to individual treatment under certain conditions. Some of these, described in the preceding section dealing with exclusive treatment

[15] Illustrations of the integration of case work and Group Therapy are given in Chapter VIII.

needs, are sibling rivalry, tapering-off treatment, and diagnostic service. Several other specific problems in which groups are needed to supplement treatment follow.

Parental opposition. Parental opposition to the agency's "interference in family affairs" is often so strong that no contact can be made with the client by the case worker. The parents, usually the mothers, view the social agency's efforts as an invasion of their realm. Resistance in some instances arises from the fact that the case worker frustrates their need for brutalizing or exploiting the child. Not seldom hostility to social workers is aroused by errors or indiscretions committed by previous workers. In such circumstances, the referring agency, like the school, is advised to suggest to the parents membership in a "club" for their child. To this they seldom object and the child is thus enlisted in a therapy group.

For several years the mother of a fourteen-year-old girl consistently refused to see a case worker or to allow her daughter to be seen by one. The family was known to a number of relief and family agencies and all saw a need for psychiatric guidance for the girl. The public school also expressed concern over the girl's behavior, but the mother remained adamant. It was finally decided that the school should refer the girl to a "club" (therapy group), and this was acceptable to the mother. The latter was so delighted with the improvement in her daughter's behavior that in a feeling of gratefulness she prepared a jar of preserves for the "club." This mother was the first one of that particular group who sent such a contribution. In a number of instances, parents were willing to refer the child for individual treatment after such an initial contact with the group.

Parents or siblings under treatment. In cases where the treatment should be centered on the parents and siblings of the child rather than on the child himself, the former often refuse to see the case worker, since that would be an admission of their failure and of their responsibility in creating the problem. They come for interviews, however, if they can be assured that they help the worker with the treatment of the client. The latter is, therefore, referred to a therapy group. This approach has value not only because it brings the relatives for treatment, but also because it exposes the child to the benefits of the group. At the same time he is under observation where his progress can be noted.

Families inaccessible. There are families where the home pathology is very intense but cannot be relieved through direct treatment or manipulation. The child cannot be institutionalized or placed in a foster home. He does not need intensive therapy, but rather affection and guidance. Sometimes these needs can be satisfied by a Big Brother or a Big Sister. When the reaction to the home (group) relations is such that the child is unable to get on with children of his own age, a therapy group is necessary as a part of the therapeutic program. If parents are under treatment, some case workers find that assigning their children to groups in the same agency increases the parents' confidence (and probably reduces their sense of guilt).

Rejected[16] and deprived children. Children who have been emotionally and economically deprived gain great satisfaction from the permissive and nurturing atmosphere in therapy groups. The record material reveals the extreme delight such children derive from freedom and acceptance. They display unmistakable surprise and gratification because they have free access to materials and tools, have food, and go on trips and, above all, because the adult in charge is kind and considerate. It would be difficult to overestimate the value in the emotional guidance and treatment of children that the feelings of acceptance, status, and personal worth arouse in them. All that is necessary to be convinced of it is to observe their growing relaxation, their friendliness and gratefulness to the adult in charge, their improved attitudes, and their increas-

[16] For definition see Chapter I, page 3, footnote.

ing warmth toward other children and adults. One of our most deprived children expressed it thus: "I am lucky, everybody is good to me now." The warmth and love he received in the group were magnified in his mind to include "everybody," as indeed it soon did. Even his "illegitimate" stepfather became more acceptant of the boy as he began to act in a less provoking and more friendly manner.

These satisfactions cannot come altogether from the individual case worker. Almost all emotionally deprived children require a close and comforting relation with an adult and they become even more convinced of the goodness of the world, as it were, when they experience acceptance and love in a group as well. In most of these cases individual treatment is necessary only to interest the child in a group and sustain him during the early period of his membership in it.

Adelaide Dorn, interpreting an experiment in the correlation of group work and case work in the treatment of problem girls in Rochester, makes a number of points that coincide with our findings relative to the value of the group as supplementary to individual therapy:

. . . group work, from the case worker's point of view, had been valuable in that the activities promoted by the group had relieved tensions, had given security, provided limitations and situations which were like the ones to which an individual needs to adjust in life but which were tempered and made easier by the presence of the leader, and had provided a wide range of interest. . . .

The experiment showed that case work in Rochester had with profit turned to group work for help. It accepted the importance of play for health development; it recognized the value of the group work program as a definite treatment tool; it saw that group work was peculiarly able to furnish situations comparable to real life experiences, lending itself as a controlled medium for providing many of the child's needs for social consciousness, security, recognition, prestige, and self-expression through developing interests.

Absence of any stigma connected with attendance at the "Y"

makes some cases more accessible for treatment to the group worker than to the case worker. Through this cooperation, success for both the group worker and the case worker is enhanced. The shy child, resisting at first, is socialized more rapidly through the medium of varied group experiences. The aggressive child is disciplined by a group. The physically handicapped child finds self-expression and friendship. The girl whose problems are deep-seated makes a better adjustment by the indirect satisfaction introduced through the group experience. The girl who goes from one school to another finds continuity in belonging to a group. Another girl finds a mother substitute in the group leader and develops friendships with other children. One finds security in the group and relief from nervous tensions.

Because of treatment the girl is receiving with the group work agency the case worker may not have to consider her as a major responsibility. In this way group work has been able to contribute to case work, and together both have been able to work out a method of treatment to meet the immediate and changing needs of the child. When the group no longer is a contributing factor in the lives of individuals, some other treatment of association is recommended, and case workers and group workers should be more keenly intelligent in their recognition of the point where treatment in one group should stop.[17]

CHILDREN INACCESSIBLE TO GROUP THERAPY

Children whom we found inaccessible to Group Therapy are grouped according to their characteristics in the following pages.

Narcissistic children. As already indicated psychotherapy is possible only when the patient is inclined to accept it. This is especially true of Group Therapy. We find that this type of therapy is not suitable where the problem is caused by the underdevelopment of the social cravings in the child that causes him to exploit the group, undervalue it, or retreat from it. Fundamentally, the prime qualification for Group Therapy

[17] An Experiment in Case Work–Group Work Correlation, *The Family,* 20: 160–163, July 1939.

is the child's desire to be accepted and become part of the group. He also must have the facility to make the initial steps in group living.

Narcissistic children enjoy coming to groups. In fact, they seldom miss a meeting except through illness or other compelling cause. They use the group, however, for their personal needs: they dominate, order the other members about, monopolize tools and materials, take supplies home with them, interfere with the work of others, arrange for the meals, and so forth. Such domination prevents the other members from developing individual autonomy and maturity; it blocks interpersonal relations and social growth. The resentment of the other children and the adult's efforts to control them seem to have no effect. Narcissism in some of these children is so intense that they seem unable to become aware of the will of others.

Such behavior may point to true psychopathy. However, in many instances, there is an underlying neurotic compulsion behind this pattern. When denounced by fellow members or taken to task by the worker, the child becomes very anxious and may go into a mild panic. He is able, however, to repress his anxiety quickly and to find a rational justification for his acts; he acts as though he had squared the matter with himself, though actually he remains quite upset.[18] Despite this, and after a brief period of quiescence, he again resumes his disturbing behavior. We have attempted to use direct restraint with a number of such children but so far have failed and have been forced to close the cases. We did this, however, after at least a year of trial. Evidently children with intense narcissism and extreme behavior disorders are not suitable for Group Therapy.

Sadistic children. In some children, the behavior we have just described is accompanied by sadistic acts against mem-

[18] See the case of Harmon Mancher, Chapter VIII, page 273.

bers of the group. In others, sadism is not a part of the syndrome and the compulsion to hurt others physically is dissociated from their disturbing behavior. True sadism probably appears in later adolescence and early adulthood and since we deal with children under sixteen, only a few children in our groups have had this manifestation. Two boys presented a more or less clear picture of sadism. They physically tortured other boys: squeezed their hands in doors, pinched and pricked them. After a series of explorations, conferences, and discussions of their problems, we found it necessary to close these cases.

Children who seek punishment. Another mechanism that makes some children difficult cases for Group Therapy is the need for punishment. Children with such a craving provoke the other members to strike and reject them; they use every means to provoke the worker as well. As a result, the group is in a perpetual state of conflict, turmoil, and disequilibrium. In milder cases this mechanism eventually subsides and the children fit into the group. Where the need for punishment, however, assumes a neurotic quality, there has been no improvement in the child. The underlying malformations in such cases require deeper psychotherapy than the group can provide.

Children who steal. One of the symptoms that needs careful analysis before a child is placed in a group is stealing. If the client steals either to express deep-rooted hostility or to activate punishment, the group is unable to meet his needs. We cannot punish him in the group, even if this were desirable; we cannot counteract the intense hostility that such stealing represents. The twig has been bent too far. Because of our inability to affect him, we are not justified in exposing other members of the group to this contagious practice.

The general criterion that can be used is the place where the stealing occurs. Stealing at home is generally (though not always) an act of retribution against unkind treatment or a

bid for affection that is not fully given; or the thing taken may
represent love symbolically. The accepting atmosphere of the
group, the family substitute, meets in most cases the love
needs of the child, and the stealing impulse subsides. However, when the child habitually steals (not as a single isolated
episode) outside the home, we can assume (though this is also
not always the case) that it is an expression of deep-rooted and
structuralized hostility toward society. Such children steal
from the group and discharge their hostility there in other undesirable ways. We have experimented with such children for
as long as two years, but up to the present have found them
untreatable through our groups. It must be noted, however,
that stealing outside the home may also be treatable by Group
Therapy, when the practice is episodic, is not too deep-rooted,
and does not represent a neurotic need.

Reuben, a boy of twelve, had been brutally treated all his life
and had developed cruel and aggressive traits. In addition he was
an inveterate thief, having begun to steal at the age of four. Individual therapy was not possible and was given up in the hope
that the boy would come in conflict with the law and be committed to an institution. It was agreed that Reuben was a case for
an institution. The parents oscillated in their attitude and finally
refused to proceed with the necessary legal action. The client was
discharged from individual treatment, but continued in Group
Therapy on an experimental basis.

In the first group to which he was assigned, Reuben was the
strongest and the most aggressive, though not the oldest or the
largest, of the boys. Because of his definite cruelty he was the
leading spirit in many destructive acts. In addition he made
Salem, a boy a year older and a good deal taller, the recipient of
his really intense brutality. Although Salem learned to resist
Reuben somewhat, the original relation between these two boys
did not change appreciably. It was felt, after a year of this, that if
Reuben were placed in a group of older and more mature boys,
they might keep him in check.

To the new group Reuben brought along a friend of his whom
he turned into a "stooge," as he had Salem previously, and con-

tinued his cruel practices on this boy. Although the latter was not
a client of the agency, we accepted him as a regular member in
another group, so as to separate the two. Having lost his friend,
Reuben, unable to take his place with the other boys, withdrew
into himself. He worked with materials assiduously throughout
every meeting. (He did not miss one meeting in three years.) The
worker once surprised him in the act of stealing. Reuben explained that he thought the worker would not mind if he took the
things, displayed no anxiety about his act, and continued, to attend meetings. On one occasion a trunk in the meeting place that
belonged to a lodge was rifled. There was little doubt in anyone's
mind that Reuben was the culprit. His stealing became bolder
and the other members referred to it by innuendo and indirec-
tion. It was therefore necessary to discharge Reuben from the
group for we became convinced that we could not reach him.

Actively homosexual children. Actively aggressive homosexuals were also found to be sources of contagion in groups.
However, children who are passive or latent homosexuals did
not prove to be undesirable. In fact, there is reason to believe that some of the boys with feminine identifications have
gained greatly from group experience and interaction with
more overtly masculine boys and from a relation with an adult
male which was not too personal. Active homosexuals of the
aggressive type, on the other hand, may involve other children in homosexual episodes or activate in them latent tendencies in this direction. In our experience with these groups,
only one actual incident of homosexuality occurred and the
activating boy was removed.

Oral aggressives. Children with the character structure described as oral aggression (Chapter III, page 52, footnote)
were found most disturbing. The quarrels and intrigues that
they set up vitiated the total atmosphere of the group and
prevented desirable personality interplay. In all cases they
were eventually eliminated from our groups.

Homicidal children. We have had a few cases of homicidal
boys. In instances where this trend has been turned into a suicidal tendency, redirected, or sublimated, we have kept them

in our group with beneficial results. However, boys who had a compulsion to burn others with hot pyrographic electric pencils, throw knives, hammers, and chairs at the other members, had to be eliminated from the groups as a safety precaution.

Extremely aggressive children. We have already described this mechanism as it relates to therapy groups in several connections in the preceding pages and will have occasion to discuss it again in the future. All that need be said here about extreme aggressiveness is that when it proceeds from sadism, homicidal tendencies, serious behavior disorders, psychopathy, and other similar conditions, clients cannot be included in groups. The case of Reuben on page 115 is one that falls into this category. Another case, rejected by Group Therapy, though an extreme one, will point up further the discussion with regard to aggression. This boy (Manfred, eight and one half years old, I.Q. 124) had been referred for group treatment. The case was summarized in the minutes of a Treatment Conference held by the case worker, case supervisor, and psychiatrist from which the brief abstract that follows is taken:

Manfred presents a pattern of behavior which generated from inner compulsion. There was very little modification of it through outside pressure. Though there had been some change with the attempt on the part of the mother to modify her handling of the child, he quickly resumed his old pattern. In his malicious, aggressive, destructive, intractable behavior in home, school, and community, the child was acting out inner conflicts. If his impulses were impeded, he would become considerably more conscious and his anxiety and fear, such as the phobic anxiety about getting dirt into his food, might take more specific, oppressive forms. The child is showing a pattern of pathological behavior which may be said to represent a character disorder. It finds its expression also in fixed phantasies which indicate distorted representations of external reality and distorted images of himself and others, as well as of his relationship to others. The acting out of sadism and open cruelty take on the quality of a perversion.

Though at a certain point in the past, about which at the present time we can only speculate, this behavior and character pattern were started as a result of external pressures and influences, it has become self-generating; it goes on spontaneously. There are gains and pleasures derived from the behavior itself, so that there is involved also the element of being "bad for bad's sake."

When behavior becomes a perversion in this way, the patient must be compelled to give it up. He is not treatable unless strong barriers are set up to his behavior and he is compelled to meditate before he acts. The behavior has gone beyond the point where the child can be induced to give it up. The mother must be instructed to check and restrain him actively. He must not be allowed to strike his brother, he must not be allowed to injure property or people, etc. The mother was not strong enough and not able to carry out the bivalent instructions such as were given previously to indulge the boy in part and to restrain him in part. Therefore, it is necessary to play down with her the idea of indulgence and stress the necessity for checking this behavior by setting up forceful barriers. If the mother cannot impede the boy's behavior, then it will be necessary to place him in an institution.

Our rejection memo stated in part:

From the description of the boy's personality, it would seem that Group Therapy would be undesirable for this client. The permissive and non-authoritarian atmosphere of our groups and the neutral role of the group therapist would only further encourage the child's destructive impulses and his lack of self-control. From the statements which you make concerning this boy, it would seem that he rather requires external inhibitions of his impulsive and irrational behavior. Our groups could not supply this. In addition, a boy with this character structure would be definitely destructive to the other children. His unpredictable behavior and his violence would be directed toward them. He would vitiate or completely prevent the formation of a therapeutic atmosphere and interpersonal relations.

I would therefore suggest that the placement of this boy in a therapy group be held in abeyance until he brings himself more under control through individual treatment.

CHAPTER V

THE PROBLEM OF GROUPING

SINCE the group is our therapeutic agent, it must be planned so as to supply therapeutic influences at every point and in every relation. If therapy is to proceed from personality inter-actions and group dynamics, it is essential that the members of the group should be chosen for the effect they have upon one another and the possibilities for group equilibrium they offer. This is the ideal toward which one is to strive. In prac-tice groupings are seldom perfect. It is difficult to envisage the effect of placing people together, even when the information about them is adequate. But when this information is inexact or incomplete, as it often is, there is inevitably a considerable element of chance. Many characteristics and overt misbehav-ior that may affect the group are frequently not known at the time of placement. Another variable to be considered is the personality of the group therapist.

Some children are *instigators*. They activate the group de-structively or constructively. If they are destructive or nega-tive influences, it is important that not more than one or two should be placed in one group. Even constructive instigators may come into conflict with one another because of jealousy or drives to leadership. Other children are *neutralizers*. They are those constructive influences in the group who have the capacity to check hostility and aggression. They help estab-lish equilibrium either by word of mouth or by some group activity or interest. Another class of children may be de-scribed as *social neuters*. They have indifferent personalities, are unassertive, and their effect upon the group is not evident, at least in the early stages of treatment.

Other children are *foci* or centers, around which two or

three others constellate. These become the leaders and may exert a very strong influence in either a positive or a negative manner. Still others are *isolates* who, because of their personality difficulties, withdraw from the group and work and eat by themselves. There are the inevitable *scapegoats* who activate the aggression and hostility of some of the members of the group against themselves; in a negative way, they are also instigators. Some children have the capacity to stimulate manual and social activity and can be classified as *catalytic agents* in a group process; others serve as *supportive egos.*[1]

In assigning children to groups many factors besides their personality patterns must be considered. Some of these will be briefly outlined here. It must be kept in mind throughout, however, that grouping for treatment purposes is still experimental and much of the material presented here is tentative.

1. The ideal number of children for our type of therapy is five or six. The number can be increased to eight at later stages of treatment. In a group exceeding this number the atmosphere becomes surcharged with hyperactivity and there are too many conflicting currents. In addition, we found therapists cannot act *in loco parentis* to a larger number; they cannot focus their attention upon individual children and their activities, and note the behavior of each child. We found that a roll of eight members brings to the meetings approximately the desirable number, though often the group becomes too large when the attendance is full or when some of the members bring along friends or siblings.

2. The basic age distribution which we employ is a two-year span. Usually groupings are made up for ages eight to ten years, ten to twelve years, and so forth. Sometimes it is necessary to digress from this plan because a child lives in a neighborhood where a group is functioning. In such cases a few

---

[1] For discussion of supportive egos, see Chapter VI, pages 153 ff.

children a year older or younger are included in the group, provided other considerations such as emotional and social development and physical size do not militate against it. Just as emotional immaturity or sophistication may interfere with group adjustment, oversized or undersized children have difficulty in finding their way into a group. Most of our groups consist of children less than a year apart in age.

In our initial work those accepted for Group Therapy were between fourteen and seventeen years of age. This brought them up to nineteen and twenty before they were ready to be discharged. We found this age level too advanced for most effective therapy. We have, therefore, lowered the age level so that the majority at present are under fourteen. The nature of the family and its influence upon younger children is such that Group Therapy which serves as a family substitute is most useful for children in the lower age brackets.

3. In assigning children to groups emotional and social development, that is, maturity of personality, must be considered. Very frequently chronological age, which is the basic criterion for grouping, must give way to these considerations.

Children who have been overprotected or whose anxieties are so intense that they revert to infantile mechanisms are not accepted by children who are of the same age but are emotionally and socially more mature. They therefore need to be assigned to groups of younger children. When they are misplaced, and they are forced to fall back on their immature behavior, their difficulties are intensified. The only way they can find their level in a group is by "playing up" their cuteness, overactivity, misplaced humor, and mischievousness; they even resort to bribery to gain status. Some of these children if misplaced respond by fear, self-effacement, submissiveness, or withdrawal, and since they make no or very little contact with the others, they gain little from the group experience.

Other children respond with rowdiness and boisterousness

or they bring friends to meetings for support. Usually these friends are persons who are dominated by the client.[2] In some instances the immature (and therefore submissive) children attach themselves to a stronger individual in the group (supportive ego) and this has proved of great value in treatment. Some feel stigmatized or inadequate when placed with children younger than themselves. On the other hand, a youngster placed in a group of less mature or physically smaller children than he, has his aggressive, extraverted trends intensified. He orders, abuses, and even torments the others.

Thus it is necessary to consider personality factors other than chronological age and clinical diagnosis. In practice, it is often necessary to reassign a child to a more suitable group after his unfitness for the first is discovered. One boy was reassigned twice, and finally adjusted to a group of children four years younger than himself because of his size and immaturity. Sometimes personal appearance, physical defects, or other stigmata have to be considered. It is for this reason that we ask for a description of physical defects in the Referral Summary. Placement in groups must be cautious as shown in the following abstract:

Placement of Tom Meyer was discussed with case worker. We indicated that this client may not fit into a group of boys because of his smallness, the deformity of his teeth, and his foreign accent. He is a child who would activate the hostility of the members of the group and would suffer only an additional rejection. Case worker indicated that this boy is in need of group experience. He agreed, however, that rejection by the group, which is quite probable in this case, would only add to the child's difficulties.

We suggested that Tom should not be assigned to a group but rather be invited by the case worker to come and see the "club"

___

[2] In practically all instances, these friendships are gradually dissolved, the client making a friend of one or more of the group members. We consider this an important therapeutic process. It involves the concept of the supportive ego.

and if he likes it he can join up; if he doesn't like it, he can drop out. This would leave the decision to him and when he feels threatened he can withdraw without losing face. Case worker agreed to this.

It was also suggested that Tom should be placed in a group of younger boys.

(Note: This boy was accepted by the group without any difficulty.)

It often becomes necessary to regroup children because they reinforce each other's problems as in the case that follows. We give here a portion of the minutes of the Integration Conference:

Shield is a very infantile boy (ten years of age) and plays like a little child with Philomar (another infantile boy of the same age in the group). It was decided to separate them, since they reinforced one another's infantilism and each prevents growth in the other. Philomar is more promising than Shield. . . .

It was also decided to place Shield in a group of boys younger than he, so that he can be the "older brother" and take on responsibility. However, Philomar is to be placed in a group with older boys because his striving is to be big and strong and he identifies with stronger people. Placed in a group with older boys, he would attempt to act as they do, as this is his pattern. Through this identification he may give up some of his infantile behavior. (Note: This arrangement worked out as anticipated. Philomar made good progress. His case was closed out by the case worker soon after and, at the end of the following year, was ready for closing in Group Therapy as well.)

4. If the grouping is incorrect, undesirable behavior and attitudes on the part of some of the members may be taken on by the others. Where the more dominant members are hostile, destructive, or otherwise antisocial, they create a destructive atmosphere that is contagious. It is obviously undesirable for children to be grouped so that some will acquire from others the very attitudes that need to be corrected. It is also important to group the members so as to prevent the dominant ones from activating criminal or delinquent behavior in the others.

5. There is always the temptation on the part of the group therapist to "protect" the sensitive and introverted individuals against the onslaught of the rough, extraverted children. This is contrary to Group Therapy practice for, as already indicated, if the therapist singles out any one member for special consideration, he stimulates sibling rivalry.

In one of our groups, the "victim" was an exceedingly weak boy, unable to resist the tyranny of some of the others. He was abused for a long time by a fellow member (Reuben; see Chapter IV, page 115), who cowed him completely and kept him on the verge of tears and in constant fear. The group therapist, a sympathetic and sensitive person himself, was at the beginning disturbed by this untoward behavior. He found it difficult to accept the situation and overcome his pity for the abused youngster. However, we recognized in the boy's relation to Reuben the *critical event* in treatment.[3] If he had been removed from the group, his old pattern of constantly escaping difficulties would have been further reinforced. The therapist's interference was, of course, out of the question. As predicted, the harassed boy finally turned against his tormentor and, on occasion, the roles were reversed. Previous to this experience the boy had been placed in a dozen or more clubs, but had attended in each case only one or two meetings and dropped out. His attendance at the therapy group was perfect, even though the treatment he received there was seemingly unbearable. He was later placed in a less aggressive group and made an excellent adjustment with good results. The newly gained power that resulted from his rebellion against the aggressive friend prepared him for normal group relations.

This boy's consistent attendance, in spite of the cruel treatment he received and his inability to accept friendlier groups,

[3] The critical event in Group Therapy is an occurrence or a series of occurrences that reach the nuclear problem of the patient.

demonstrates a major requisite in psychotherapy. The patient's needs must be met if he is to accept the therapist and the treatment situation. In this case the client had masochistic cravings which were not satisfied by other groups. The present group satisfied these cravings and he willingly exposed himself to its influences. However, he experienced here positive as well as negative relations. The therapist's basic kindness and constructive contacts with the other members, except Reuben, seemed to recondition his disposition, and he was later able to accept normal group relations. The boy in question was of very low intellectual capacity and limited in power and personality resources. Because of this we carried him in groups for four years (an unusually long time) as supportive treatment. According to the case history the boy has made an acceptable adjustment in the community.

In another similar situation where the bigger boy of the two employed the smaller one as an object of his cruelty and we felt that there was no likelihood of the roles being reversed, as in the case just described, the situation was handled in the following manner. *In the presence of the entire group* the aggressor was asked to stay after the others had departed, and the group therapist had a talk with him about his responsibility to the group as one of the bigger boys. After this conference not one single instance of the conflict occurred until the group was discharged more than a year later.

6. There must not be too many aggressive children in a group. Aggressive members inevitably reinforce each other's trends with detrimental results. In a therapy group where the number of such members is excessive, behavior approaches the point of group hysteria. In one of our early groups the mutual reinforcement of aggression became so great that the boys consistently drove nails into window sills and chairs (with the sharp ends pointing upward), plugged up key holes, threw missiles, water, and chemicals from windows

at passers-by. When their aggressiveness toward their environment ran itself out, they attacked each other; they threw one another's coats and hats out of the windows, often on top of parked trucks, so that the articles of apparel were lost as the vehicles moved away. We had to disband this particular group and reshuffle its members.

Even overaggressive groups usually come to terms with their environment and bring themselves under control. Group control, however, is greatly delayed, and some of the members (usually the infantilized and spoiled children) continue in their original pattern indefinitely. They require a more maturing group environment.

Our observations lead us to conclude that a therapy group of eight should not have more than two very aggressive and hostile members. Three or more create turmoil and tension and vitiate the therapeutic atmosphere of the group. However, it is sometimes necessary to add a third to break up the clique that the two may form. The number of active children can be larger.

Gil was the most tyrannical, aggressive, and domineering boy in his group. Although some of the other members were also aggressive, Gil controlled them and blocked the interpersonal process. As a part of his own treatment and to protect the other boys, Gil was transferred to a group of boys older and bigger than he. The reaction of the remaining members is revealing as to the importance of proper groupings for the purpose of therapy. The following is an abstract from the group report:

Julius and Hugo continued playing handball against one of the walls. After a while they tired of this and both boys sat down and talked about camp. Suddenly Julius turned to worker and asked, "Where's Gil?" Worker replied that Gil was no longer a member of the club; he was transferred to another club. Julius jumped up, laughed, danced about, clapping his hands, and said: "Oh boy, that's great. Now we're rid of him." Then in serious vein, he turned to the worker and said, "You remember I always used to tell you I was sick when I couldn't come to the club? Well, that wasn't the real reason. It was because Gil was in the club. He always used to pick on me and made me mad. Oh boy, now that he isn't here, we can have some fun. And I'll be coming every week from now on." Upon hearing the news that Gil was no longer a member of the group, Alvin looked up from his work and smiled broadly and said, "That's great." Brent and Hugo both seemed happy about the news. Brent said, "Yeah, that guy used to think he was tough." Hugo merely said, "That's a good thing. I never liked that guy anyway."

Girls are not as aggressive physically as boys, though they are often as boisterous as boys when in groups. Witness their behavior in a train when on an outing. Girls' hostility to one another is expressed orally. Only in very few instances was there an actual physical encounter among our girl members. Among boys, on the other hand, fights are not uncommon at first, though a definitely infrequent occurrence later.

The following, an abstract from a group record, describes what is perhaps the most extreme example of oral sadism in our groups and is taken from a record of the Girls' Group in Chapter III:

Mary arrived. She greeted worker, welcomed Gladys significantly. The latter seemed to turn slightly pale. She stooped over her drawing a little more and ignored Mary's greeting. Mary sat down heavily, without removing her coat, and began to talk about school. Worker had to leave the room for a moment to get another chair. When she returned Mary was asking Gladys where Miss Kemp, former group worker, lived. "On River Parkway, two doors away from my aunt." "What is the number?" "Well, my aunt lives at . . ." and Gladys gave the number. "I'm going to see my aunt on Sunday and I'll get it [Miss Kemp's number] then." (Note: This is pure phantasy as Miss Kemp lives in another part of the town.)

"Are you in the main building at J— High School?" Mary asked Gladys. "Yes, I am," replied Gladys rather defiantly. "Strange I never see you there," Mary remarked. "What are your hours?"

Mary insisted. "Oh, from one to about five or a quarter to five, whenever I get out," Gladys replied. "But there is no session at that hour," Mary informed Gladys. (Gladys seemed to become increasingly nervous and belligerent with each question. Mary remained "terribly" calm.) "The afternoon session is from ten to four," Mary continued. "That is not afternoon session," replied Gladys, "that is mid-session." Mary continued to insist that the main building did not have any session that met at the hours between one and five. Gladys maintained that it did. "All right. You don't believe me. I'll get six girls from my class here next week and prove it to you," Gladys replied, getting more and more excited.

"Show me your program card, that'll prove it to me," Mary replied. "I have it at home. Where is yours?" Gladys asked Mary. Mary did not have hers, either.

"Who is the assistant principal?" Mary asked Gladys. "Oh, I forget," said Gladys. "You can't tell me. You don't go to that school. You're sixteen and not in the sixth term. You're not in your right term and you're ashamed to admit it." "That's what you say." "Will you shut up, Mary?" said Ann. "Are you starting in to fight again?" "Yes," said Gladys, "she always starts in to fight with me."

"Who is Mr. Harris?" Mary persisted. "What does he look like?" "Oh, if I'm not mistaken he's medium height, wears glasses, and is slightly bald," Gladys answered all in a rush. "He is nothing of the kind," replied Mary. "He is tall and is hunch-backed." Gladys remained silent. "What does he teach?" "He teaches English," came the quick reply. "He teaches French," said Mary with mocking sweetness. "He teaches English also," maintained Gladys. "He does not. He only teaches French," said Mary. "What are you doing, starting in to fight again?" asked Ann. "Yes," said Gladys, "she's always picking on me, always fighting with me."

"Who is Mr. Zimmer, what does he look like?" demanded Mary. "He's small and wears glasses," replied Gladys. "He is nothing like that. He's a cripple," retorted Mary. Jean looked up from her leather work in amused surprise and said, "All the teachers in her school are cripples." "You're crazy. He is not a cripple," replied Gladys. "You're telling me?" said Mary. "He is my grade adviser, and I see him practically every day, and you are telling me he is not a cripple." "Oh, you're crazy," repeated Gladys. "If you go to the main building," said Mary, "come up to my house on

Sunday. Mr. Harris will be there and you can prove to me then that you go to that school." "Sunday?" asked Gladys. "All right, I will. I'll be up there with six girls from my class. I'll prove it to you."

Then Gladys turned the tables on Mary and began quizzing her, asking her where the girls' infirmary was, certain offices, the dentist's office, etc., to all of which Mary replied calmly, Gladys usually disagreeing with her. Finally Gladys in desperation, with tears in her eyes, exclaimed, "I don't want to talk to you, Mary. I don't want to fight with you, do you hear? I'm not talking to you any more!" And with that she stooped over her drawing.

Throughout the meeting Mary was almost offensively aggressive and domineering. She dominated everyone, worker not excluded, and every situation. She had evidently consumed a considerable part of the cookies and candies she had bought for the group, because the quantity she brought in was very small, and certainly appeared to weigh less than Mary claimed it did. It would appear that Mary's labeling of the other group members as "sweet tooths" is applicable principally to herself.
(Note: It was a mistake to allow Mary to make the purchases, because this distinction seemed to increase the girl's aggressiveness. It is also possible that the theft of the cakes increased her anxiety and also her hostility toward Gladys.)

7. Groups consisting entirely of self-effacing and withdrawn children were found ineffectual for therapy because the essential group dynamics are not set up by them: each pursues his own special occupation and remains largely isolated from the others. In such cases active and aggressive children are added to set up interpersonal reactions.

8. Intra-group balance is achieved when the membership consists of aggressive, active, withdrawn, and average children approximately equal in number and in intensity of characteristics, for this tends to establish an equilibrium. One excessively active child can disturb a group more than two children under less pressure. Some of our groups had one member so disturbing and "playful" that constructive work on the part of the other members was at a low level, and very fre-

quently impossible. He would constantly move about and playfully disturb others at their work, push them around, make provocative, humorous remarks, talk excessively, whistle, start fights, quarrel, and bang things. Evidently a group with three or four such infantile individuals cannot get to first base. However, the problem is usually not such good-natured fun-making. More difficult are the hostile, actively destructive, and domineering children. Since the adult in charge of the group cannot continue to restrain them without disturbing the other children and his relation with them, there must be restraint from the group itself. This can be accomplished through intra-group balance and the controls that come from such a balance. In a group of eight there should be two aggressive and three withdrawn members and three who tend to fall between these two extremes.

We found that one or two children who are fairly stable set a pattern for the others. In many instances the less controlled boys and girls seek out the friendship and approval of the more stable ones. In some instances they attach themselves to the more balanced members, who may act as supportive egos or neutralizers, as the case may be. They are obviously important factors in developing a *group super-ego* and in helping others to attain self-control.[4]

9. We found it advisable to confine the membership of our therapy groups to one sex. Recently we have experimented with a mixed group of eight and nine-year-olds. This group is directed by two group therapists, a man and a woman, which makes the group even more like a family. The policy of setting up one-sex groups has not been arrived at pragmatically, but rather adopted arbitrarily, and therefore requires empirical confirmation as to its validity. Our experience with older boys and girls between the ages of fifteen and eighteen, in a cor-

---

[4] For a discussion of the group super-ego, see Chapter VII, pages 229 ff.; see also the case of Paul Schwartz, Chapter VIII.

rectional school, leads us to the tentative conclusion that mixed groups of problem children create serious difficulties. This may not hold for younger children.

10. Among the elements to be considered in grouping children is the composition of the group. It is a question whether a therapy group should be composed of individuals who have had no previous contact or of those who know one another already through other associations, in school, at camp, or on the block. It is felt at the present time that the former plan is preferable because in addition to supplying an opportunity for a new orientation it provides a new basis for group adjustment. Since Group Therapy is also a form of reeducation in social attitudes in the new type of environment, it is advisable that former relations and attitudes be eliminated as far as possible. If early patterns of behavior and old relationships are continued they preclude or block the reeducational process.

For the same reasons siblings are discouraged from joining the same groups. Family situations and therapy needs frequently make it impossible to exclude them, however, or the exclusion of one may mean losing the other. Usually each sibling is assigned to his own age group.[5] Sometimes even twins are separated, though we always find them resistive to separation, since they have been accustomed all their lives to being together.

11. Members who bring their friends often create a dilemma for the therapist. Because of the prevalence of this practice, we evolved a loosely applied rule. It seems that all members want a "small club," and since the "club" would become too large if each brought friends, brothers, and sisters, the rule is that only occasional visitors are acceptable to the group. This arrangement seems satisfactory to all and mem-

---

[5] It is sometimes necessary to place siblings in the same group for treatment reasons. See the case of the two sisters in Chapter IV, page 104.

bers invariably adhere to it. The therapist does not put the rule into effect; the group members do it, or it is done through "the office."

There are, however, instances when the rule is conveniently overlooked, as when therapists feel that unless the friend is permitted to come a child will drop out. Sometimes a child is too frightened to attend meetings alone; sometimes a domineering child needs his "stooge," without whom he would not come at all.

Margaret, aged fourteen, would never come to meetings without Jessie, a girl of her own age. Margaret addressed and treated Jessie as her slave. She came from a rather complicated family background. Both she and the mother refused individual therapy. Jessie was a constant companion without whom Margaret would not move anywhere. We suspected from the material presented in the group records that if Jessie continued coming, she would throw off the yoke of her friend. It took more than a year before this occurred. Jessie found her own orientation in the group, developed friendships, and rid herself of Margaret's domination, so that Margaret was forced to make a new adjustment. This was the critical event in the treatment of these girls.

12. In order to increase our clients' adaptability and to test their growth, we provide for them experiences in more than one group or modify the group to which they belong. When a child makes a satisfactory adjustment in one, we transfer him to another, add new members to his group, or change the group therapist. This is usually done at the beginning of a "club season." Adjustment to one group cannot be taken as evidence of improvement. Rather the child just gives up some of his symptomatic behavior. Just as the family is a haven of security, a group, too, may be adopted by a child as such a haven. After the initial difficulties and conflicts the client may accommodate himself to his new social matrix without further emotional growth. Growth implies ability to

adapt to new situations. After a period of time, varying in length with the readiness of each individual, the security and comfort derived from the group are disturbed. The child is exposed to new experiences in a different setting, and again guided and helped to make an adjustment. It is to this *variety* of adaptations that we must look for final socialization and maturity and not to one successful group adjustment.

For the same reason, in nearly all cases, we discharge our children to neighborhood centers either in groups or as individuals.[6] The proof of successful therapy is the child's ability to get along in ordinary situations. The therapy group is only a preparation for life in the community.

But even before we discharge our groups or transfer clients to other therapy groups, some experience in readaptation is provided by the introduction of new members to existing groups. We aim first to solidify the group (like a family) by isolating it from the impact of the outside world. Our members experience the feeling of "belonging" for the first time in their lives. But this insularity is only temporary. The group and the individual members must become more receptive to the world. Eating in a restaurant, trips, visits, and excursions to various points of interest are among the first steps in this direction. The next step is to arrange trips for more than one group together and only later we add new members.

This practice is valuable for at least two reasons: first, because it increases in our clients their receptivity to other children and helps them to develop a socialized disposition; second, because it offers diagnostic possibilities. Children who feel secure and emotionally satisfied in a group, for example, readily accept a newcomer and make him comfortable. The older members are friendly and helpful. They talk to the new arrival, exhibit the materials and their work. They tell him of the opportunities of the group and generally make him feel at home. If, on the other hand, they are still insecure or if an

---

[6] For discussion of transitional groups, see Chapter IX, pages 326 ff.

undercurrent of hostility or anxiety permeates the group, they are not ready for newcomers.

These reactions are a replica of sibling jealousy in the family and are indications of the degree of emotional maturity.

13. After a considerable number of meetings, small sub-groupings within the group begin to appear spontaneously. This is usually an outcome of common interests and mutual needs. A grouping may center around some powerful individual who attracts the less strong personalities, or it may consist of those who reinforce each other's infantile behavior—boisterousness, mischief, or aggression. Other children combine to reinforce one another in hostility and delinquent behavior,[7] to annoy a scapegoat, or to form an alliance in the struggle for power or out of a common jealousy. Sometimes a common interest, like scientific experiments or making the same objects, serves as the motive for a more or less permanent sub-group formation. Deeper emotional factors, however, determine more enduring and more effective groupings than activity interests.

To illustrate this process (as well as the interpersonal dynamics) the following is taken from an analysis of the early developments in one group of boys after the tenth meeting:

Edward and Murray were the only boys present at the first meeting of the group. At the second meeting Robert and Nathan came, but the other two were absent. This may have caused the formation of two distinct cliques. Edward and Murray continued their friendship at later meetings, while Robert and Nathan formed a separate unit. Another factor in this group formation may have been Edward's natural preference for Murray and, since Edward was the strongest boy in the group, Robert and Nathan were inevitably thrown together.

[7] The number in this grouping is usually very small, because the boys and girls usually commit antisocial acts by themselves or with their intimates in their neighborhoods and friends outside of the group. Sometimes, however, they bring these partners to the meetings as guests or constant companions and steal materials from the group.

At first Murray was very aggressive and overactive but, as he came under Edward's influence and related himself to the other boys, his hyperactivity subsided. At the same time Robert, who was at first withdrawn, became more outgoing and friendly. This change in him brought him closer to Edward and Murray, leaving Nathan alone.

Nathan was rather inhibited and, being an isolate, did not enter into many of the group activities. After two months, however, he became quite active and tried to outdo the other three boys. He apparently hoped in this way to become a part of the group. In spite of this he was not accepted by the others.

The addition of several new members, especially Sol and Craig who were very active and disruptive, disturbed the equilibrium of the group. This tended to throw Edward, Murray, and Robert together to an even greater degree than before. Edward's antagonism . . . is now transferred to the two new boys. As a result of the emotional tension and a feeling of isolation, Nathan has been forced to make a bid for the group worker's affection by helping clean up and wash dishes. To him, the new members were an additional threat.

14. There has been considerable distribution in the intelligence quotients of clients as derived from psychometric tests; the distribution extends from 59 to 162. The I.Q. of the largest number of children is between 70 and 100. We have found that the intelligence quotient is not an important criterion in grouping maladjusted children, nor are their manual skills significant. Rather it is their fitness to relate to one another, in terms of the mutual immediate or prospective therapeutic effect, that needs to be considered.

The most important of all considerations in grouping children is to prevent them from re-living in the group the traumatic relations and the problem-producing atmosphere of the home and school. This must be considered as an imperative condition in Group Therapy. A child who has suffered at the hands of brutal siblings cannot be exposed to the same type of rejection and cruelty from his substitute siblings in the early stages of treatment. One who has failed socially and in activities must be so placed that he is accepted and is successful in whatever he undertakes, and the therapist must help him in this. We must also prevent children who have been stigmatized because of physical defects, intellectual inadequacies, or emotional immaturity from being discriminated against in the group. An effeminate boy is made more guilty and anxious when in the therapy group he is referred to as "sissy." The appellation of "shrimp" to an undersized boy is of little corrective value. It is for this reason that we require a statement in the Referral Summary concerning such matters.

The further traumatization of children in a group that repeats earlier patterns can be prevented by detailed information on the character structure of the child, the social pathology of the home, school, and other relations, and a thoughtful matching of these against the personalities and backgrounds of the other members in the group. One child in a group may be so destructive as to prevent any therapeutic experience for several others. It should be kept in mind that what the child needs is a haven of security and relief from his past pressures. With some exceptions, Group Therapy aims to substitute pleasant for unpleasant experiences and to compensate the child for his earlier sufferings. If we fail in this, we fail in our chief objective.

CHAPTER VI

THE FUNCTION OF THE ADULT

THE prime condition of psychotherapy is that the client must establish a positive relation with the therapist. Without entering into a discussion of the extremely complex dynamics involved here, it may be said that a client who is unable, for whatever reason, to establish such a relationship is not accessible to treatment. This transference situation is the pivot of all reeducation. Freud states that the "ego-neurotic" cannot be treated by psychoanalysis because of his inability to relate himself to the therapist. The therapist's personality must become meaningful to the patient before emotional activity can be set up. The patient's attitude toward him may oscillate between savage hatred and intense love, but the positive elements must eventually predominate, or therapy is impossible.

In general terms, transference consists in the patient's directing of the feelings which he has for his parent, be they positive or negative, to the therapist. The therapist employs these ambivalent feelings and attitudes as means for helping the client mature beyond the point of his traumatic fixations at an earlier age. However, the therapeutic situation becomes effective at the point where the transference is a positive one. When the positive transference is established, the client, having accepted the therapist as his parent, aims to please him as he aimed to please his real parents when he was a child.

This is to a certain degree true also in Group Therapy. We have ample evidence that children accept the group therapists as parents. We read in one report for example: "The boys who pass by the open door stop to look in. One of them says, 'You have a nice-looking teacher.' Gladys answers, 'She is not our teacher, she is our mother.'" In another group: "Marian turns to worker and says, 'You are my new mother.' " A boy walking with the therapist announces, "I'm walking with my pop," or when they stop for drinks at a stand the boys say, "Pop will pay." We have already reported that a large number of the boys addressed the therapists as "Pop" and "Unk," and in one instance the male therapist earned the appellation of "Mom," because to this boy, the son of an extremely dominating mother, only a woman could be in authority.

The children strive for acceptance by the group therapist as in individual therapy, but the process in Group Therapy is vastly modified and complicated by the presence of the other members. From the very outset, the child has to accept the fact that he must share the adult with others. Not all children, however, are able to fit into this communal attitude toward the substitute parent. They make a bid for his favor, create all sorts of difficulties, demand attention, ask for help with their work unnecessarily, attach themselves to the group therapist on trips or when the group walks down to the station. This situation is fraught with difficulties. But because the adult remains passive or divides himself equally among his charges, the children come to realize that it is useless to make such demands. The destructive behavior which is a reaction to this seeming indifference goes unchallenged and unquestioned so that it brings no satisfaction. The child must, therefore, grow up and become one of the siblings instead of an only or a preferred child.

In individual therapy, the client relates himself to the therapist; in Group Therapy the intent is that *the child should relate himself to the group* as well as to the individuals in it. The therapist's role is that of catalytic agent in this process. His attitude of acceptance, friendliness, and appreciativeness sets up like attitudes in the children toward one another. The group therapist is also a *synthesizing influence* for the group. Though neutral and usually passive, he is the center around which the group constellates and to some degree also integrates. The group may be too pressing a reality to some children and the function of the adult in such instances is to relieve such pressure. This must be done with care and infrequently, lest the members of the group interpret it in terms of their feelings toward their own siblings. The therapist prevents failure in whatever the clients undertake to do by help and suggestion. Frustration to an already frustrated individual is of no great value. We must rely upon successful achievements and satisfactions. The group therapist supplies the least complicated materials and situations and helps individual children when they show signs of stress or fear of failure. As tolerance to frustration is increased, the children are allowed to fail and discover their limitations.[1]

Because no discussion takes place, the therapist must represent positive elements in the life of the client through his attitudes.[2] He must become the *ideal* parent possessing all the desirable characteristics that the real parents may lack. Thus the child by the nature of the circumstances has a composite parent consisting of two persons, in many instances with antithetical characteristics. The real parent may represent the negative, prohibitive, and rejecting forces. The group therapist counteracts these by *being* a positive, sanctioning, and accepting person. Thus he supplies the elements which are lacking and establishes a balanced parental picture. One of the girls in the discussion group (Chapter IX, pages 325 ff.) became aware of her attitudes after several analyses of the relations between parents and children when she said, "I guess my ideas about parents and families are cock-eyed."

This anomalous position of the group therapist is not simple. The adult has to counteract by his attitudes negative reactions to other adults. The abstract that follows not only

[1] For discussion of self-acceptance, see Chapter VII, pages 197 ff.; and for discussion of frustration tolerance, see Chapter VII, pages 219 ff.

[2] By "positive" is here meant accepting, permitting, and not *active* as differentiated from *passive*.

illustrates destructive feelings that children have about teachers, but also the very significant fact that they trust and confide in the group therapist:

The boy was playing with simple chemicals. He suddenly turned to the group worker: "What is the most poisonous thing in the world?" "I don't really know," said the worker. "There are a number of things that are quite poisonous." "I'd like to put something in my teacher's glass so that she'd die." "Why?" questioned another member of the group. "Is she mean to you?" "Is she?" came the reply. "She is the meanest woman in the world. She screams and scolds like a crazy nut." "Mine is pretty mean, too," the second boy said thoughtfully. "Sometimes I'd like to punch her in the nose."

Confidence in the group therapist is also illustrated in the following abstract:

Joseph and Robert told worker they were going to take the street car home. They never paid fares on the street car; they slipped in without paying. There were always a lot of people getting on, and in the crowd nobody noticed two boys of their size. They saw a car and told worker they had to run ahead, said goodbye, and told him they would see him next week.

In order that the therapist may appear in a positive role, *he must accept the personality of the child unconditionally, but not necessarily his antisocial behavior*. Dissocial acts are symptoms of emotional disorder as physical pain and fever are symptoms of a physical illness. A physician who became annoyed or lost his temper with his patient because of the latter's temperature would be a poor physician indeed. It is more difficult to tolerate cruel, unjust, destructive, and disruptive acts than it is a rise in temperature, but it must be done. The behavior of our clients is frequently hard to stand. Someone who read our group records expressed well the strain under which group therapists labor. She asked, "How can an adult sit through all this and control himself?"

But the personality of the child must express itself in some way. It is an entity that cannot be ignored or rejected, directly or indirectly. We cannot expect to correct it by intensifying a feeling of rejection by further repressions. It would be deleterious if the expression of the infantile impulses were *sanctioned*, that is, overtly or covertly approved. This would only reinforce these impulses, and they would become the sole controls of the child's life, preventing the development of a super-ego. At the same time the adult cannot actively disapprove or reject behavior, for that would place him among the "oppressors"—parents, teachers, policemen. He must let the child become aware of a *contrast of attitudes*. Hostile, destructive acts and peculiar behavior go unnoticed. Withholding recognition is a form of disapproval to the child, but it does not set up hostility and resentment as would expressed disapproval. The adult still remains the ideal parent, but the child *feels* that his own behavior is unacceptable. Thus imperceptibly his super-ego is built up. It is even more strongly established when other members of the group restrain him as well.

Although the group therapist strives to be passive, the children themselves do not permit him to remain so. They turn to him for help with their work or for materials that they may need. Some children whose affect hunger is intense or *frustration tolerance* is low attach themselves to the adult or make a strong bid for his attention and support. In his relation with the children the therapist aims to accomplish three things: 1) to accept the child, but at the same time 2) not to feed his dependence, and 3) to prevent the jealousy of other children and their consequent aggression.

Often there are situations that require direct participation by the adult. We give three examples (Alice, Gladys, and Harmon, each in a different group) that emphasize the discrimination with which situations must be handled:

Alice, Johanna (both eleven years old), and the worker were playing jacks. While taking her turn, Alice touched the jacks and should have given up the ball, but she continued playing, pretending not to notice it. Alice is in intense rivalry with a brother two years older and is unable to take defeat. Apparently she was in conflict between her need to be on top and the guilt due to her cheating. She resolved this conflict by turning to the worker with the question, "Did I touch it?" The worker replied, "Did you?" Alice said, "I don't know" and continued to play.

The group therapist might have responded to the girl's evasiveness in a number of ways: 1) she might have said that she had not seen whether the girl touched the jacks; 2) she could have told her outright that she had; 3) she might have thrown the responsibility upon Alice by asking her what she thought; 4) she might have expressed doubt and suggested that the point be played over again; 5) she might have pretended not to hear the question; or 6) she might have turned to Johanna and asked her what she thought.

The course to be taken in such situations is determined by the need of the child. If the girl is rejected at home, sensitive, and self-protective, any suggestion that may imply disapproval as in plans 2), 3), and 4) would be undesirable. If the girl is neurotic and anxious, 3), 5), and 6) would be particularly unsuitable: to be called upon to decide for herself as in 3), being threatened by being ignored as in 5), or being judged by another child as in 6) would greatly increase her anxiety. On the other hand, if the girl is secure, is not very sensitive, or needs external authority to make decisions because her super-ego is defective, 2) is a method that could be employed with profit.

In the particular instance cited, the latter method would have been appropriate since Alice is naturally not sensitive but rather aggressive and tends to be egocentric. When we permit her to ignore the rules of the game and take advantage of her playmates, we are feeding that egocentricity. The important consideration is, however, that this girl is not generally overanxious but is able to face the restrictions of reality.

The therapist met the problem in a neutral manner. The motive in Alice's asking the question of the worker may have been a) to resolve her conflict by shifting responsibility or b) to test the adult as to the degree of her permissiveness and acceptance. From our knowledge of the client's history we can conclude that a) was the case.

Alice is the middle of three siblings in a family where no adequate restraint is exerted and she is considerably infantilized. Like her mother, she is quite aggressive and domineering. She is in conflict with her older brother and dominates her younger sister (who is now a member of the same group for therapeutic reasons). As the mother is an all-pervasive person, there is little opportunity in this family for the children to take on responsibilities and mature. We also know that Alice is quite secure with the therapist and knows her place in the group, as she is in the second year of treatment. All facts seem to indicate that the motive was a shift of responsibility rather than a test of the therapist.

It is sometimes necessary to help a client to escape the pressure of his impulses from which he cannot extricate himself, as in the following:

Gladys threatened to break Mary's skull. When challenged by Mary, Gladys held up the hammer with which she was working and held it poised over the other girl's head. After several seconds, the worker calmly asked Gladys to give her the hammer as she needed it. The girl seemed quite relieved and turned the hammer over to the worker.

The manner in which the therapist dealt with the situation was quite appropriate. She relieved the girl from her conflict. Gladys had a great deal of repressed hostility and had a genuine desire to strike Mary.[3] Her fear of consequences prevented her from doing so but the fear of being defeated if she gave up, defeat being her difficulty at home, impelled her to pro-

___
[3] See also Chapter V, pages 127 ff.

ceed. She was evidently in a state of conflict and anxiety. The group therapist resolved the conflict by asking for the hammer.

In the following situation direct assertiveness on the part of the leader was not necessary:

Harmon challenged Paul[4] a number of times and insulted him. Harmon, a very intelligent boy, had once touched Paul's nuclear problem by referring to his mother's rejection of Paul. Paul was incensed, but was too hurt to act on his feeling at the time.

In Supervision Conference the group therapist's attention was called to the fact that Harmon's remark would eventually lead to a fight, with Harmon the loser; but it was considered that such an event would be a desirable development in Harmon's treatment. Harmon often boasted that he was a "genius." Once in anger Paul took out his pocket knife, opened it, placed the blade against his heart, and challenged Harmon to "push" the knife. He did this for a considerable time, with no response. The worker knew that Harmon was incapable of such an act of violence and did nothing. Had the situation been reversed, however, the worker would have at once removed the knife, as Paul, who was at that period of treatment in a state of irritability, would have pushed the knife into Harmon. Later Paul beat up Harmon rather severely.

UNCONDITIONAL ACCEPTANCE

At the outset, all children test the group therapist to see how genuine is his permissiveness. Those clients who have been habitually restricted or rejected cannot quite accommodate themselves to a free environment and a non-restricting adult. They attempt to activate the therapist by extreme aggressiveness to fellow members, by unreasonable demands for materials, money, or service, and by other forms of extravagant behavior. It would seem that they would like to make certain of the therapist's sincerity and it is his function to convince them of it. The demonstration of unconditional accept-

---

[4] For Harmon's case, see Chapter VIII, pages 273 ff., and for that of Paul, see Chapter VIII, pages 288 ff.

ance is at first disturbing to the child. His set attitude that all adults are his potential enemies against whom he must keep his hostilities mobilized is shaken. He has gained security in the past through hostility. When he has no cause to use it, as in the group, his security is threatened and tensions are set up. In some extreme instances considerable inner conflict results as well.

A boy thirteen years old often urged the worker to be "strict" with the boys. He told worker on a number of occasions that the other boys were "not worth it." One day, after a "treat" in an ice-cream parlor, the boy snuggled up to the worker and said, "I can't make up my mind if I should kill you or love you to death."

From the case history we know that there is no outstanding homosexuality in this boy. This was a spontaneous verbalization of a conflict that originated in guilt because he was not punished by the adult for some of his acts for which he was accustomed to receive punishment. In some cases the withholding of punishment may be a frustration, but such instances are comparatively rare. In nearly all cases children become accommodated to the adult's permissiveness and this also happened to the boy in question. When children no longer need adult control—admonition, sanction, and punishment—they have gone a long way toward maturity. The need for it is one form in which infantile dependence manifests itself (in addition to deeper character disturbances, such as masochism).

The therapist's unconditional acceptance of every form of behavior continues for a longer period with children whose hostility and aggression are reaction-formations to early rejection and brutalization. In the case of overprotected, infantilized children this period is much shorter. The latter have a real need for external control. Without it they become increasingly overactive, hilarious, and disturbing, and as a result their personalities cannot integrate. They remain immature and maladjusted, and some experience intense anxiety. This is alleviated and corrected through external control which comes from the other members of the group and, when necessary, also from the therapist.

In a group situation control need not necessarily come from the adult. The reader will find in this book a number of typical instances of control by other members, a procedure that is less threatening to the child. Occasionally when no protest is forthcoming from members of the group,[5] the adult in charge calmly but firmly calls the child's attention to his behavior. It is of the utmost importance, however, that this course should be taken on the basis of a careful diagnostic decision.

Kurt, a boy of eleven, was very hilarious and annoying at the group meeting, behavior which was particularly bad for Vlad, older than Kurt but mentally inferior and very insecure. At one point when the situation became quite difficult for Vlad the worker peremptorily said to Kurt, "Why don't you stop this business? Haven't you had enough of it?" The boy stopped abruptly; his mood of hilarity changed instantly into one of depression; he dropped into a chair and remained almost immobile during the remainder of the session.

Kurt's behavior in the group seemed more normal for a number of weeks, but the experience was a traumatic one. The boy's manic behavior had a neurotic component. Hilarity was a deep-rooted need to discharge emotional pressure as a defense against depression. Kurt had no satisfactions in any areas of his life and the only release he had was in the group. The group therapist was of greater importance to the boy than he suspected, for Kurt felt accepted by an adult for the first time in his life. Now this security was suddenly snatched from him. When a child has few or no satisfactions, it is of the ut-

[5] This is one indication that the group personnel is not properly constructed.

most importance to give him as many of them as possible during therapy. In addition to other values, this decreases his resistance and he becomes more accessible to treatment.

DEFEATING THE THERAPIST

The group therapist should not place himself in a position where he can be defeated. It is to be expected that many children will be hostile to adults and desire to challenge and defeat them. The attitude of the therapist tends to allay this desire, but the drive persists in many children. Defeat of the therapist can be achieved by stealing, disobedience, challenge, command, demanding, cajoling, nagging, ingratiation, name-calling, general disturbance, and physical attack. When the challenge is a subtle one, such as wheedling, cajoling, and excessive demands, the response is suited to the child's needs at the time. Frequently, it may be necessary to accede to such demands. This may be of special value during the early period of treatment when the child is testing the adult.

However, when he challenges the therapist overtly by disobedience, swearing, or physical attack, he is asked to leave the room for the rest of the period. If he refuses to go, it may be necessary to eject him, but this must be done calmly and without anger or disturbance.[6] Before any action is taken, however, the child's basic mechanisms and motives must be understood. We must anticipate such developments, as they can be dealt with much better when the worker is prepared. As already indicated, one of the functions of the supervisor of Group Therapy is to recognize such trends in advance. However, under no circumstances should retaliation be the motive in treatment. The therapist's neutral attitude prevents

[6] Only once was it necessary for one of our group therapists to ask a boy to go home. His provocative behavior had been almost unbearable to the other members for a long time, but when he turned upon the group therapist and called him "dirty" names, it was necessary to take this step.

situations that may lead to his defeat. When an aggressive act is being committed by a child or a group of children, the therapist ignores it. He must not look in the direction where it occurs. Unless he is ready to stop it, his witnessing it may spell approval. However, hostile children almost always interpret the therapist's tolerance in this situation as a defeat of him.

Harmon employed a particularly interesting plan to defeat the adult. He was an especially uncontrolled and disturbing boy of thirteen, whose average demerits at school for misbehavior were seven a day. He tried every means in his power to make the group therapist express disapproval of him. He would create chaos in the room and then turn to the therapist with such remarks as, "Aren't you annoyed with me?" "Don't you dislike me?" "You don't? Everybody dislikes me. Don't you?" "Don't you care what I do?" "I drive my teachers and my mother crazy. Don't you care?" The boy was always assured that the therapist liked him and was not annoyed with him though there was no expressed or implied approval of his behavior. Had the therapist expressed disapproval or shown irritation, Harmon would not have curbed his behavior (as he eventually did) since he would have derived satisfaction from it. It would also have eliminated in Harmon any reason for improving since the adult was "bad" to him, as were his father, mother, and brother. A clear case of defeat of the therapist is given in the following abstract from a record of a meeting:

Mary was very restless, wandering around the room, giving orders to everybody to do things for her. Soon she also began to paint, and proceeded to flick water at Mamie. Mamie laughed and ran away, which started Mary off. Mamie had run out the door. When she was outside, Mary flattened herself against the wall near the door and when Mamie opened the door threw the entire contents of the cup at her, splashing the floor both in the room and in the hall. Mamie escaped most of the water. Worker told Mary that the floor would have to be wiped up. Mary said, "All right," and took some large white sheets of drawing paper and dropped them on the wet spots, making no effort to wipe the floor. She then sat down at the table and began to do copper work.[7]

Sometimes children use profanity in an effort to disturb or challenge the therapist and they succeed with some young and immature adults. It is of the utmost importance for the group therapist not to fall into this trap either by direct response, facial expression, grimace, or postural reaction. Once they discover the adult's weakness, group members make good use of it in all their future relations. Perhaps the best example of an excellent handling of such a situation is the following episode. We once took over a gang of young hoodlums who were harassing a neighborhood center. One of the toughest boys, aged about fifteen, combined the figures 6 and 9 so that they resembled male genitals, and came to the therapist with the question, "What does this look like?" The therapist calmly looked at it and in a matter-of-fact tone called it by the commonest name employed in the street and as imperturbably returned to his work. He never had any trouble again on this score. He had passed the test.

RELATION TO PARENTS

Because of the place of the group therapist in the life of the child, he is not permitted to meet the parents. The parents are not welcome at meetings and the therapist does not enter into the client's family circle in any capacity or in any relation. Group therapists have to arrange their time so as not to be able to accept invitations to parties in the homes of the children or to graduation exercises, "just to visit," or to allow group members to visit them. They have to find some means of discouraging the parents from visiting the group, though this has been

[7] Although violently aggressive, Mary seemed to grow afraid of her act and escaped from further attempts to provoke the group therapist by constructive work. Note, however, that she chose an occupation of an aggressive nature (hammering on a piece of copper).

necessary only very rarely. The reasons for this rigid separation are several. 1) There is the inevitable jealousy that a parent, especially a mother, feels toward anyone who displaces her, which may lead either to direct unpleasantness or to such hostility on her part that she will not permit the child to attend the group. 2) Seeing the two "parents" together may cause confusion in the child's mind as to the part each plays in his life. 3) Of even greater danger is the possibility that the child may associate the therapist with his home and parents, so that he becomes an integral part of that configuration. 4) The child may suspect the group therapist and the parent of being in collusion against him. This eventuality would cause the therapist to become associated in the mind of the child with the repressive and rejecting adults in his life.

We have found it better policy to keep the two relations entirely apart and to prevent them from touching at any point. In fact, when a case worker or a psychiatrist is treating a child who is also a member of a group, he refrains from discussing with the client his experiences in the group unless the child brings them forward as interview material, and then this material is treated as any other that comes out of the child's daily life. The group itself is not projected into the individual treatment. As far as the child is concerned, there is no relation between the two. When asked point-blank, both individual and group therapists state that they do not know one another.

One of the interesting observations made during our work is that each member accepts the therapist as a substitute father or mother irrespective of his sex. The choice is made in accordance with the child's need. In instances where the child needs a mother's affection, he draws upon the therapist for such affection, even if the latter is a man. On observing the male worker setting the table for a meal, a boy new to the group said, "You are just like a mama." The boy referred to earlier who spoke to the therapist as though he were a woman

made a similar remark the following year in a group with another therapist. We quote from the record:

When worker brought cocoa to the table and poured it for all
the boys he remarked rather breathlessly, "Isn't this nice, fellows?
Jay [group worker] is our mama; she is cooking for her four
children." The boys laughed at this and he winked at the worker.

Others follow a habit. If they have been pampered by the
mother, they accept the male worker in the place of the
mother and seek like treatment from him. These attitudes will
require further observation and study. The technique of neu-
tralizing early influences by a substitute parent of the opposite sex and to what extent the substitution can be employed
as a part of the treatment process will also need further examination.

Authority

Since the aim of group treatment is to help the client establish himself in a normal environment and to submit to the reasonable authority of persons and situations, the therapist's
role as authority is of paramount importance. However, before we proceed with a consideration of this specific area, it
may be of value to discuss, briefly at least, some general aspects of the question.

Character is formed through internalizing restraints and
controls imposed by the outside world. The inhibitive principle which conditions one's reactions and behavior is established by accommodating oneself to the pressures from the
outside, be they circumstances or people.[8] When the child
makes a positive identification with parents or others, he also

[8] We cannot eliminate, of course, original dispositions, emotional and
physical tolerance, and numerous other factors and latencies of the personality. They are the foundations of character, but the modifications in them
and their strengthening or weakening are the result of experience and circumstances.

accepts them as authority. In addition to these personal sources of authority, there are numerous pressures of customs, ethics, social necessities, economic needs, and cultural climate to which accommodations and adjustments must always be made. These pressures are applied in constantly expanding areas and under wholesome conditions, with graduated severity.

In Group Therapy the client comes under pressure of authority from five distinct sources: 1) other children; 2) activity and materials; 3) group mores; 4) the supportive ego; and 5) the adult.

1. The presence of authoritative elements in the group will become quite clear from the record material in this volume. After the early stages of the group's existence, children are constantly exerting an inhibitive or releasing influence upon one another. In one of the records of a meeting we read:

While Harris was at the closet getting the leather binding, an argument started between Martin and Frank as to who should use the paints. Martin had the paints in his possession, although Frank said that he had taken them out before, but had gone to another task and had left them for a while. Harris said to them, "You dopes, why don't you both use them?" Martin, who was the more aggressive, said, "That's an idea." Both boys took the paints, brushes, water pans to one side of the room, brought over two chairs, and proceeded to paint.

A similar instance in another group is the following:

Max (eleven years old) happened to sit down at the same table where Pete (about ten years old) was working. Pete happened, at the moment, to be using the electric saw. Max looked up angrily at Pete and told him to move, as the vibrations of the saw disturbed him. Pete blushed and replied angrily that he would not. Max said, "You better move, or I'll move you!" Pete said, "Oh, yeah? I'd like to see you." Max jumped up and pulled out the plug of the electric saw and pushed the saw away. Pete angrily lunged at Max and started to swing at him. Max stood back and swung back at Pete. Barry (about eleven years old and in his third year of treatment) looked up and saw the fight. He walked over and stepped between the boys and said in a somewhat serious tone, "Now, now, boys, stop the fighting." Pete turned to the worker and said, "Bill, you make him leave me alone." Max said, "Yeah, I'll kill him, if he gets in my way." Barry said, "What's all the fuss about? This little saw? Here, I'll show you what to do." Barry took the saw, moved it up to the other end of the table where there was another outlet, and plugged it in. Barry then turned to Pete and said, "There you are, see? You can work, and you won't be near him. O.K., boys? Go back to work. That's settled." Pete mumbled something under his breath and then sat down and continued his work. Max sneered at Pete and waved his hand at Barry and continued with his work on the key case.

2. Materials and tools have characteristics of their own to which the child must accommodate himself. At first children are very impatient with the resistance they experience in materials. They may impulsively break or throw aside the object they are making when they find it difficult. Though it takes longer in some clients than in others, we found that frustration tolerance has in all cases increased and that different children require a different amount of encouragement and help. All, however, eventually acquire the ability to start and finish a project. This development is evident in a large number of the abstracts from records appearing in this volume.

3. Sooner or later the group develops mores of its own, instances of which will also be found in the records. We term these the *primary group code*.

4. One member of the group frequently attaches himself to another because of insecurity, an awareness of some common characteristic or interest, or the threat of attack. The individual with whom the alliance is made we have called the supportive ego and is of incalculable value in interpersonal therapy. The child *freely chooses* his supportive ego from the group during the early stages of therapy and uses him to sat-

isfy some emotional need. The supportive ego may also be a friend whom the child brings to the group or the therapist himself. In the case of Harmon the supportive ego was the therapist. Because he was completely rejected by the members of the group, he had to turn to the adult. Ivor's supportive ego was the case worker (Chapter VIII, pages 259 ff.). Boys and girls, however, usually turn to their fellow members for this support (Ray Rosen's supportive egos were Tess and Jane, Chapter VIII, pages 237 ff.) and often bring friends for the same reason. Usually these relations give rise to considerable restraint and authority that the children exert upon one another.

The function of friends at meetings varies greatly. In some instances they are a source of security to the client. In others they are the recipients of extreme domination and abuse. Sensitive and frightened children bring others to support them in this new situation. Where aggressiveness is a reaction to deep-rooted insecurity and fear, boys and girls bring along friends toward whom they direct their aggression.

Outside the group Benjie was dominated by Les and he brought him along as a guest for many months. Here he was boss. It was *his* club and Les had to do *his* bidding or he would not allow him to come. Benjie held the threat of banishment from the group over Les's head like a whip. To counteract this, a letter was sent to Les from the office, not from the group therapist, inducting him as a regular member in order to confront Benjie with a new situation. Benjie had to make a new adjustment in his relation to this friend and to the group. He did not have as difficult a time of it as we thought he would. Having experienced power over his friend in the group, he was now able to give it up easily.

This is an illustration of how one child gains status with a stronger friend through a group, while the latter rids himself of the need to satisfy his cravings for power and self-assertion. Such interpersonal relations contribute greatly to the correction of defects in character structure.

Sylvia was much more aggressive and "tough" to everyone when her friend was with her. She used the visitor to reinforce her self-confidence and to relieve her fears of her own aggressiveness in the group. We saw that Benjie directed his aggressiveness toward his friend only; Sylvia, on the other hand, left her friend alone, but the latter helped to release Sylvia's hostility to the others. Jean, a member of the same group, had her friend come with her to the meetings regularly because she actually was afraid of a group situation. She, too, was more talkative and outgoing in the presence of her friend, but this was due to the fact that, usually a shy and quiet girl, she felt more secure when her friend was there.[9] The following two quotations from records illustrate further the value of a supportive ego:

Alan began to bring his friend to the meetings, and now brings him regularly. It seems that Alan is helped by his friend in that when he works on a project he is more self-reliant. He comes to worker less frequently for help and advice. Before Alan brought his friend his work was not as constructive. Although he did finish some projects, it was only because he had come to the worker frequently for help and advice.

The two boys live in the same neighborhood and are of the same age and size. The friend is a little, quiet, withdrawn boy. He is quite the opposite of Alan who is aggressive, talks a lot, runs around, jumps off and on tables, and runs up and down stairs. His friend seems to stabilize Alan when he works on materials. They now work together all the time. The friend looks up to Alan and expresses his admiration for his projects.

The group worker praises Alan also, but it seems that he gets more support from his friend and as a result he now feels accepted by the group as well.

This seems to be a relationship of opposites—an extravert and an introvert—in which each would like to be what the other is. This is evidenced by the fact that Alan seems calmer in the presence of his friend, after whom he attempts to model himself. On

[9] The three illustrations above show the different values of a supportive ego in therapy.

the other hand, his friend admires Alan's achievements. They seem to balance each other. (Note: Since the above was written, Alan has become more mature in his behavior and is accepted by the group. He no longer brings his friend.)

Sidney began bringing his friend to the group at a time when several of the boys were bringing theirs. Sidney was a very restless, overactive boy. His friend was the exact opposite. He was very quiet and accepted with graciousness whatever the group offered him. When Sidney worked with his friend, he quieted down. Previous to this, Sidney, who was the most dependent child in the group in his work with materials, would always come to the worker for help. He did not do this when his friend was present.

When Alex made the rest of the group stop bringing friends to meetings, Sidney was at first very much disturbed. He asked the worker to ask "the office" to make a special rule for him. Worker told him later that the office informed him that they could not make a special rule for one boy. Sidney finally agreed that, as long as no one brought a friend, he would not bring one. As a result he urged Chris to go home with him. This Chris did. Chris is very much like Sidney's friend. He is quieter and less restless and is easier to get along with than any of the other boys in the group, who are on the aggressive side.

The factors that determine the choice of a supportive ego are as yet not clear to us, beyond what has already been indicated. We find that there is a tendency on the part of sensitive members to pal together or turn to each other, though this is not always the case. An aggressive child who does not feel at the moment capable of challenging another member allies himself with him. In either case the members of these combinations act as supportive egos to each other and exert authority over each other.

5. Lastly, the adult acts as authority under specific conditions. Even without the use of direct pressure, the adult, by virtue of being adult, represents authority to the child. As an infant he is dependent on the care of an all-powerful adult,

his mother or nurse; later he comes under the control of other grown-ups, like teachers. Because he is so much smaller and weaker than they, he feels inferior, and naturally accepts the adult as authority. Psychotherapy aims to diminish this sense of inferiority and the consequent resentment when they have become unduly exaggerated and when violent reactions to them are formed. The child must come to accept adults as friends and not as potential menaces to security and happiness. The acceptance of an adult as a friend and as a source of security and satisfaction is the first and most important step in Group Therapy as it is in individual therapy. It is for this reason that group therapists create a permissive environment and are themselves permissive individuals. Even acts of vandalism have therapeutic value if committed in the presence of a permissive adult. The aim of the group therapist is to alter the perceptions of the client, but try as he may, he cannot succeed in *completely* eradicating the symbolism built up in the child's mind concerning adults.

If the adult is a mature and peaceful person, he represents to the child authority which he can accept. He exerts a steadying effect upon the group when he maintains an attitude of equanimity and poise. Generally speaking, the rules in our work are: *Don't do anything; don't say anything; when in doubt, don't!* The permissive attitude, however, used indiscriminately may be deleterious, and even dangerous in some instances. Three examples of the bad use of permissiveness by a worker in training will illustrate what is meant.

Larry said to worker, "Are you allowed to mix these things?" Worker said, "Everybody can do whatever they feel is right."

Such a blanket statement is not only dangerous, but not true. In the first place, it is not true that everyone can do whatever he likes. The group sets limitations. The statement gives the child a wrong notion of his omnipotence, injures his growing sense of reality, and negates the authority of the boy's contemporaries and of grown-ups as well. A blanket permission such as this can be applied only when a child asks whether he can make something from the materials supplied in the group. We then say that he may *make* anything he likes. There is no moral (interpersonal) factor involved here, and it is quite true that the child is free to use the materials. This is not comparable to giving blanket permission to *do* anything a person thinks is *right,* because "right" has a moral element.

In another instance a boy discussed with the worker the matter of "throwing out" a fellow member. The worker said that it was the boys' club, and *they could do* whatever they liked. This is again permissiveness carried too far. In the first place, the worker himself is a part of the group and shares the responsibility of membership; moreover, if a member did whatever he liked, he would be denied the therapy that he needs, for he would acquire a distorted concept of reality and group life. It would be quite different if the worker had said, "If you think that is what you want to do, talk it over with the other boys." In a few instances groups have hounded out particularly annoying members. But this was done without the consent of the worker.

Hart asked the worker if he could take a piece of wood home. Worker said, "You can take anything you want to." Hart said, "Yes? Stand aside." He made believe that he was going to dive into the cabinet of materials and tools and take them all with him.

In this situation, too, there was an excessive degree of permissiveness, which was not true to life. If members took everything they liked, other members would be inconvenienced; it would interfere with the other groups that use the same materials, and it would feed the predatory trends of many of the members.

Here we have three distinct situations in each of which the permissive attitude of the group therapist has to be used differently. 1) In saying the child can *make* anything he likes, the therapist avoids giving his sanction to what he *does.* 2) The group has the authority to do whatever it likes about members, and the adult does not give or withhold his consent but reserves his right to disapprove. 3) With regard to taking things home from the group, permission must not be a blanket one, but confined to the specific matter in hand. We must differentiate between acceptance, tolerance, and sanction. *We accept everything, tolerate much, but sanction little.*

We found it a general practice among the boys to steal rides when going on trips. They would sneak past the station agents, or two boys would pass through the turnstile on one fare. The therapist in such instances does not call the attention of the children to these infractions. Instead, in their presence, he inserts the additional fare and turns the turnstile. This method has proved effective.

When the members feel sufficiently secure with each other and with the adult, the latter employs restraint when necessary. This is done gently without disapproval or rejection. It should never be tried, however, before the therapist is absolutely certain that he is fully accepted by all the members of the group. Some of our therapists feel that restraint should never be used if one of them takes a group from another either temporarily or permanently, but this cannot be made a general rule. For instance, a substitute therapist asked a boy to wash his cup. The boy refused and the adult did not insist. This is a clear case of defeat of the adult.

Another factor is the differential maturity among the members. Some can accept authority, others become disturbed or hostile. In a group where there are aggressive, tough, sensitive, and rejected children together, the use of authority must necessarily be adjusted to the condition of each child. In some children the slightest manifestation of restraint produces panic; others gain enough security from the group situation to enable them to submit to authority from either the group or the adult; the character structure of others is such that they react negatively to authority or to restraint. Where the child's impulsive behavior already creates excessive anxiety, any expression of censure will have serious consequences.[10]

Authority has to be related to the age of the children as well as to the other factors indicated. Very young children—under six or seven years of age—need external restraint, especially when they are overaggressive and destructive. Because of their age, they have not developed inner controls; they are still self-centered and dependent and look for approval and disapproval from adults. Their aggressiveness and uncontrolled impulses feed upon themselves, as it were. Unless these children are checked by someone outside themselves, their aggressiveness gains momentum and increases in intensity. The situation is considerably altered with older children, especially during puberty and early adolescence. At this age, children are very much aware of authority. Physiological changes and psychological growth accelerate self-determination and personal autonomy. These and sexual awareness make adolescents more sensitive to being exposed to public view or having attention called to themselves. In exerting restraint we need especially to be aware of the growing drive for personal autonomy in children as it becomes more pronounced and more significant with age. The invasion of the child's personality and the blocking of his will meet with increasing resentment and resistance. It is therefore necessary to employ with older children only as much authority as is essential.

In only one instance has restraint taken physical form and in this case the worker was a student in training. Because of intense rejection by a psychotic mother and a weak, passive father, Albrecht (Chapter IV, pages 99 ff.) felt great satisfaction from the acceptance he received in the group. This made him less withdrawn. He was very fond of the worker and once on a trip, feeling happy and released, he put his hand on the adult's face. The student worker, not realizing the significance

[10] Note Kurt's reaction to restraint, page 146.

of this gesture, took Albrecht's hand and, removing it, said, "Don't do this again or you won't be able to come on trips." An expression of deep pain passed over Albrecht's face. He withdrew into himself. Realizing his mistake, the student tried to make up for it and when the boy was leaving the trolley he said, "Good-bye, Albrecht." Albrecht did not answer or look at him, although he had always been friendly and ingratiating before.

The rule is that therapists do not come in physical contact with the children and must not let themselves be touched. Adults have to maintain their status of an ego ideal. However, in this particular instance, the boy's impulsive gesture was an act of love and confidence and a deep desire to make contact with a person whom he loved and with whom he could feel free. This was of great value to the boy. The student missed the significance of the episode.

The following illustrates the poor use of denial. A boy of fifteen took a roll of bandage from the first-aid kit and asked the group therapist if he could have it. The latter told him that he could not because the group needed it. When we read this in the record we asked why this step was taken. The therapist replied that since the boy had been under treatment for several years, he believed he would be able to accept this denial. The boy was described as having no constructive elements at any point in his life. He was emotionally probably the most deprived child we had under treatment and we predicted that he would not return to the group. Though his attendance in years past had been very good, the boy absented himself for six consecutive weeks, and the group therapist was instructed to write to him very friendly letters each week in long hand (not typed). We stated that if the boy did not return the therapist would have to call for him at his home, even though this was against our general practice.

Evidently the asking for the bandage was symbolic of asking for love. When the therapist denied the bandage, he denied love. The boy must have been under a special strain on that day as a result of conflict at home and particularly needed reassurance at the moment. The therapist had failed him and this made it impossible for him to accept the group. (Later the boy returned.)

Denial and restraint must be very carefully considered. Premature or poor use of it may be harmful to individuals and to the group. In one instance the children (eight to nine years old) decided to go through the entire settlement house and investigate "everything." The group therapist did not refuse this request and took them on the tour. Had he failed to do this, he would have recalled to them the prohibitive adults with whom they were in daily contact. Because he acceded to their request the children did not touch anything or create any disturbance, for, as one boy said, "You can use anything you like in this room [their meeting room], but once you get outside of this room, you must watch out."

When a child has to be denied or restrained as in instances of excessive demands for money, taking tools and materials home, going to movies or on trips too frequently, or bringing too many friends to meetings, the therapist employs "the office" as the authority. He conveys to the children the fact that there are limitations placed upon him by the agency as to the quantity of supplies the group can use, the money that can be expended, and the number of children that can come to meetings. This recourse to external and impersonal authority has many values: 1) it permits the exercise of restraint when it has therapeutic value without arousing hostility toward the adult; 2) it applies the pressure of reality through limitations and denial; 3) it shows that the therapist, too, must submit to authority and does so without resentment or complaint; 4) it builds up frustration tolerance; 5) it creates situations for resourcefulness in supplying other gratifications for those that are denied.

When children ask the therapist after going to a movie if they can go again at the following meeting, he says, "I'll have to ask the office if they will allow us the money for it." One group of older girls insisted on going to the movies every week. After three or four successive trips to the movies, the group therapist received a letter from "the office" informing her that she was spending more money than the agency could spare for her "club," and no money could be allotted for movies at the present rate. She left the letter on the table.[11] When the girls read it, the group discussed the problem and compromised on going to the movies once a month. The following year, they went to movies only a few times.

It is sometimes necessary to defeat the children's need to beg and wheedle by offering them some privileges or pleasures before they ask for them. This is sometimes done after a prolonged period of denial. A case in point is the above group of girls. The year after they were denied weekly movies, they proceeded to nag the new therapist for movies. She was prepared for this and said that she had asked "the office" for money, and she would inform them as soon as she received word. For several weeks the response from the office was withheld. Gradually the girls forgot about movies and became interested in other things, including the activities in the settlement house where they met. Four or five weeks after interest in the movies had subsided, the therapist announced that she had received permission for the group to go to the movies.

Letters are also written to groups whose members have adopted a pattern of borrowing or taking tools and materials. When it occurs occasionally or is resorted to by a client because of an inner need, it goes unnoticed. When it becomes a general practice, however, the group therapist receives a letter stating that the other "clubs" who use the same supplies

[11] Such letters are not handed by the therapist to the children directly as he must not become the transmitter of denial. After reading the letter which is addressed to him, the therapist leaves it unfolded on a table. One of the members of the group invariably picks it up, reads it aloud, or passes it on to the others.

and tools have complained that they have insufficient materials. The letter goes on to say that for this reason, if materials are being taken away, it must be stopped.

Some children cannot accept even this remote authority and a few become quite violent and abusive toward the collective entity, the office, or the person who signs the letter. Most seem to be able to accept this limitation if the restraining authority is impersonal and absent. In all instances groups and individuals have adjusted themselves to these denials, with good therapeutic results.

It must be noted that impersonal and remote control is not the only method used. The group therapist sets up intentionally frustrating situations; he refers matters to the group for decision and sometimes exerts authority directly. Examples of frustrating situations are the introduction of new members into a group, reshuffling of members, limitations placed upon the quantity of materials and the number of trips. As the children become ready to withstand frustration, even greater denial is imposed: food is eliminated from the meetings, materials are not replaced as they are used up, the worker comes late to the meetings, or turns up without the keys to the cabinets so that there are no materials available at all. These measures serve not only as forms of denial, but also as tests of the children's readiness for personal interaction without the intermediary of manual activity. Progressive steps are taken in accordance with the degree of maturity of the members, the degree of integration of the group, and the group therapist's position in it. Such limitations are also placed upon transitional groups (see Chapter IX, pages 326 ff.).

Despite such devices and artifices, the most important service of groups to clients lies in what may be termed *situational restraint*, as differentiated from the direct or passive personal authority described. It is necessary in our work first to create a living situation in which the child will make desirable adaptations to satisfy his instinctive need to survive as a social atom. Such adaptations are more deeply effective with the young child than are any number of "techniques" used by the therapist, and techniques must be considered only supplementary and secondary to the major factor—the therapeutic situation. Throughout this volume there are numerous examples of situational restraint. Much of it grows out of interpersonal reactions among the children and the leader. However, the physical environment must be planned with forethought. The variation of environment with different groups is briefly discussed in Chapter IX. There are some specific matters, however, that must be considered in the set-up. In fact, when these receive adequate thought, the need for personal restraint is reduced.

Finger paints, for example, are overstimulating for most children in our groups. They are also conducive to disorganization since they suggest throwing colors at one another and smearing one another with them. Overactive groups should not have sharp or pointed tools that may be injurious if used without self-control and discrimination. All such materials are therefore removed from the supply closets. A good example of situational restraint is the following:

A little girl of seven moved the windows in the room up and down with a large window pole. She did this at every meeting for long periods of time. The windows reached to only a short distance from the floor and there was danger that the girl would topple and fall out. The worker watched her from a distance without saying anything or displaying concern, but was poised to act in any eventuality. When she discovered that this occupation became the girl's regular activity at the meetings, she closed the bottom halves of the windows before the children came into the room. Without noticing it, the child continued to play with the upper half of the window.

Such an example, taken from numerous similar instances, demonstrates how by thoughtful planning the need for direct denial, inhibition, and discipline is avoided until such time as the children are ready to accept them.

In analyzing the behavior of a boy in one of our younger groups, it was discovered that the permissiveness of the group caused confusion in his mind. The boy's father and mother were both hard, rigid people and disciplined him severely. He was pronounced "hopeless" by a teacher who used progressive and free methods, but he got along somewhat better in a traditional classroom setting. His unrestrained infantile behavior in the group and his reaction in the free classroom were evidence that the boy was unable to bring himself under control and needed external authority. This is more or less true of all infantile children, but in the case of this boy an additional factor was present. Freedom was inconsistent with his experiences everywhere else. To him life was a hard, inhibiting, frustrating reality, and the therapy group seemed to confuse him in this conviction. As a result the boy was on edge and unable to make constructive use of the freedom he was offered. It was recommended that the group therapist first use restraint on the child and gradually relax its intensity. Thus he would be led toward freedom and personal autonomy through adult control. In a sense, this reverses the basic process of Group Therapy, but in this particular instance it seemed advisable.

We quote below some instances of restraint exercised by group therapists, chiefly when other members were involved in the situation, thus making it indirect and impersonal. However, even this mild and, to the child, understandable control was not used before the relation with the children was secure.

When the opportunity arrived worker told both Harvey and Miles, individually, that it was perfectly all right for them to bring their brother and sister to the group as visitors once in a while, but he felt that there were too many children to have them come all the time. They both said they understood it and would not bring their sister and brother regularly any more.

Harvey took a hammer and saw. Robert and Joseph wanted to borrow the hammer for their friend who was visiting that day. Harvey (in a loud voice): "You can't have it, I'm using it. You can't touch any of these things." A heated argument ensued. Worker went over to the group and Harvey told him that he did not want to give the hammer up. Worker asked him if he was using the hammer and the saw at the same time. He said no, he only used one at a time. Worker then asked him if he couldn't lend the hammer while he was using the saw and then get it back when he needed it. He thought he could and turned the hammer over to Robert and Joseph (twins).

Joseph and Robert immediately noticed the other cabinet in the room which was identical with the one this group used. It belonged to another group that met Thursday evenings. The boys said, "We have a new cabinet." Worker informed them that it did not belong to them but to the other club that met in the room. They wanted to know when the group met. Worker told them. They asked, "Is it like this club?" Worker said not quite, because the boys in that group were older. They wanted to know if worker went to that group, too. He told them that he did not. Robert went over to the cabinet and opened it. He said, "They have a lot of the things that we have" and proceeded to take some of those things out. Worker told him he thought it would be much better if we didn't touch those things, and just used our own. There was a horseshoe magnet in the cabinet. Robert took it out. He said he liked it better than the one we had, and wanted to play with it. Worker told him that if he would like one like it, we could get one for our own, and asked him to put that one back. He did so.

Then Joseph looked in the cabinet and said, "It's better than ours; it's bigger." Worker told him that they were exactly alike. But he insisted that the other cabinet was larger and took a pencil and measured both cabinets. Presently he said, "You're right; they are the same." He scrutinized the cabinet further. "Their door closes better than ours." Worker pointed out to him that their cabinet was not as full as ours. He looked inside and said, "That's right; we have more stuff in ours." Robert went over to the cabinet of the other group and proceeded to take some drawing paper from it. Worker told him that he could not take anything from that closet. Robert: "Aw, let me take a piece. If you let me take it, I'll be a good boy." Worker: "But you *are* a good boy." Robert: "No, I'm not. I'm bad. But if I can have a piece of this paper I'll be good." Worker told him that the paper did not belong to us and therefore he could not give it to him. It was late anyway. Next week he would have some new paper. Robert said all right, if worker could not give it to him, he would not take it, but he should buy two pads next week. He went back to the group and continued to look at the drawings with the others. When they came to one that worker had made, Robert said, "This is the one our teacher made. Isn't it best?" The boys seemed to be taking a lot of pride in each other's drawings as they showed them to visiting friends and commented on how good they were.

(Swimming party.) Worker told the group that he was going in to get dressed, and that when he came out in his street clothes, it would be time for them to leave the pool. They asked him if they could stay another half-hour. Robert begged. Worker told him that that would be too long, but he would make it twenty minutes. They all agreed to do this. When worker came out all dressed, the boys at once left the pool without any argument and got dressed.

Harvey took one of the cutters and proceeded to cut the box in which the tools were stored. Worker asked if he'd mind not spoiling the box as they needed it for the tools. He stopped and said he just felt like cutting today. Worker told him he could have some paper or scraps of wood to cut, if he liked.

(Trip to marionette show.) All the boys ran down front to take seats but worker took a seat several rows back. Several of the boys came back to ask him why he did not sit up front. He said he thought the front rows were reserved, as indicated by the slips of paper on the seats. Miles, James, Benjamin, and Sol came back to sit with the worker. The other boys, singly or in pairs, walked around the auditorium and looked at the paintings on display. Sol pointed out to worker the pictures he thought expressed most imagination and beauty.

Murray had been painting at the window in a new room which overlooked the street, and having a little dish of water, decided to have some fun. This fun consisted in pouring water down on the passers-by. Philip, too, thought it would be huge fun to do this and both ran into the hall to get more water. Worker stopped them at the door and told them that pouring water from a window might lead to our losing the privilege of using that room. They drank the water instead.

FAMILIARITY AND HUMOR

It cannot be too strongly emphasized that in his effort to be accepted, the group therapist must not come down to the children's level. Humor, playfulness, jokes, and banter are not permitted him. In the first place, this camaraderie would leave the children without an external frame of reference for their behavior. If they discover that their infantile lack of control and absence of serious attitudes are indulged by the adult, they will accept them as right and will continue with them. This will prevent growth in the individuals and in the group. The second danger lies in the fact that unless the adult retains his symbolic value to the children, they may turn their aggressiveness (humor, sarcasm, direct challenge, disobedience) upon him. He would then cease to be important. Since the therapist represents the ego ideal for his clients and acts as the group's super-ego, it would not do for him to become personal, playful, or humorous. It is hoped that the above will not be construed to mean that the group therapist is aloof, superior, unfriendly, or impersonal. On the contrary, his attitudes are the very opposite, but at the same time he is controlled and poised.

Occasionally humor can be used to relieve tension as in the following instance. In a group of thirteen-year-olds, two boys began to fight. Soon the entire membership was boxing and fighting in pairs. The worker said, "I think we'll have to get a license from the boxing commission for this club." The boys burst into laughter and the fighting stopped at once.[12]

---

[12] Another situation where humor was used constructively is recorded in Chapter III, pages 56 and 64.

We take the following from a Supervision Conference that deals with this question:

Group worker must be careful not to become too friendly with Gladys. The girl is making a bid for the worker's friendship and is becoming too intimate. If she succeeds in this, she will redirect her hostility toward her mother upon the worker. This she will probably do in a chummy, but derogatory, humorous manner and through sarcasm, and the worker's value to Gladys, as well as to the other girls in the group, will be negated. She will no longer serve as an ego ideal. The worker must, therefore, pretend not to hear the humorous and personal remarks that Gladys directs to her. She must not fall into the trap of the girl's basic hostility even if it takes the form of jest. However, the worker must take steps to reassure Gladys, to compensate for her unresponsiveness. The girl is sensitive and intensely rejected by her mother, and a like pattern must in no way be suggested in the group.

It has been our rule not to touch or pat clients, shake hands, or come into any form of physical contact with them. To the introverted and sensitive child, physical contact represents an invasion upon his privacy. It may set up or reinforce unconscious or active homosexual impulses. In extreme instances it is symbolized as an actual attack. Some children become quite upset by it; others become fixated upon the worker. It acts as a bid for attachment and retards emotional maturity. As a general rule, intimate physical contact represents a lack of respect, and since our purpose is to build up self-respect and help maturity, such practices are ruled out.

PRAISE

We have already indicated that the attitude of acceptance and friendliness that pervades the group is an irradiation from the group therapist. This is particularly evidenced by the praise that becomes a rule of group life. The group therapist makes a point of praising every deserving creative effort (but not social acts) and calling the group's attention to it. Very soon, the members quite spontaneously begin to notice one another's work and praise it warmly. We consider this development important, for to be able to praise is not only an indication of social development, but of self-acceptance as well. The unconscious reaction to giving praise is the feeling that the praised person is placed above the one who praises. To praise others full-heartedly, therefore, implies self-confidence.

In our work with emotionally deprived children, both in the therapy group and at correctional institutions, we were rather surprised to find an abundance of generosity. Readiness to praise one another and insight into one another's problems are among the outstanding results of group life and must be considered indications of healthy character and of social growth. The tendency to praise, however, disappears when the members become sufficiently free and accept one another fully, because the need to hurdle the barrier between individuals no longer exists.

We ought not to leave a discussion of praise without indicating a very important aspect of it. Many of our children found praise from an adult embarrassing. They reddened, stuttered, and felt generally uncomfortable. In one instance a thirteen-year-old boy said, "If there is anything I hate, it is dishonest praise." This embarrassment and anger reflect discomfort and a fear of the unfamiliar; praise is interpreted as an aggressive act or an exposé of inadequacies. Children who have not experienced approval or who have suffered rejection are actually frightened by praise, as they would be by any strange or threatening phenomenon. Some do not trust the adult's sincerity because they feel undeserving of recognition. The writer once had the opportunity of awarding a prize in an oratorical contest in a school for "delinquent" youths. The winner had histrionic ability of a high order and a very impressive stage personality. The boy later came up and asked quite seriously, "Did I really deserve the prize, or are you trying to boost up my spirits?"

The therapist must be aware of the condition of the child and to what extent he is able to accept such an overt, friendly advance on the part of an adult. It may be necessary in some cases to assume an *attitude of approval and praise* rather than express it verbally. An approving nod or a whisper of affirmation may be more appropriate. Open praise is often too difficult to bear for the rejected and persecuted. It is only when the child is certain of being accepted by the group therapist, and especially by the group, that he can take praise. Our observation indicates that children who have been most persecuted and rejected respond more intensely, positively or negatively, to praise than do those who have been pampered and infantilized. The ability to accept it with ease is one of the symptoms of improvement.

The generosity among the members that is undoubtedly a reflection of the therapist's own sometimes takes other forms. On a number of occasions members brought children to the groups out of a recognition of the latters' needs. We read in one of the records the following:

Bernard brought a boy to the meeting. He called the worker aside and said to him, "I asked Joe to come to our meeting because his mother works and he is alone all the time. He has no friends, and nobody plays with him. They are very poor and Joe is undernourished. He really needs the milk we have here. Do you mind if he stays here?" Throughout the meeting Bernard took care of Joe. He made him feel welcome, helped him with the work, and saw to it that he got enough to eat.

The group therapist's skill and his generous attitudes are reflected in the child's freedom to express his emotional tensions in his presence, to confide in him, and to establish a rapport with him. Positive feelings toward adults are aroused through the relations in a therapy group and this is an important step in character reconstruction and social orientation.

We give here a few examples as they manifested themselves in the conversations of children in groups:

After the boys left, Moe waited around to accompany worker to the basement to return the brush and dust pan. He couldn't seem to leave. He insisted upon coming back the following night just to see worker, who told him that he didn't think they would permit boys of his age in the settlement house during the evening. In addition, he said he would be too busy the entire evening. Moe, however, insisted on coming back and asked again if he couldn't come and talk and be with worker for a little while the following day. Worker agreed to see him for a short while at 7:30 the following evening. At this Moe's face brightened, his eyes widened with glee, and he warned worker not to forget. Upon leaving he shook hands with a very tight grip.

Miles: "I hate to think of you spending money." Robert: "That's not his money; it's the agency that is paying for this." Miles: "Oh, then it's all right."

Gladys, Ann, Jean, and Mary were already present when worker arrived. Mamie came just a few minutes later. The girls waited in the lobby with worker while the janitor who had the keys was being located. Mary said, "She chased us out of the room," and Gladys added, "She wouldn't let us stay there and she locked us out." Worker asked who and Mary said, "Porter, I think that's her name." [She was referring to a staff member of the settlement house.] Jean: "Yes. She was mean. She made Mary take her dress out of the room and locked the door and our coats and hats are in there." It was cold in the lobby and some of the girls were huddled together. Worker: "Well, perhaps it would be better for you to wait down here for me after this and we'll all go up together." Mary: "Oh, she's all right [referring to Miss Porter] when she sleeps. They're all alike. How about you, Miss Kemp?" Jean: "Miss Kemp is different. She's *always* nice."

Worker walked down the street with the girls, Ann on one arm, Jean on the other. As Ann quickly grabbed hold of the worker's arm, Jean walked over to the other side of her and asked her if she could take the other arm. Worker said, "Certainly."

In one instance a worker who became annoyed with a client's prolonged destructiveness during the refreshment period said impulsively, "Why do you grab like this? You wouldn't do it at home." The boy turned crimson with anger and snapped back, "This isn't home!"

QUALIFICATIONS AND TRAINING OF A GROUP THERAPIST

As a result of careful observation of successful group therapists, the following personality traits are at present offered as criteria for qualifications for this work. A group therapist must be: 1) sensitive not only to himself and to his own feelings, but also to the feelings and needs of others; 2) fundamentally un-hostile—one whose adjustment to life is on the side of masoch-ism rather than sadism (such persons are sometimes charac-terized as "saintly"); 3) of few words and of good judgment in the use of language; 4) of a placid temperament—one whose manner and speech are relaxed, quiet, and comforting to others, or what is sometimes referred to as a "therapeutic per-sonality"; 5) positive in his approach to life—he cannot be cynical or destructive; 6) objective—though fond of children and interested in them—for he cannot become involved in the emotional stress of his charges or develop favorites in the group; 7) possessed of what is known as "psychological in-sight," the capacity to recognize and observe the latent con-tent and meaning of what appears to be ordinary behavior; 8) able to meet unusual problems and resourceful in devising psychological and physical conditions to cope with difficult situations; 9) handy with tools and able to learn easily crafts and other art and mechanical occupations to meet the needs of the group; 10) receptive to suggestions, emotionally re-sponsive, and intellectually hospitable, not on the defensive and unable to grow in his work. There is no room in Group Therapy for the compulsive, the paranoidal, the rigid, or the moralistic. The adult must be psychologically free and recep-tive in his attitude toward his charges and toward conditions that may contribute to his own development and effective-ness.

A statement by a group therapist summarizing his own impression of his job after five years in this work may be valuable:

Basically, the group therapist is a scientific observer and reporter. His contact with the members of the group is very personal, yet he must remain in the background and outside the sphere of direct influence, since the greatest therapeutic value is derived from the children's contact with each other. As an observer, he must watch most carefully all the actions, statements, mannerisms, and behavior manifestations of his charges. He must record his observations accurately in a written report, supplementing them with his own conclusions, and then confer with the supervisor on the progress or immediate needs of the group. As a result, new procedures or practices are put into effect as the needs of the group require them.

The qualifications for leadership in Group Therapy are more diverse than in most branches of social work. The therapist is a combination parent-teacher-counselor-caseworker. The parental love and understanding which are lacking in the life of the average delinquent or problem child are qualities that are most essential in him. The teacher quality is necessary in order to create situations, plan the timely introduction of new activities, and assist children in difficult problems where failure would prove a further setback to them. The very nature of the group meeting requires the group therapist to be a club counselor of a sort, although these meetings are not conducted in the manner of a settlement club. To give the entire project meaning, the therapist must be able to understand the psychological import of the behavior and conversation of the group members.

Many of the qualities desirable in a group therapist are not those that can be acquired. Such characteristics as love for children, patience, forbearance, an equable temper, and inner peace are inherent. It would be futile for one lacking such traits to attempt Group Therapy, whatever other scholastic or scientific proficiencies he may possess.

Other qualities, which are largely technical, may be developed through adequate training. Since group meetings are conducted on an activity basis, the therapist must possess or acquire the ability to perform such activities or execute such projects as the group may undertake. A group member often turns to the therapist for advice, criticism, or help in some work at hand. Failure to receive satisfactory advice or assistance may often result in definite harm. The child may assume it to be a personal rejection, which may be disastrous, or lose his interest in the project with a resultant increase in his sense of failure. In addition, all feeling of respect and love for the therapist may disappear as a result and the child will withdraw from the group or become more hostile to the other children and to the surroundings. It is important for the therapist to acquire a knowledge of arts and crafts.

Over a period of a year, a variety of projects will certainly enlarge the children's experiences and give them more ground for common interest and freer conversation. This is bound to involve all the children. There are available many simple books on arts and crafts which could be of utmost use for the workers and the groups. Such books, together with various magazines, may become the basis of a group's library.

The therapist's psychological understanding can be developed through suggested reading, discussions of books and papers, and analysis of actual cases in current active groups.

To report correctly the progress of work, the therapist must view the group psychologically. All behavior, both at play and at work and during accompanying conversations, must be interpreted so that the conditions and motives that prompt it are understood. The ability to give meaning to apparently meaningless things can be developed by the study of the fundamentals of depth psychology.

Technical skill in arts and crafts can be developed only through *doing*. Whether the project is to be clay modeling, puppets, or airplane models, the therapist should prepare himself before the project is introduced into the group. He should actually *model* in clay, *make* puppets, and *construct* airplane models, at home or at workers' meetings. He must know names of parts, techniques, "tricks," and "short-cuts" to encourage children who are awed by something new. The therapist's own work may be used for illustrative purposes to enable the children to visualize the object in a finished or half-finished form. The work need not be perfect; as a matter of fact, it is better if it is slightly crude so that the child may feel he can do "as well" and not be afraid to try. But when the child seeks information or help, it *must* be forthcoming.

It is evident from the foregoing that the proper choice of group therapists is the pivot of this work. The atmosphere which the group therapist creates through his own attitudes and the skill that he uses in dealing with situations as they arise are the foundation of the therapeutic effectiveness of a group. We are not as yet clear as to the type of background training that would be most valuable in this work. It is the temperamental quality that is important rather than specific knowledge. We have already discussed the manual skills and aptitudes that are necessary. We have also stressed the need for "psychological insight" and judgment of group interpersonal situations. We can draw some conclusions from our experience with more than forty workers, but they are necessarily of a very tentative nature.

Persons trained for teaching and especially those who have had prolonged teaching experience are usually poor material for Group Therapy. They are unable to remain as neutral as is required in this work. Perhaps, also, the conditions under which the average public school teacher functions are frustrating and make him irritable. There may be exceptional teachers who could readapt themselves.

Our experience with the eight case workers who directed therapy groups has not been encouraging, either. They seemed to find it difficult to reorientate their attitudes toward interpersonal therapy and to accept the fact that therapy can take place without direct participation by the therapist and without verbal communication and confession on the part of the child. The case workers had it fixed in their minds that no therapy was possible unless there was "insight" and "understanding." As already indicated, this is no doubt true of older adolescents and adults, and in some cases also of children. However, there are many children in treatment who must have direct experience and need to adjust to the impact of actual situations; they need situational therapy. Referring case workers are aware of this and accept it as true in theory.

However, because of their training and practice in interview therapy, those who worked with us were unable to make the necessary functional reorientation even though they had intellectual comprehension of the theory. The difficulty may have arisen from the fact that the case workers in question attempted to conduct groups while they were engaged in their regular work. The functions in psychiatric case work and activity Group Therapy are in great contrast. It is difficult to make the transition from one to the other.[13] The psychiatric training and field work which some case workers now receive would be of great value for group therapists. They must, however, devote themselves exclusively to Group Therapy and absorb its spirit as well as learn its techniques. It can be assumed that, by eliminating this conflict, case workers with psychiatric training can be drawn on for this work.

The worker who supervises group activities in settlement houses is trained for direct participation and active leadership. Ordinarily, psychiatric understanding among such workers is not very high, and there is no need that it should be. Their concern is with the "average" child or youth whose adjustment does not present excessively difficult problems and they do not need to be psychotherapists. Although modern group workers are trained in progressive methods and social work practices and are aware of individual differences and needs, they do not and should not think in terms of pathology. The treatment of pathology through groups is a specialty that should be reserved for a special type of group worker whom, for lack of a better name, we have called group therapists.

A promising field from which group therapists could be drawn is that of occupational therapists, provided they have

[13] This does not hold to the same degree in interview therapy with groups and the combination of activity and interview described in Chapter IX. Enough difference exists between these types of Group Therapy and straight case work, however, to require considerable reorientation here also.

also had psychiatric training and understand abnormal behavior and its meanings. Still another profession that may be fruitful is the nursery teaching group. The training of nursery teachers is such that it qualifies them to understand infant behavior and its meaning, and it is arrested development at the infantile stage that causes problem situations in therapy groups. But the training of nursery school teachers would have to be supplemented by studies in abnormal psychology, case work, and elementary psychiatry in order to qualify them to serve as group therapists.

However, it is our conviction, based upon our experience in Group Therapy in institutions, in social work agencies, and in the education of backward and handicapped children, that only in-service training is effective in this work. Background knowledge is important, but essential skills and judgment can come only from experience.

The procedure which we have employed has been to train workers in seminars after a careful preliminary selection of the group to be trained. The training has consisted in reproducing the actual setting of Group Therapy. The candidates worked with the same materials that children use, in a room like the therapy group room. When they felt unable to cope with a situation, they were not helped right away but allowed to experience the anxiety children suffer when they are threatened with failure, and their relief when aid is offered. We have observed that much of the interpersonal process that occurred in these groups was the same as in therapy groups: antipathies and attractions developed, friendships were made. At the beginning trainees worked as individuals, but gradually they grouped themselves in accordance with common interests and personal preferences. The group consisted usually of about fifteen persons. The training period gave us the opportunity to observe the temperamental constitution of the candidates. The few who could be entrusted with a therapy group were finally selected as a result of these observations. Usually not more than two or three out of the already selected group of fifteen were found suitable to take charge of groups.

At each meeting, after an hour or so of manual work, records of actual groups were read and analyzed by the trainees. The procedure employed was to ask the trainees to list 1) significant situations in the group, 2) mistakes made by the therapist in dealing with situations, and 3) manifestations of skill and insight on his part. They were also asked to deduce a child's problems from his behavior, reconstruct his case history, and interpret the meaning of his acts in terms of his personality. Their conclusions were then checked against the actual case history. This part of the meeting usually took about an hour, after which the group prepared and served refreshments. It was interesting to note that the group gradually took on the responsibility for clearing away materials, setting the table for refreshments, and cleaning up, just as in a therapy group of children.

The training course consisted of twelve to fifteen sessions. At the end of this time, those selected as possible workers attended for several months weekly conferences with the supervisor at which they discussed group records and case histories they had read in advance.

We feel, however, that the real training comes from taking charge of groups, writing extensive and detailed weekly reports, analyzing them with the supervisor, and discussing with him the therapist's behavior and attitudes during the group meetings. The first two years a group therapist is not allowed to meet with a group before a Supervision Conference is held on the preceding meeting. The supervisor *makes definite, concrete suggestions* as to methods of dealing with individual children, anticipates developments in the group, and interprets children's behavior. It is essential to prepare the novice for possible developments in advance and instruct him as to how to handle them until he acquires judgment and the capacity to make quick adjustments to situations as they present themselves.

After two years, Supervision Conferences can be reduced to alternate meetings and group reports submitted less frequently. However, even with the most experienced workers, it is necessary to follow through critical situations in groups that require particular care to avoid destructive developments. It sometimes needs the combined thinking of several people to prevent such difficulties. In addition to the supervisory discussion, a continuing seminar in Group Therapy is held at regular intervals. Our present seminar is in its fifth year.

CHAPTER VII

THE THERAPEUTIC PROCESS

Up to this point, we have discussed Group Therapy as a functional procedure. We have aimed to describe the various elements that go into the making of a therapeutic group complex—the members, the adult, the activities, and the situation as a whole. Questions that may have arisen in the mind of the reader are: What specifically takes place which helps the child to make new and more acceptable adaptations than he has been able to make in the past? What occurs within the child and what is it in these experiences that leads to change? The present chapter will be devoted to answering these questions briefly.

The major result of correcting personality malformations is a decrease in the child's problem-producing propensities. By this we mean that because of the decrease in his own hostile attitude and other psychological pressures, he does not activate the hostility and counter-aggression of parents, siblings, teachers, playmates. Maladjusted persons, especially those of the aggressive type, are problem-creating entities. They do things to people that arouse resentment and hostility. A frustrated and unhappy child comes home from school where he was a failure that day and picks a fight with a sibling or a parent. This gives the evening at home a wrong start and a series of conflicts ensue which mount in intensity and recrimination. These are continued the next day and the next in an endless chain, since emotions have a strong carry-over. What is necessary in such a case is to break the vicious circle. Either the attitude of the parents and teachers has to be changed, or the client's need to discharge his destructive emotions has to be eliminated. If we can succeed in giving him the kind of satisfactions that release his tensions and anxieties, he will not attack the world and set in action this vicious circle.

Another result of emotional relaxation is that with it resistance to the world is decreased. We have already indicated that maladjustment in the majority of problem children springs from the fact that they reject or resist the influences of the outside world. When we dispose the child to accept the reality and restraint of this world, we set the basic condition necessary for psychotherapy. When an individual does not respond to external (educational) influences but resists or defies them, there is indication that his character is malformed and that it needs correction either through psychotherapy or, in cases of organic malfunctions, through medical treatment. The aim of therapy is to correct the structure of the character or the ideological and perceptual attitudes that make satisfactory social adjustment impossible or difficult. The function of psychotherapy is to make the client accessible to external influences by eliminating the blockings and resistances set up in his early life and to release him from his emotional encapsulation. The perception that the world is hostile and threatening must be removed. We must convince the patient that he need not protect himself against it by either withdrawal or attack. These reaction-formations are corrected by the psychotherapist through the establishment of a pleasant mutual relation. The patient establishes (perhaps for the first time in his life) a constructive rapport with another human being, an emotional experience that tends to change his perception of people, the world, and other aspects of reality. It dissolves antagonism and fear, producing a state of mental health.

In the past, therapy consisted chiefly of discussion, advice, and manipulation of the client's environment. The advent of psychoanalysis and the light it brought to bear upon the unconscious sources of behavior made it evident that in many instances intrapsychic tensions must first be removed before the reeducation of the emotions is possible. Interpretation is effective only when a certain relation exists between the client and the therapist. This relation must be satisfying to the client. Here the therapist serves as a catalytic agent causing the flow of unconscious and repressed material toward the traumatic center. The therapist guides the client in evaluating (on an emotional as well as on a rational level) unconscious content and interprets the significance of the traumata, and the consequent aberrations and abreactions, in the light of the client's maturing personality. We have already indicated that because of the age of the client, his low mentality, or his refusal to participate in the therapy process, this is frequently not possible.

The discussion of one's reactions and problems implies a recognition of the existence of a problem. It also assumes a desire to be helped. Such purposiveness is rarely found in young children. Because children lack the "understanding" of their own difficulties and tend to consider themselves in the right—which is characteristic of children's primary egocentricity—direct therapy often fails. It is difficult for a child to understand his own inadequacies, and even when he is led to recognize them, the desire to correct them is not always present. Situational therapy such as a therapy group provides, as differentiated from confessional interviews, is indicated in these cases.

REDUCTION OF ANXIETY

Group Therapy, like all other types of mental treatment, seeks to reduce the inner stresses of which undesirable behavior is only a symptom. It deals with the sources of anxiety that arise from destructive impulses, on the one hand, and the fear of punishment or rejection, on the other; that is, it seeks to recondition the ego structure.

The ego can be viewed as the arbiter or synthesizer of the undifferentiated, instinctive part of the personality and the social strivings of the individual. Studies lead to the conclusion that the disharmony or imbalance between the social trends (super-ego) and instinctive or egoistic trends (id) is the most frequent cause of dissocial behavior. Interestingly enough, unsocial and criminal conduct may be caused either by a laxity in these internalized controls (super-ego) or by their excessive severity. When the checks of the super-ego are too weak, they are unable to cope with the overpowering drives of the primitive and undifferentiated instincts, and dissocial conduct results. On the other hand, when the regulative and inhibiting forces are overintense, they set up anxiety, which is often resolved by antisocial acts.

The vicious circle that is thus set up, in which the child's anxiety impels it to destroy its object, results in an increase of its own anxiety, and this once again urges it on against its object, and constitutes a psychological mechanism which, in my view, is at the bottom of asocial and criminal tendencies in the individual. Thus, we must assume, that it is the excessive severity and overpowering cruelty of the super-ego, not the weakness or want of it, as is usually supposed, which is responsible for the behaviour of asocial and criminal persons.[1]

While we cannot fully accept Mrs. Klein's statement that *all* criminal behavior is a result of an excessive rather than a weak super-ego, studies of the psychological constitution of *some* criminals at least confirm her theoretic formulations.[2] An overintense super-ego begets guilt feelings in respect to even normal impulses. The desire to rid oneself of these disturbing guilt emotions makes one seek punishment through criminal or unsocial acts. The training of the ego so that it may

[1] Melanie Klein, The Early Development of Conscience in the Child, *in* Sandor Lorand, ed., *Psychoanalysis Today*, New York, Covici, Friede, 1933, page 153.

[2] See August Aichhorn, *Wayward Youth*, New York, Viking Press, 1935; Franz Alexander and Hugo Staub, *The Criminal, the Judge, and the Public*, New York, Macmillan, 1931.

accept in a wholesome manner both its negative and positive components is accomplished, in accordance with the principle of displacement, when parents, educators, and society use persuasive rather than punitive and frustrating methods. Excessive punishment and frustration induce either rebellion or guilt and anxiety.

One of the aims in the treatment of maladjusted children is to release the tensions created by the conflict rather than to increase them through constant correction, fault-finding, or punishment. This is particularly true of neurotics. The atmosphere of a therapy group is such that at first it completely suspends social restraints and the child feels free to behave without fear. He returns to a state of irresponsibility and infantile patterns, but because the group sets up a primary group code, he gradually reconstructs his impulses (id) so as to be accepted by the therapist and the other members of the group (superego).

Another source of anxiety is the primary and acquired aggressiveness which the individual seeks to curb so that he may gain the love of others and be accepted by the group. But where the ego structure is defective, the individual cannot rely upon his inner restraints to achieve this—it is as though he were afraid of himself—and as a result his anxieties are increased. This is clearly shown in shy and submissive persons. Along with submissive behavior, we usually find in the inner layers of personality a surging cauldron of repressed, hostile tendencies and drives. The function of psychotherapy in these instances is to eliminate the conflict that results.

By accepting the child's hostile behavior in a group[3] his ten-

---

[3] This acceptance is fraught with great danger. If the patient's basic character structure is a criminal one or if constitutional factors are present which make reconstruction of character problematic, the release of guilt is not desirable. Without restraint the client becomes an active criminal and a menace to others. Sometimes it is necessary to turn the delinquent into a neurotic, temporarily at least. If there is no possibility of accomplishing this, a criminal free of all restraint may be dangerous indeed.

sion is released. External imposition, social control, judgment, and censure are removed. Indeed, the therapist feels he has succeeded rather than failed when the child, who has shown evidences of inner tensions caused by inhibited aggressiveness and hostility, expresses his aggressive tendencies freely. This is activity catharsis and has been found to be eminently successful with neurotic children. The patient throws over the tyranny of his super-ego, feels the release of freedom of action without conflict, relaxes, and becomes amenable to the influences of the group and the therapist and later also to the wider culture. Thus a new and healthier super-ego is built, devoid of fear and anxiety.[4]

The center of disturbance in many patients is their fear of losing the love of their parents and other persons, or resentment at having already lost it. The resultant anxieties are probably the most terrifying of all. Sometimes rejection is real; at other times it exists only in the imagination of the patient. In both instances, the patient must enter into a relation with someone by whom he can feel completely accepted. The psychiatrist and case worker satisfy this affect hunger. A therapy group serves similar ends. Here the child is accepted not only by an adult, but also by a group of peers, a substitute family, one more reason why the child's hostile aggressiveness must be accepted in Group Therapy, for acceptance assures him of unconditional love.

There was a bureau in the room the two top drawers of which were assigned to the group for materials. Harold said, "They have no right to gyp us like that; all the other drawers have two knobs on, and ours have only one." He decided to take a knob off one of the other drawers and put it on ours. Joseph helped him. Harold to worker: "You see I am breaking the dresser." Worker told him he wasn't breaking it. It evidently did not make any difference which

[4] The change in the ego structure which is marked by the transition from the infantile (parental) super-ego to the group super-ego is discussed on pages 229 ff. of this chapter.

drawers had the knobs on, and the boys were merely changing from one to another.

Murray called Alter a "dope" and said that he had no brains. As Alter passed Murray he picked up the bundle of grass rope and hit Murray on the head. The latter picked up the bundle and hit Alter over the head several times, chasing him around the room and out into the hall. They must have had a fight there, for Murray came back hastily and locked the door on Alter. Moe now joined in with Murray, holding the door for him against Alter. When Murray resumed his work, worker pretended to go out for something in the next room, allowing Alter to come in.

Throughout the remainder of the afternoon Mary and Rose were engaged in rather good-natured battling. The slightest remark started them off, Mary usually doing the chasing. Rose would run around the room, then out the door. The two of them would reenter a few moments later, all smiles and no resentment. Once on her way out after Rose, Mary picked up a bottle of yellow water color, which she evidently threw in Rose's direction. Rose escaped being soiled, but the floor in the hall was liberally splashed. . . . Later Mary went to Rose's bag and removed a note. Rose besought her to return it, but to no avail. Mary absolutely refused to return it. Rose did not at any point become angry. She merely begged and pleaded, saying that she must have that note, and that she wouldn't leave without it. Mary finally returned it just before the group disbanded.

Murray held Alter down across two chairs and held a large knife threateningly over him. At this point Hal decided to annoy Alter, too, and while Murray had him down, attempted to remove his shoes. This continued later in the outer hall, even while the refreshments were being served.

RELEASE THROUGH ACTIVITY

It can be said that modern man's energies and interests flow toward a number of centers: family, vocation, avocations, political activity, friends, economic security, recreation, and others. These interests vary with the individual in number and kind and also in the degree of importance attached to each.

Everyone has one or more major or focal interests and a number of minor or peripheral ones. It is to be expected that the former will be more meaningful and charged with greater emotion than the latter. The person with a healthy character directs interest into a number of channels. Single-interest persons—those who are excessively preoccupied with one interest to the exclusion or neglect of others—are not adequately adjusted. Such hyperemotivity may be symptomatic of anxiety, insecurity, the need for escape, and similar pathological causes requiring correction.

Activity[5] is so important that many persons suffer from what are known as "Sunday neuroses." While this particular disturbance appears to result from idleness, it may have other causes, such as a break in routine and in the rhythm of life, hyperemotivity, hyperkinetic tensions, early associations, or hostility to persons in the home. Whatever the reason, the fact to be noted is that it is interest and activity that hold the threads of living together and keep people in a state of effective function and seeming normality. The experience of one of the colleges in Oxford University[6] bears closely upon the question under discussion. Two groups of workers were equated as to intelligence, but the members of one group were employed while those in the other were out of work. All took exactly the same courses. The unemployed seemingly had more time in which to study, but they failed in their examinations. Also, a larger ratio in the employed group attained "honors" than in the group who had no jobs. The conclusion of the Master of the college based upon these results was expressed in the cryptic statement: "Jobless men are only shadows of their real selves." While the elements of social rejection and the paralyzing effects of insecurity are factors to be reckoned

[5] The concept "activity" is employed here to designate all human functions (physical, aesthetic, emotional, intellectual, and social) and not merely manual or physical activity, the sense in which it is often used.

[6] Quoted in S. R. Slavson, *Character Education in a Democracy*, New York, Association Press, 1939, page 41.

with, there is no doubt that the lack of energizing stimuli as a result of inactivity played its part.

The most obvious means of evolving a balanced field of interest in the child is to provide him with a many-sided education and a variety of active experiences. Activity has guidance value as well as direct therapeutic possibilities. It is effective, however, only when it meets certain conditions. 1) It must be appropriate to permanent interests (due to disposition) and to temporary interests (due to growth). This means that the child must discover these interests by himself on an exploratory basis. 2) In therapy, work is initiated and carried out by the child unblocked by the therapist. The latter participates only when necessary to achieve a reasonable degree of success and satisfaction. 3) Activity is carried on in a group setting *but not necessarily as a group project*. The presence of others has a socializing effect through spontaneous mutual help, admiration of the work done by others, cooperation of two or more in a group project, pleasurable feelings that come from constructive effort in a group, and the gradual development of an awareness of the need of others.

One of the chief values of such activity is that it is *libido-binding*: it gives form, organization, and direction to the otherwise dispersed and disorganized urges, impulses, and desires. Libido-binding interests, such as love, earning a living, a social interest, or a creative effort, are not only essential in the therapy of the neurotic (for they are among the major realities to which he has to adjust), but are also excellent preventatives of neuroses. Their value lies not in reeducation alone but in education as well.

Some activities produce quiet, sedentary response from the participants; others release and stimulate. The two extremes are crocheting, in the first category, and basketball, in the second. Between these extremes range such occupations and games as weaving, basketry, clay modeling, painting, wood work, metal work, finger painting, quoits, tenpins, baseball, cops and robbers. The quieter activities can be described as *immobilizing;* those that activate more or less intense response as *stimulating.*

The withdrawn child prefers the immobilizing occupations such as leather work, pyrography, sewing, knitting, drawing. The aggressive and hyperactive child usually chooses the more lively and noisy forms of expression. Active games, metal hammering, wood work, bell ringing, and the like are his starting point. In a therapy group, these peak activities tend to meet at an average level. That is, extraverted children become increasingly interested in the quiet occupations, while the withdrawn and self-effacing gradually join their more active fellow members. The balance in activity is undoubtedly indicative of intrapsychic growth and personality balance as well.

In activity therapy the hyperactive child starts with stimulating activity, but the objective is to help him reach a point when his energies can be focused and he becomes less active. In the case of the hypoactive clients, the aim is to extend and diffuse interest and group participation. By choosing immobilizing activity, the hypoactive child isolates himself from the group. This need for isolation may be caused by fear or lack of experience with groups. A large proportion of children in therapy groups begin with *isolating activities.* But the atmosphere in the group, the physical arrangement, and practical necessities—such as sharing materials and tools—encourage them to take part in *socializing activities.* Later these assume more purely socializing forms such as quarrels, fights, games, hilarity, horseplay, cooperation, and friendships. Davis presents in graphic form the same development in psychoneurotic and psychotic patients (see accompanying figure).[7]

[7] John E. Davis, in collaboration with William Rush Dunton, *Principles and Practice of Recreational Therapy for the Mentally Ill,* New York, A. S. Barnes, 1936, page 92.

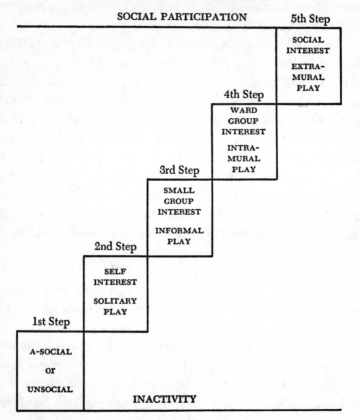

INTEREST AND EFFORT

SOCIAL PARTICIPATION 5th Step

SOCIAL INTEREST

EXTRA-MURAL PLAY

4th Step

WARD GROUP INTEREST

INTRA-MURAL PLAY

3rd Step

SMALL GROUP INTEREST

INFORMAL PLAY

2nd Step

SELF INTEREST

SOLITARY PLAY

1st Step

A-SOCIAL or UNSOCIAL

INACTIVITY

Represents theoretical steps for the utilization of available motives leading to resocialization with possible concomitant exercises. Theoretically the patient might be progressed from inactivity through solitary play to social participation by utilizing the progressive motives of self interest, family interest, small group interest, and finally social interest.

It is fundamentally important to emphasize the social nature of the behaviour disorders and to seek in the play situation the highest available motives for resocialization and the control situations which will enable the therapist to assist the patient to become more social. The regressed patient may first be inducted into solitary play and as he becomes more at ease and confident enlarge his social activity until he can engage in progressively larger group adaptations.

From Principles and Practice of Recreational Therapy *by John E. Davis*
Copyright 1936 by A. S. Barnes and Company

This movement from self to non-self is demonstrated in the several short quotations from reports of the meetings of therapy groups which follow.

Hal, in carrying the can of red water-color paint, spilt it accidentally on the floor, on one of the chairs, a considerable amount on Simon's pants, and a lesser amount on Alfred's. The boys realized it was an accident and did not scold him, and Hal went out with Simon to the sink in the hall and began to remove the spilled paint from Simon's pants. He worked at this for quite a time.

Harold took his airplane model out of the closet and asked Richard to help with it. Richard, who was busy with his own job, promised to do so later, which he did. . . . Richard asked worker if he could go down and get himself another plane. He said he could. Teddy asked if he could get one for him, too. Richard asked Teddy what type of plane he wanted. The latter told him. Richard invited Harold to go along with him and both left.

Hilary said it would be very good if the boys had a work bench. He suggested that they start making things for themselves. All could get together and make a bench for the group to use. The others agreed to do it.

One of the men in the building came in and gave worker a big box of cup cakes, telling him he could have it for the boys. They all ran over to look at it. Worker told them they could each have one to take home, since they had just had their milk and crackers. They counted the cakes and discovered that after each one took a cake there would be six left. Richard suggested that worker leave these six remaining cakes, with a note, for the other group. The boys all agreed, saying, "That would be fine."

The psychotherapist recognizes that all behavior and impulses have etiological significance and that the patient's acts and conversation are the path that lead him to the center of his problem and to a probable resolution of it. In individual therapy this is achieved largely through the medium of language. In Group Therapy the child is encouraged *to act as well as to speak freely*. He is released through activity catharsis.

The impelling drive of hate is to destroy the object of that hate. Hate cannot be as easily satisfied as love. The fear of punishment and the pressure of the super-ego check the destructive impulse. One cannot kill, for example, without dire results, but one can love. Love is acceptable to society and to its internalized representative, the super-ego or conscience. This may be the reason why hate is so much more consuming and more lasting an emotion than love: it cannot be satisfied; and why love wanes so readily: it is more or less easily satisfied. But when hostility and hatred are redirected to other objects as substitutes, the patient feels relieved. In Group Therapy we supply opportunities for such substitutions and sublimations. The following abstracts illustrate ways in which this happens:

Robert said he would make something later. He took the piece of wood he had cut and said it was a spear. He walked around with it saying he would kill anyone who crossed his path. Joseph told worker to walk in front of Robert.

Harvey was unusually restless that afternoon. He annoyed everyone and touched everything. He did not seem to find anything to do with the materials. He said all he did at home and in the street was play with guns. That was the only thing he liked. Worker asked him what type of games he liked to play with guns, and he said, "Just fighting." Worker asked if it was supposed to be a war or something like that. He said, no, they just had two gangs of kids and shot at each other. That was the game they played and that was the only thing that he liked. . . . At the meetings Harvey very frequently picked at other children's work with a knife, tore paper, broke pieces of wood, or just threw knives to the floor cutting into it. Today he did the latter. Worker explained that he was cutting up the floor and that he could have some wood to cut if he liked. He said there wasn't any wood in the closet, but worker showed him that there was, and he took a big piece of wood and just kept cutting it.

During the evening, for no apparent reason, Mary would suddenly scream at the top of her voice and stamp her feet as if in a rage. The girls looked at her in surprise and at the worker as though expecting her to interfere. When the girls saw that the worker paid no attention to Mary's behavior, they told her to "shut up" and to "stop acting crazy." . . . After each screaming episode Mary would look at worker and laugh. Worker paid no attention to this.

Intellectual and manual activity (and often social activity as well) may be a form of aggression, and in some instances also of hostility. A young student who makes hydrogen by destroying zinc derives as much pleasure from destroying the metal as from creating the gas. In fact, on numerous occasions, the object of the experiment is abandoned and the pupil spends a great deal of time in merely watching the zinc disappear. This he repeats many times. It is still difficult to determine what it is that pleases the child more: the cutting up of boards or constructing the shelf. In fact, the numerous complaints on the part of teachers in shops where free activity is permitted, that so many of the children do not finish what they start out to do, may indicate that the destructive phase of their projects is more captivating to them at that particular time than the constructive.

Creative effort, such as painting, clay modeling, and carpentry, by relieving unconscious and inner pressures, has therapeutic value for the same reasons as aggressive behavior. In many instances our clients make clay figures and jab at them with knives with expressions of anger and hate on their faces. Breaking and mutilating doll figures is also common. Older children frequently discharge their hostility on tools, materials, and windowpanes.

An eight-year-old girl, rejected intensely in favor of an older sister who was much brighter and more socially acceptable, was once playing with a window pole. She turned to the group worker and said, "I'm going to throw this down [out of a seventh-floor window] on the head of someone whose name begins with E." Her mother's name was Edith.

A boy of fourteen made a corpse with arms crossed over the chest from green plasticine and placed him in a coffin with a pink cover made of the same material. The quality of workmanship was quite high and he was profusely praised by the other boys. His response was, "You ought to see my brother do clay work. He is much better than I." (Note: The brother was a preferred sibling of whom our client was very jealous. He was very hostile toward his brother, which had made him withdrawn and anxious. There is little doubt that the corpse and lidded coffin expressed our client's hidden wishes in regard to his brother.)

Activity balances emotional pressures because it serves some specific corrective needs of the client. Attack upon materials and surroundings by emotionally disturbed children proves quite conclusively that children redirect their hostility upon the inanimate environment in accordance with the principle of "dispersion of emotion" and gain considerable release through it.[8] Dr. Oberndorf has found that "activity which admits free play of repressed aggressivity unconsciously permits a beneficial egress of the hostile affects." It may be thought that such unimpeded activity has only release value. But that is not the case for, by allowing a disturbed child to act as he pleases, we assure him of our love and of acceptance by the group. The effect is a diminished need for further aggression. We have already quoted one boy's definition of love: *"When people let me do what I want to do, then I know they love me."* We must accept at first even this distorted idea of love until the client is ready to see it in a more realistic light. The following conversation during a trip of one of our groups illustrates the same idea. One boy said to another, "I like this club. There are no bosses here." The other replied, "Yes, but Joe [group therapist] is a boss." "Yes," said the first, "but he doesn't tell you what to do." Unconditional acceptance serves to attenuate hostility to (what the client feels to be) a persecuting and rejecting world.[9]

---

[8] In a study made by the author (unpublished) we found instances of permanent and temporary recovery in delinquent children in an institution as a result of hostility-diverting effort.

[9] "Normal" children in free-activity schools also improve both in attitudes

Free play and work, therefore, have no therapeutic value if carried on in isolation. Their value in therapy springs from the fact that others witness it and do not restrain or punish. In fact, a hyperactive child may seek to draw other persons even into the individual therapy situation: he may stop adults who pass by, or invade a room where there are other persons in the hope that the therapist will follow him there. Once in the presence of a third person, the child tests out how far he can challenge the case worker, that is, how completely he is accepted by the substitute parent.

In the early stages of Group Therapy, therefore, children are allowed to do whatever they please. The new family is kind, accepting, and approving, and offers the things that one craved but never found before. *Hostile and aggressive acts have therapeutic value only when they are permitted and not merely because they are committed.* What the disturbed child needs is the assurance of his personal worth, of his value as an individual. It is to this as much as to the release value of activity that we can attribute improvement. Where he can get recognition for constructive acts, therapy is furthered. It must also be kept in mind that a child's hostility is really counter-hostility to a world at whose hands he has suffered. Even when the perception of this antagonism is phantasied, it is real as far as the child is concerned. A destructive act alone, therefore, does not satisfy the inner cravings to be loved. It is only when the act is accepted by some adult that it releases tension and sets the stage for emotional reorientation.

DEVELOPING SELF-ACCEPTANCE

When the child is not censured and his personality is accepted, his attitudes toward himself are also altered. The all-

and in health, an improvement which can be attributed to two causes—the setting up of an organic balance through activity, expression, and group participation and the feeling of being accepted and approved by adults and peers.

pervasive dissatisfaction with himself, self-hatred, is displaced by self-tolerance and a hopeful attitude. A child who has been rejected seldom escapes self-blame for he is consistently reminded that he is "bad" and that because of this badness he is punished. Even when he resists and evolves a self-protective righteousness, there lurks deep in him a feeling of guilt and inadequacy. Not to be loved comes to mean to the young child that he does not deserve to be loved. Even when hostility is directed toward the parent because of his rejection, the child blames himself for not being different, better, like the boys and girls who are loved, so that he too would be loved. But still, he feels, the parent ought to love him anyway.

This vortex of conflicting emotions torments him. He feels lonely, uncertain of himself, insecure, and hopeless. To counteract the confusion and to restore his sense of self-worth, the child represses this self-censure. He becomes introspective, restless, tense, and nervous. He abases himself or finds relief in delinquency and criminality. Various types of aberrant acts serve as ways of escaping the tension that comes from the contrast between the child's ego ideal set up by his infantile super-ego—what he ought to be—and what he is. Being debased or punished gives him the relief that the neurotic is always pursuing but seldom finds.

When the guilt due to inadequacy and badness is too well repressed, as in some types of behavior disorder and in psychopathic personalities, treatment becomes difficult and even problematic. Since such persons have rejected almost completely the restraints of parents and teachers, and with them the outer world, there are no controls or sanctions within themselves. The child returns to a state of infantile autoeroticism. In some instances he regresses to a condition of polymorphous perversion and becomes inaccessible to Group Therapy.[10] In less seriously disturbed children the conflict be-

[10] For discussion of such a case, see Chapter IV, pages 99 ff.

tween self-love and self-rejection is more on the surface and can be reached.

It is our belief that if such a character anomaly is intense, as in the case of neurotic children, correction cannot be achieved until the client has first accepted himself as he is. The conflict between the ego and the ego ideal must first be resolved and when this is done a new superstructure is built. As the child acts out his conflicts in the group he is also aware of the other members as they are and as they react to him. In such cases Group Therapy seeks to prevent the child's being censured or rejected. The personnel of the group must be so planned that no further tension or self-rejection is induced. Rather, the group experience must be comforting so that the client can evolve a feeling of self-worth. With some exceptions the aim is to give constant satisfactions rather than to create outer discord and inner unhappiness. We consistently help those children who need it to accept themselves and thereby to be accepted.

Another condition that aids the process of self-acceptance is the discovery on the part of members that they are not as different and unique as they had felt. There are others (the members of the group) who act in the same way they do and are in the same difficulties. This reduces considerably feelings of difference, consequent anxiety, and reactive behavior—a process that has been observed in all group treatment situations such as reeducational institutions, "reform" schools, therapy camps, and in our groups. This point is also made by Mrs. Gabriel when she states that "the children [in her group] realized they were not different from other children" and that as a result their compensatory behavior was diminished.[11]

There are of course many cases where direct impeding of

11 Betty Gabriel, An Experiment in Group Treatment, *American Journal of Orthopsychiatry*, 9:146–149, January 1939. See also Chapter IX, pages 316 ff.

aggressive behavior is indicated. In cases of prolonged infancy, pampering, and emotional exploitation there is a need for the child to discover the reality of human relations. Provided social hunger is present in these clients, they give up their domineering, provocative, and narcissistic behavior if it is not accepted by the others in the group and by the adult in charge. As they adopt more acceptable means for communicating with the world and gain satisfactions through them, their attitudes are altered. In some instances deeper personality changes also occur as a result. The following excerpts from records illustrate how self-acceptance gradually grows out of group activities:

Toward the close of the meeting, Jerry showed his ring to worker. He was enthusiastic about his work and remarked, "Boy, isn't this coming out swell! Now I'll have my two sisters on my neck for it." He placed the ring in his pocket and began to assist worker in cleaning up the room, placing the materials in the cabinet.

The worker asked Sam how his folks liked the copper plaque he made at the previous meeting. "Nobody believed I made it," said Sam smilingly. "I could hardly believe it myself. I never tried anything like that before." . . .
(A few weeks later.) Sam looked again very intently upon his finished project in admiration, slowly shaking his head from side to side, and said, "Gee, who would ever think it." After a while he added smilingly, "Nobody'll ever believe I made it."

Harold was left at the table alone. He showed worker the glider, saying that it wasn't any good, one wing was larger than the other and now it wouldn't fly. Worker asked him to try it. He threw it up in the air, and it flew a little distance. Worker commented on how nicely it worked. He said, "Yes, but it would go better if the wings were even." He seemed disappointed. Worker asked him if he had made many planes. He said, "No, this is the first one I ever tried." Worker told him he thought it was very good for the first one; considering the fact that it was a first attempt, it couldn't possibly be perfect. Worker was sure when he got more practice he would make them more the way he would like them to be. Harold put the plane down and went over to watch the checker game. . . .

(Two months later.) Harold took his plane out of the closet and began to work on it. With great surprise he told worker to look. "I can work on it myself now, I know how to do it."

Robert came in without his twin brother Joseph. The boys greeted him. They all sat down at a table and talked about the circus. Robert said he wasn't going because he didn't want to miss school. The others told him they didn't mind missing school, they were going. Robert, without any feeling of embarrassment, said that if they were as dumb as he was in school, they wouldn't want to miss either. Maybe they didn't get "D" on their report cards the way he did. He'd like to go, but if he missed school, it would be hard for him to make it up.

Hal drew quite accurately, and when worker remarked upon how perfect his reproductions were, he said, "Yes, I like drawing and I am pretty good at this kind of work."

Jean, formerly a withdrawn and inferior-feeling girl, held up her copper ash tray, and asked worker if the design was all right. Worker admired it, saying that it was very effective. She smiled happily and said, "Do I have enough time to make another one? I'd like a pair of them to give to my mother."

Developing Acceptance of Others

As anxieties are reduced and the child grows less tense and less self-critical, he is also able to accept other people, for the inability to accept others arouses counter-rejection and counter-hostility on their part. Basically, one is rejected by a group because one rejects it first, either by withdrawing from it or by attacking it. "The life of the party" is usually one who exploits the group for his emotional needs. The ascetic gains his ends by rejecting the group entirely. Rejection of a group can be expressed overtly through quarreling, taking issue, stubbornness, or domination, or by non-cooperation and indifference. Direct domination destroys the group's autonomy; the less direct means threatens its stability and survival. In either instance the group reacts by threatening or rejecting the divergent individual. The value of group experience to such persons (if they can adapt themselves to it) is apparent. Here they have the opportunity to reexperience group relations in a new light and evolve a better adjustment to social situations; they can acquire new habits in line with new feelings and attitudes. To accomplish this the group must be so balanced that it does not threaten or frighten the child. Our records show that Group Therapy has been eminently successful as a social reconditioning experience. Boys and girls who were isolated and unable to get on with people before have become progressively more mature and better adjusted in groups.

The ability to relate oneself to other persons is the crux of human happiness. To many all relations have brought unpleasantness. The prime aim of psychotherapy is to help the patient establish constructive relations first with the therapist, later with other people, and finally with the larger world. We have already mentioned in preceding pages the universally accepted fact that when such a relation (transference) cannot be established between client and therapist, treatment cannot be continued with profit. Some children are so suspicious and apprehensive that they are unable to establish a direct transference to an adult. They can, however, slowly relate themselves to children of their own age in the group, and later to the therapist, because neither constitutes a threat. The group does not invade the intimate precincts of personality, deep anxieties, and traumata. A therapy group provides latitude: the child can keep to himself, work by himself, evade contact with other members. The group stimulates activity, yet makes no direct and immediate demands upon him. In this way, he can establish relations at his own pace.

George, with an attitude of assurance, began work on his airplane. His work was of a slow, steady, planned type, which indicated experience. Throughout the evening he offered help and advice to the other boys. Simon, who worked with Hal on a boat model, withdrew and took up an airplane model for himself. [These boys have become inseparable friends.] With advice from George he kept working on this model all evening. Alter, too, came to George for advice. Further advice was forthcoming from Philip's friend [a visitor], who gave it voluntarily to the other boys. This information, though not asked for, was quite agreeably accepted by all the boys, all of whom were very much absorbed in what they were doing.

Esther promptly offered her services in cleaning up. Both she and worker went down to the kitchen to wash the dishes. Esther insisted upon washing and drying them by herself. When they returned to the room, Mamie told worker that they had been discussing the name of the club and the fact that they wanted to purchase sweaters or jackets of some sort with the name of the club across the back.

Ann and Gladys talked about school, Regents' Examinations, and camp. Ann asked Gladys if she would go out with her to get the refreshments. The latter said she would. Ann took out the certificates she had received from her high school for perfect attendance and punctuality and showed them to Gladys. She also displayed her sunburn. This she did as each one of the girls arrived at the meeting.

Worker had drawn a picture of a woman's face. Richard looked at it very closely and told worker that it was lopsided. He agreed with him and Richard told him how to fix it up. . . . The cocoa was upset. Teddy and Harold came running over to the table. Teddy commented that the cocoa was wasted. Harold: "You fool, why do you talk about that? He [worker] might have burned himself. Maybe he did." He asked worker if he was hurt. Worker told him he was not.

Worker suggested that the girls discuss where and when they would meet to go to the theater the following Wednesday. The girls said they could meet in front of the building. Mary said maybe her brother-in-law would drive her down in the car. Worker: "I could meet you about 1:15 then." Gladys: "You wouldn't have to come all the way in to meet us. We could meet you near the theater." The other girls agreed that they could do that. . . . Worker was clearing away the materials, and Ann, Jean, and Rose helped. Ann: "Who is going to help rinse the cups?" Worker went over to cabinet and took out the dishes to be rinsed off. Ann said to Jean, "You help her with it." Jean went along with the worker and rinsed out the dishes as the worker dried them.

After the card game was over Richard looked at the paintings the boys had made and suggested that they have an exhibit of all their work and invite their friends and relatives. All the boys agreed that this would be very nice.

Sue, who had nailed a piece of copper onto a wooden frame last week, told worker that she had drawn a picture on the copper and that everyone at home had admired it.

This is the third meeting at which Gladys mentioned the fact that her father used the sponge she had made out of spongex.

One of the most important single factors that help members of groups to relate themselves to one another is free, unimpeded communication. It has been noted by students of behavior that communication is an imperative need of the human being, and indeed of all animals. Exchange of ideas and emotions arouses creative and social impulses. Language is an expression of man's dependence upon man and it is a form of power, a source of security, and a mechanism of evasion. Its importance is attested to by the jealousy with which it is guarded and controlled by tyrants and dictators. Control of communication is the most reliable means of checking subversive developments. Solitary confinement (removal of the possibility of communication) is the severest punishment next to physical torture.

The communicative drive is especially strong among children. The results of a study conducted by the present writer of the frequency and types of communication in a group of fourteen children between the ages of four and ten reveal its importance. The study was made in the course of a year in a combination workshop and simple science laboratory, designed for individual use rather than for group projects. Stenographers recorded the children's remarks and described and made sketches of their work at various stages. The room was at all times the scene of intense activity. Although the projects were largely of an individual nature, there was constant intercommunication among the children. Of several thousand contacts noted, 87 per cent were verbal communication. These data, which are confirmed by many observations in less controlled situations, indicate that verbal communication is a primary need of man.[12] We have also noted that this need varies in degree with different individuals. Our observation of problem children both in therapy groups and in institutions leads to the conclusion that free access to one another and free exchange of views and feelings have unsurpassed therapeutic value. In Group Therapy there is full freedom for interaction and communication, which provides the members with the opportunity to relate themselves to one another.

When one overcomes the tensions that impede or vitiate human relations and finds the much needed group acceptance by such means, a foundation is laid for total adjustment. The child is now prepared to find for himself a satisfactory place in the many areas in which he has to function in modern society. He can get on with his family, in school, with his playmates, on the job, and, as he grows older, in more intimate personal relations.

(Minutes of one of the Integration Conferences.) This was Benjamin's first group experience and case worker felt that the boy had been much freer in his interviews since he had attended the group.

(Report of a trip.) The boys were continually talking to each other. Richard said to Robert, "Do you remember when we were enemies?" and both burst into good-natured laughter.

(Indoor swimming party.) There was an entirely different feeling in the group at this meeting. For example, the boys accepted Robert and Joseph. This was clear by the way in which they

---

[12] The corollary of this observation is the imperative need for a change in educational practices, both in school and out, which insist upon quiet and receptivity on the part of the pupils instead of allowing expression and free communication.

talked to them, no longer criticizing everything they did. Worker noticed the boys patting one another on the back and putting their arms on one another's shoulders. Their acceptance of one another was also indicated by the intonation of their voices. When they went to see Jumbo, a few months before, there were many strange boys, but they paid no attention to them. While in the swimming pool today, they talked and played with all the other children there. They played tag and ball in the pool in a friendly manner, and no arguments or fights arose.

We started the trip by walking toward the Battery. Hal, Phil, Alter, and Simon walked ahead, with Hal always managing to stay closest to worker. He pushed Simon out of the way several times to walk close to worker with his arm on the latter's shoulder. On turning back to see how close the other boys were, worker saw Alfred walking between George and Murray, their arms on one another's shoulders.

ADJUSTING TO AN EXPANDING ENVIRONMENT

Psychotherapy and psychoanalysis assume that when character distortions are corrected the client finds his own way in the world. However, because of its special field and nature, social case work has to deal with the total situation as well as give direct psychotherapy. The client must be helped to get himself accepted by his social environment, and case workers alter the client's environment in accordance with his needs. They help with school placement, jobs, recreational and other social outlets; they manipulate and correct the home setting. The two aspects of psychotherapy (and this is especially true of psychiatric case work) are 1) to readjust the personality of the patient so that he may become acceptable to others, and 2) to manipulate, when necessary, the external environment so that it will accept him. Sometimes it is necessary to expose the client during the course of treatment to groups of attenuated social pressure where he may adjust with a minimum of fear and strain, or to place him on a job where not only the occupation itself is suitable, but also the relations with other people are not too threatening or irritating. This is equally true of recreational and other social contacts. Agencies that are of service here are the schools (through their special classes), correctional institutions, resident clubs, and neighborhood and recreational centers.

Group Therapy meets these treatment needs by exposing children to an ever widening social and physical environment as they become ready for the experience. They are also given the opportunity to activate the world and to suffer the consequences of their undesirable behavior. On trips rowdyism in trolleys and trains, for example, is not stopped by the group therapist. Rather he ignores it by reading a paper or carrying on a conversation with one or more of the quieter members. Other passengers complain and restrain. The only person who is not allowed to use violence against the children is the conductor. When he attempts it, the therapist goes over and announces the fact that the children are with him. It is gratifying to see how rowdy and uncontrolled behavior in public conveyances gradually subsides until it altogether disappears after four or five trips.

Trips, picnics, excursions, movies, concerts, theater parties, bicycle rides, and similar diversions are introduced to provide variety as well as new experiences, and about one meeting in five or six is held outside of the regular club room. The value of these activities lies in widening the children's social horizon and supplying direction toward the larger world. Children who cannot participate in direct personal relationships find it easier to go out with the group on trips and excursions and, according to reports from case workers, gain considerable satisfaction and security through the experience. Some children, however, are too frightened to venture beyond the confines of the club room. Trips are particularly meaningful to children from economically deprived homes and neighborhoods. A report of one of our early groups reads:

It was evident at the start that in spite of their age (seventeen to eighteen years) the members knew nothing of their city. Their life did not extend beyond their immediate neighborhoods. The trips seemed to unfold a world of new ideas and interests to the girls. Their spontaneous exclamations and questions indicated that they were literally spellbound by everything they saw. Upon seeing Radio City, all of them declared that they never thought such things existed.

The girls displayed equal enthusiasm and wonder when they went to museums, swimming pools, picnics, transatlantic steamers, and similar places. These outings were pleasurable to the girls and it was a revelation to the worker to find that they had had so little constructive guidance in the past. All the girls had lived in New York all their lives and had never before seen the Public Library.

During these trips it became evident that their value to the girls was more than mere pleasure and enlightenment. From the very outset the girls made their own decisions. The worker suggested possibilities and described briefly the places to which they might go. The decision rested with the girls themselves. The experience of making decisions gave them unmistakable satisfaction. Not having participated before in a positive manner in groups, the pleasure of getting together and doing things with others under the guidance of a friendly and sympathetic adult had telling results.

A further value of trips lies in the fact that they satisfy the children's need for new experiences and change. Aversion to monotony and repetition proceeds from a general instability and low degree of frustration tolerance. Trips such as we have described should therefore be utilized for their value in treatment as well as in the development of social maturity. Our transitional groups described elsewhere in this volume (Chapter IX, pages 326 ff.) also serve the ends of social acceptance. The members are gradually introduced into the activities of a neighborhood center either as individuals or as a group and are helped to fit into the larger social environment. This is especially necessary when the child, because of his early memories, is afraid to make the first step in this direction.

Another way to make the transition from the protected

therapy group to wider social acceptance is to combine two groups of children about the same age for trips. This has to be done cautiously, however, as it may result in conflicts and jealousy or prove threatening to some clients who are still fearful of social contacts.

The acceptance by the group of a new boy, who was extremely deprived and neglected at home, is well illustrated in the incident given below. This acceptance is a necessary preliminary before the child can venture into the larger environment.

Hy completed his telegraph set that evening. He had difficulty getting it to "click" and asked the worker to help him. He seemed a little abashed when worker removed the insulation around a wire which prevented electrical contact. Once this was done, Hy proceeded on his own. When the apparatus began to respond to the key, Hy's eyes expanded with joy, and there was a grin of elation on his face. He jumped up and down, clapped his hands, and called on the other boys to come and see the set he had made. It was genuine ecstasy. He sang, he jumped, he showed his set around the room, and then settled down to work with it. He experimented further and described to the worker his plan for installing a light which would synchronize with the click. Even aggressive, critical Ben admitted that it was good. He looked at the apparatus in silent admiration and voiced congratulations which added greatly to Hy's joy. Sandy: "How do you make a thing like that?" Leo: "That's good, that's as good as a regular set." Manny: "He's all right, isn't he?" Ted and Bernie looked on astonished and admiringly. But Ben, the final authority, said, "I didn't think you'd be able to do it, but it's pretty good."

We give the following rather lengthy abstract which describes a boy's own effort at widening his social contacts as soon as his basic personality difficulties were decreased:

Moe was referred for treatment because of extremely aggressive behavior at home and at school. He had misbehaved so badly that he was put out of a settlement house. When he first came to the therapy group he was withdrawn and frightened, fearing to reveal himself and suffer the inevitable consequences of his acts.

As he became more secure, though the boys did not fully accept him, he became quite aggressive and fresh, and talked back to adults in the building and to the children. This was a decided change from his original behavior. . . .

(Eighteenth meeting.) When worker arrived he learned that Moe had already been in the building for more than an hour. Coming out of the story-telling room he met worker and said he liked the activities at the settlement house so much he intended to come earlier and oftener from now on and take part in them (something which he would not have done before his therapy group experience).

Although all the boys were busily occupied with their work there was a free flow of conversation. Moe, Sandy, and Alter were working at one table, Simon at a desk nearby, and Murray at a wall shelf which he used because of its softness. He needed a place into which he could stick pins. It was the most orderly meeting so far.

(Nineteenth meeting.) When worker arrived at 5:15 he was informed that Moe had been in the building since four o'clock, participating in the other activities. He was at present making a reed basket. He told worker that he had joined the basket-weaving class and was now making a square basket because last summer at camp he had constructed a small round one. Back at the group, Moe spent most of the period painting his airplane. While waiting for the paint to dry, he asked if he could go back to his basket making. This he did despite the jeering remarks from Hal and Simon, who called him "sissy" and "pansy" because of his interest in it. His answer to this was that he made baskets at camp and it was a boys' camp.

(Twentieth meeting.) Moe had been coming regularly to the settlement house, arriving at four o'clock in the afternoon. . . . Everyone in the room was busy at his work, and there was quiet conversation throughout most of the evening. The interest in their own jobs and in the jobs their neighbors were doing kept them quite occupied.

(Twenty-third meeting.) Moe was with the children's rhythm orchestra connected with the settlement, of which he was now a member. He was very quiet and well behaved, following directions as well as any of the more experienced participants. He smiled at worker when he saw him from a distance. After the rehearsal, he said that he had just joined up. Although he would not perform with the orchestra at its next recital, he would be considered a regular member in the future.

Moe's self-control and maturity are the result of slow adaptation in other and narrower relations. Adjustment to the therapy group came first, later his relation with his sister had greatly improved, and now he was making an adjustment to a wider social environment where he had failed before. With reference to his attitude toward his sister we read in an earlier report:

The gym became available to the group. . . . All but Moe went. He insisted on completing the valentine for his sister. He had never before sent her a valentine, and was very anxious to finish it today. . . . When the boys and worker came down from the gym, Moe had completed his valentine, folded it, and written: "To My Valentine—To Mildred from Moe." He seemed very happy and remarked several times, "Boy! Won't she be surprised!" He asked for a clean sheet of paper in which to wrap it. . . . Mildred appeared at the door to take her brother home. He grabbed the valentine and hid it behind his back and hurriedly left with her. He came back to bid worker good-night. Worker heard him remarking to his sister how much he had enjoyed the meeting and how anxious he was to come back next week.

Overcoming the Feeling of Sexual Inadequacy

One of the most common sources of anxiety and social rejection is the feeling of sexual inadequacy. It has been observed that most neurotics are unable to live out satisfactorily their biological destiny. Men are unable to carry out the functions and responsibilities imposed by nature and by social conditions. They are either weak, timid, submissive, and dependent, or overcompensate for their sense of inferiority by swashbuckling, arrogance, domination. Women rebel against their inevitable part as wives and mothers and their recessive role in society. These inabilities have characterological foundations and are sources of serious dislocations and confusions.

Children of such parents suffer particularly, and usually present serious problems in almost all areas of their lives. Many delinquents and criminals are impelled by their distorted sexual attitudes to antisocial acts as a substitute gratification or as a means of self-assurance.

A major responsibility of therapy is to set straight attitudes toward this basic function in life, for distortions here have repercussions in all other adjustments. Many of the boys referred to us for treatment are emasculated through their early relations. These boys come from homes where there is inadequate masculine identification for one or another reason: an ineffectual father; an overaggressive or domineering mother; only boy among many sisters; rejection by parents in favor of a girl sibling; a bid for attention from the mother by being like her; identification with a feminine imago. The girls' confusions come from fixation on a father or brother or from latent homosexuality because of the absence of a male in the family. Serious difficulties arise with girls who tend to use their sex as a bid for attention and acceptance.

We find that preoccupation with sex is repressed in most instances. The relations in the group, the attitude of the group therapist, and the total setting are important here because they release this repressed material. Release comes through symbolic expression in painting and modeling, but later it also takes verbal form. Since members in our groups are of the same sex, they talk about their adventures, their dislike of kissing, their attitudes in relation to members of the opposite sex, and similar topics. Such conversations rarely take place in boys' groups, but almost invariably occur in groups of older girls. Both boys and girls indulge in lewd jokes and equivocal references. Some of the members who are not so ready to bring such material to the surface are chagrined and upset.

When the conversations are serious, the group therapist participates. The aim is to demonstrate to the members a natural and easy attitude toward sex and to have them experience freedom and candor in this regard on the part of an adult. All our members had previously felt shy about discussing this (to them) all-important topic with an adult, except, in some instances, with the case worker. Many who could not bring themselves to talk about it even with the case worker were later able to do so as a result of the release and security they achieved through the group. Since all are preoccupied with the same problem, guilt on the part of each is relieved. Guilt is even further reduced by the fact that the adult neither prohibits nor restrains nor feels shy or embarrassed. The heretofore prohibited thoughts and feelings can come to the fore without fear or anxiety.

When sex is treated by the children with humor, derision, or profanity, the group therapist ignores the whole proceeding. It is very important that he should not react in any way by facial expression, grimace, or gesture. Passivity on his part is essential here for if the group members discover in him either disapproval or shock, they use it as a weapon against him.[13] Group therapists must, therefore, be prepared for developments in this area so that they will not register any reaction.

In addition to verbal release a therapy group should provide parties and trips for older boys and girls under conditions that do not challenge or threaten them. This also helps the process of social acceptance and reduces inner tension. All but a few of the girls in our groups who reach the ages of fifteen and sixteen years make friends with boys and constantly talk about them at the meetings. Those who do not have boy friends overcompensate for their feelings of inadequacy by becoming "run-arounds," boasting of their successes with men and boys, and employing similar forms of self-maximation. To make the transition to a mixed group, the group therapist arranges parties to which clubs of boys from settlement houses

[13] For discussion of contrast of attitudes, which is employed in such situations as a form of passive restraint, see Chapter VI, pages 141 ff.

are invited. The boys chosen are usually a few years older and of a somewhat higher intellectual and cultural level, though of the same neighborhood backgrounds as the girls. In all instances the girls were delighted at being acceptable. Several of these groups of girls have later functioned successfully as regular clubs in neighborhood centers during the transitional stage.

Girls in our therapy groups are usually inferior to the average in every way, physically, intellectually, and culturally. It is, therefore, necessary to spare the boys who are invited disappointment, and the girls the pain of being rejected. Unless the boys are apprized of the fact that "these are girls who have few friends," the parties may end in disaster, as our first one almost did. As soon as the boys came into the room and saw the girls they exclaimed that they were "stuck." We had anticipated difficulties, though we did not know what they would be, and had one of our own male therapists attend the party in addition to the woman group therapist. He had had considerable experience with boys and knew how to prevail upon them to stay. It turned out that all had a good time, and the girls talked about the event for weeks. These parties supply us with valuable diagnostic material as to the capacity for adjustment and the maturity of our group members. We take the following from a report of such a party which concerns a girl who had been shy and withdrawn and still considered herself too fat and not attractive:

Deby, fifteen years old, arrived at about a quarter of eight. She had expected to make a grand entrance and was rather taken aback when she found that the boys had not yet arrived. Deby came to the party dressed in what she called a sport outfit, a skirt and shirt waist, anklets and flat-heeled shoes. She wore a red ribbon in her hair and looked particularly attractive. However, shortly after she started to dance she was a little embarrassed because the seam in her skirt began to open. She came to the worker and asked if she had a needle and thread. Worker gave them to her, Deby mended her skirt, and then went back, forgetting completely about her appearance.

Deby was active and pleasant throughout the party. She joined readily with the boys in the group, danced, sang, in fact was the leader during the games of truth and consequences and charades. This is quite an advance over her behavior at the party last year for then she was perhaps the shyest girl of the group, sat quietly in a corner, spoke very little, and seemed confused and upset. She showed no confusion at all throughout this party and seemed to be having a very good time. Later in the evening after the ice-cream and soda were served, Deby stood at the sink helping the worker wash the dishes.

She remarked that she had had a good time. She said, "You know these boys are so different from last year. I don't know whether I had a better time last year or this year. These boys are richer and more refined. They aren't as smutty and dirty as the other boys. You know the other crowd is from Third Avenue. These are so much nicer." Although Deby did not say it in so many words, it was apparent from the way she spoke that what she meant was that these boys were nicer because they had not played kissing games, but she wasn't sure whether she enjoyed this party more than that one last year where she had joined in the kissing games very readily. Most of the boys seemed to enjoy Deby's company. They danced with her and one of them asked to take her home at the end of the party.

On occasion a "mixed party" may cause suffering to a member as the abstract from the record below shows. Usually boys and girls who are unable to face the situation absent themselves.

Fannie, a very shy and withdrawn girl of sixteen, new in the group, was extremely ill at ease while the games were being played. She could not dance and was so fearful that she went out of the room and walked around the block on four different occasions. The worker met Fannie just as she was leaving for one of these walks. Fannie said to her, "I don't know how to dance, I'm scared." She had fear in her eyes and spoke in a choked voice. Worker explained that she ought to stay anyway. Fannie said, "No, I must walk around the block and get up enough courage."

Lucretia was with Fannie and went out with her at this time. Later, while the game of truth and consequences was being played, Fannie became terribly upset again. Her hands shook, her face twitched, and she became hot and flustered. It happened that the boy who was acting as leader selected Fannie as the first of the girls to punch the board. She did so with much difficulty, but could not even unfold the little slip, let alone read it. After considerable hesitation and fumbling she threw it with a great deal of force at the boy who was sitting alongside of her. As much force was used in throwing this small slip of paper as might have been in throwing a ball clear across the room. The boy opened it and read it as directed by Fannie. She was asked to name ten parts of the body. However, she became terribly upset and could not name them. It took her a long time finally to list such obvious things as hair, eyes, ears, nose, and fingers.

Later, when there were no general games, and everybody stood about talking, dancing, or singing, Fannie seemed to become a little more secure. She managed to go from one girl to the next, but stayed mostly with Lucretia. She came up to the worker several times to announce that she was having a good time. Worker believes that she really was having a good time and that her excitement was due to the fact that she had never before been in an organized group activity with boys. Worker also thinks that the anticipation of the party had been a great strain on Fannie. The sex drives and conflicts that underlay her problem caused the fear that almost overwhelmed her. However, the desire to be at the party was greater than her fear. She had not looked in her letter box for the notice of the party and fearing that she might miss out, called her case worker and asked her to find out where the party was to be held and the hour it was starting.

The emasculated boy corrects his deficiency because the therapy group supplies him with masculine identifications and a supportive ego either in the person of the therapist or another boy.[14] Though the group therapist may at first be accepted *in loco feminae*, the feminine image is gradually dis-

[14] For discussion of Group Therapy and emasculation, see Chapter IV, pages 98 ff.

placed and he comes to be recognized for what he is. The group also provides a masculine environment and the satisfactions that come from boys' games and occupations. Ivor Brown (see Chapter VIII, pages 259 ff.) wore aprons, did housework, and made paper flowers. This was his bid for attention from a rejecting mother. As a result he could not participate in boys' activities and played only with little girls. The case worker was also a woman. In the group his occupations were almost entirely of a feminine nature. For more than a year he made no contact with the other boys though he never missed a meeting except through illness. The critical event in his therapy occurred when he was accidentally pushed by two other boys who were in a scuffle. The following week he played ball in the room with the boys. Soon after he climbed a Jungle Jim in the park and began to play boys' games. One of the sources of Paul's difficulties[15] lay in the fact that his younger sister had been a cardiac from infancy and therefore received special attention from the mother.

Similarly Melvin, whose sister was preferred to him by his mother because she identified him with her much disliked husband, found his masculinity a threat and acted like his baby sister.[16] When he found assurance in a group of boys he improved. Ray's growth (Chapter VII, pages 237 ff.) was partially due to the fact that she related herself to a group of girls and later to boys through the parties arranged by the group therapist and through membership in a neighborhood center. The chief reason for arranging the parties was to give the girls sexual assurance.

When our adolescent girls begin to reach out into the community through their interest in boys but have not corrected their bad habits in dress and personal cleanliness, they are re-

[15] See also Chapter VI, page 144, and Chapter VIII, pages 288 ff.
[16] C. Miller and S. R. Slavson, An Experiment in Integration of Case Work and Group Work Treatment of a Problem Boy, *American Journal of Orthopsychiatry*, 9: 792–797, October 1939.

ferred to the Big Sister Department of the agency. The majority of our group members have unattractive personal habits at first. Many of them improve these quite naturally as a result of group association. Where home conditions and facilities are such that the girls do not improve in this respect, and the group therapist cannot directly criticize or suggest, a supplementary and more personal relation with a Big Sister is usually a good corrective. The following discussion was held on the advisability of assigning Deby (see page 214) to a Big Sister. There was no case worker, the girl being treated exclusively by Group Therapy.

The request was made because Deby dressed very poorly even for her social and economic status, did not bathe sufficiently, and smelled bad. This made her adjustment difficult to boys and girls in the settlement where the group met. At the same time she was submissive and ingratiating, characteristics which carry with them a social risk in that the need for acceptance may motivate a girl to become a sexual delinquent. She may submit sexually in order to be accepted. It was felt that a Big Sister who was too well bred and with too high cultural standards might accentuate Deby's feeling of inferiority and inadequacy. She would not be able to make contact with such a person. It was therefore thought advisable that the Big Sister should be drawn from a cultural group closer to Deby's own social background.

The question of approach was also discussed, that is, how contact should be made with the girl. What would be the excuse for asking her whether she wanted a Big Sister? It was suggested that she should be called in on the pretext that all children were seen from time to time by someone in the agency so that they could make any requests they wanted to and the agency could learn how they were getting along.

Subsequent reports indicate that this worked out well. The girl eagerly responded when a Big Sister was suggested and the contact was easily made. We learned from the group therapist that the girl dressed neatly and was clean. The case was closed out from Group Therapy as the girl no longer needed this service having made a good social adjustment.

Increasing Frustration Tolerance

The ability to withstand innumerable minor and major frustrations in life is essential for healthful living. One faces from early infancy restrictions upon motor activity, verbal expression, creative effort, and personal autonomy. Group life demands that we inhibit and control our behavior to conform to traditions, mores, rules, and laws. In the more intimate relations of the family, also, the child is hemmed in on all sides by restrictions which are later incorporated into the pattern of his life. The degree to which one can tolerate the frustration of impulses and power drives is determined to some extent by constitutional factors, but this capacity is undoubtedly increased or decreased by early experiences and satisfactions. Relationships in a family where the child is excessively repressed and humiliated tend, in most instances, to reduce tolerance for such treatment in later life. Failure is calamitous; it produces panic and rage. Such persons are on edge and in a perpetual state of anger. The greatest responsibility of education, in the home and out, is to transform and shape the child's impulses into acceptable social behavior without such destructive by-products. Ordinarily the child is disposed to accept inhibitions because of his positive attitudes toward the person who imposes them; or he willingly patterns himself after the adult because of identification with him. Under such favorable conditions, the capacity to withstand frustrations in the future is enhanced, and the individual is able to bear difficulties and failure without undue shock and loss of self-regard.

Most of the children in our groups had experienced excessive frustration since early childhood. A few were not adequately inhibited. Some who had suffered from too much restraint had succumbed to it, and had remained weak, had developed feelings of debility, and had become submissive and self-conscious. Others had become touchy, aggressive, and intolerant. Still others who had not been adequately controlled in the past remained without the capacity to accept restraint or failure with equanimity. The inability to submit to a normal amount of frustration and control incidental to life in a group and in a culture is a form of autismus that requires correction, and permissiveness is essential in the early stages of therapy. It is important to convince the child of the therapist's friendship and regard for him, and thus to undercut overt or covert hostility toward the restraining agent.

Increase in the capacity to accept frustration is, strictly speaking, not a direct aim of Group Therapy. Rather, it is a result of the many forces operating in the experiences inherent in such groups. The client's emotional and physical set for self-protection, his perception of being rejected by everyone, his expectation of attack are reduced through the relations and the atmosphere in the group. As his anxieties concerning his status with others are removed, the resulting relaxation disposes him to accept a reasonable amount of domination, control, and denial.

As the children's frustration tolerance is increased, the group therapist exposes them consciously to limitations as a test. He does not allow taking tools and materials home. He announces that because of lack of funds, no food will be available at a particular meeting. Or he does not have on hand materials that were requested by some of the children, so that no work can be done at a particular meeting. Change in workers, transfer of members from one group to another, addition of new members are also frustrating situations to which adjustment has to be made.

The record material is replete with situations in which frustrations of various forms and intensities grow out of the group itself. The records in Chapter VIII also demonstrate this point, especially those of Ray Rosen (pages 237 ff.) and Harmon Mancher (pages 273 ff.). We cull the following from the report of one of our earlier groups of which Paula, Joan,

Rosalind, and Marjorie (Chapter I, pages 13 ff. and 23) were members:

The socializing influence[17] of the group experience was made evident also in other ways. The individual girls were generally unable to submit to the group without irritation. There was, therefore, considerable squabbling whenever a decision had to be made. On one occasion the girls and worker went to Indian Point on a Hudson River boat. While there they wanted to go in for a swim. The worker explained that the fare was so costly, the agency could not pay the admission to the pool as well. The girls accepted this without protest and enjoyed the day without further regrets. Even Rosalind did not demur.

It would seem that the frustration tolerance of these girls had greatly increased if one is to judge by their reactions to deprivations at earlier meetings.

It is impossible to overstress the danger of applying even mild frustration without first understanding its possible effect upon individual children. The slightest denial may constitute a major rejection to an intensely deprived child.[18] Test situations can be applied only after the group therapist is certain 1) of the children's attitude toward him as a permissive person; 2) of their security in their relation to one another; 3) of their perception of the world as friendly; 4) of the general emotional state and sensitivity of each member; 5) of the therapist's own motive in imposing restriction. A test situation in frustration and denial may have to be applied to a group when the members who are known to be unable to accept it are absent from the particular meeting. The question of denial was fully discussed in Chapter VI, pages 161 ff. The transitional groups (Chapter IX, pages 326 ff.) represent to the cli-

[17] The use of the concept of socialization by the worker in this connection is a generic one. Socialization results from increased frustration tolerance, among other factors. See also fuller discussion of this concept in Chapter IV, pages 87 ff.

[18] See situation described in Chapter VI, pages 160–161.

ents a form of frustration. Many of the "privileges" that resemble the feeding and nurturing of the child by the parent and the protective atmosphere of the family are removed. The members are placed in a position of independence and self-reliance. As already indicated, some of them cannot meet the test and have to be returned to therapy groups.

Helping the Personality to Mature

In orderly development the child is helped to grow physically through appropriate food, intellectually through teaching and drill, emotionally through self-expression and human relations. But growth cannot occur unless opportunities are provided for expression appropriate to a given stage of maturity. It is not enough to have ideas and desires; one must also have the facility and the technique for carrying them out. Unfortunately the physical and emotional settings provided by modern homes and formal schooling are repressive and frustrating to a larger extent than is usually realized. As a result, not only is emotional development arrested, but also the means of making one's impulses and interests manifest are blocked. In many instances language facility, manual dexterity, and the ability to form relationships grow inadequately because the child is not encouraged or challenged, is not exposed to sustaining and driving interests, and does not share or assume responsibilities. There are rarely adequate provisions to keep pace with the growing powers and interests of the child. He is infantilized and his dependence and immaturity are prolonged by the home and school as his bids for independence are blocked or punished. The rejected and deprived child also tends to remain emotionally immature. Thus in either case a child remains incapable of meeting the more complex and more difficult situations that life presents. Facility and skill should keep pace with growing powers and desires, for when a stage in development is not permitted to run its full course, it persists beyond its appropriate period and, as a result, one remains weak and immature.

Traditional education suppresses the play impulse to the point of danger. The manipulative and exploratory phases in growth are almost wholly neglected. Instead of playing with fire, water, mud, and mechanical objects, the average child is taught to read and write and figure. His need for free play and free group contacts is grossly neglected and instead he is forced into organized games and formalized gymnastics. It may be said that education forces creative and assertive trends into patterns of submission and complacency. The healthy personality, however, requires that these two opposing sets of impulses—expression and submission—complement rather than displace one another. At first, activity is tied up with the child's sensations, as when he accommodates himself to changes in temperature and variations in his physical environment. As he grows stronger he seeks to control his environment by attacking it. He bites the breast or the rubber nipple, scratches, throws objects, and makes noises. In the crawling stage, he pulls and pushes, bites and strikes. As a toddler he moves things, pounds objects, builds and arranges. To the adult all this multifarious activity has little or no purpose. The child, however, always has a purpose.

The function of home and school education is to transform the undifferentiated aggressiveness of the child into forms appropriate to life in a given culture and to canalize it into acceptable and constructive effort. The child's predilection for pounding, which gives him a sense of power, can be utilized by letting him drive nails to make a boat or a box. His screaming propensities, through which he also gets a feeling of power, can be turned into an interest in speaking, reciting, singing, whistling. The interest in mud and "messing around" is a direct predecessor of clay work, sculpture, and painting.

The points we are attempting to make here are: 1) that

every drive or tendency in the child must find expression in an act; 2) that education must provide suitable opportunities and conditions for such expression; and 3), which is most important for the maturing personality, that there must be *growth in the ways of expressing oneself*. With reduction of anxiety, attainment of mature desires, and acquirement of better facilities to communicate oneself to the world, the fear of growing up is overcome.

People retain infantile emotions because, on the one hand, they had no opportunities for expression in increasingly mature ways, and, on the other hand, to grow up meant to lose status in the family because of rivalry with siblings or other similar factors. Many children retain an infantile character and its outward manifestations because they can hold their parents' love by such means. It is as though they hope that if they prolong the baby period when they were loved, love will continue to be showered on them. Because of their emotional needs for a baby some parents encourage their children to remain immature. Rejected children, with their love needs unsatisfied, are of necessity emotionally infantile and children whose parents are in conflict with each other are not only fixed in their infantilism as a result, but use it to exploit the two parents as they play off one against the other. In other cases immaturity is perpetuated by mothers who activate their sons sexually at a very young age.

Because of these and similar conditions of early life, the infantile character structure persists and the fear of growing up emerges. Extreme retardations of psychosexual development require deep psychotherapy, but lesser distortions can be corrected when the necessity arises to take one's place with one's peers. Social hunger and the pressure of the group situation are enough to produce the desired results. In other cases, a combination of individual and group treatment is necessary. Many of our clients cannot relate to others of their age and either play by themselves or stay indoors, reading "funnies" or listening to the radio. Among our group members were children who were able to play in the neighborhood but could not establish more intimate and closer relations such as exist in a therapy group. They escaped from these relations by joining athletic teams which do not bring the members into close emotional interaction. We quote from the report of an Integration Conference that illustrates this point:

This boy does not seem to have a serious character disturbance, but is rather reacting to his home environment. He remains in a state of immaturity, and group experience is indicated for him. Attendance in the neighborhood center may be a sign that he has achieved sufficient security with children through Group Therapy and is now able to participate in free group play. However, the boy may be escaping from the therapy group into a club where the emphasis is on athletics, with few interpersonal contacts. It has been observed that children who are afraid of intimate relations join athletic groups, because these are emotionally less threatening. It would be best to wait and see before closing the case whether he comes to the therapy group. In view of his home problem (infantilization and overprotection) attendance would be very desirable. If he fails to attend, it may be that he no longer has a need for this type of group experience or that he cannot face it because of his immaturity. Treatment of this client should be planned on the basis of future diagnosis.

Because of inadequate play outlets, one of several pathoplastic conditions in childhood, the infantile methods for discharging aggressiveness persist in most of our group members. Our clients are in almost all instances unable to enter into a constructive play relation with other children. The home conditions and school equipment, being impoverished, fail to mobilize powers and to give adequate, constructive, and socially approved outlets for play and for other forms of social contact. A therapy group provides play opportunities with a view to developing in children facilities for more mature and more acceptable self-expression. Tools and craft materials also help to develop in a large number of cases mature and permanent interests. Satisfaction from achievement, praise from the worker and other members of the group, and recognition in the home and school spur children on in their work. In one group the therapist's suggestion to go to the movies was rejected for six consecutive weeks. The boys wanted to stay in the room and work. Other therapists record many similar occasions when boys and girls chose to work with materials in preference to trips, movies, and other "privileges" that would at first seem to be of greater interest. As the members of our groups became more mature they were able to balance these pleasures against other things.

The maturing process is also made manifest by the children's growing sense of responsibility about their physical environment. A group that met in an office building almost tore down the place during the first few months. The boys invaded the dozen or more private offices, ransacked desks, appropriated candy, toys, and other objects, pulled telephone plugs, shouted profanities into dictaphones, clogged toilets, broke the panes of glass in doors and windows, hid papers and window poles, scratched walls, and burned paper and wood on the floors. This exceedingly aggressive behavior, however, completely disappeared after a few months, both because the therapist stood the test and because the boys discovered the use of the tools and materials and the satisfactions they could derive from them. In fact, when a boy was later found in a private office (instead of the meeting room or passageway) he was upbraided by the others. An atmosphere of constructive effort, active though quiet, pervaded nearly all of these groups some six months later. The boys had matured in their way of using their powers and talents. They had sublimated their aggressiveness. What is more important, they had discovered within themselves new powers and new ways of gratifications.[19]

[19] This development is illustrated in the record material throughout the book. See especially the cases of John Sloan and Paul Schwartz, Chapter VIII.

Group Therapy provides for the assumption by its members of an ever increasing area of responsibility in the conduct of the group. From the very start the members decide for themselves on trips or outings; later they assume responsibility for the condition of the materials, tools, and meeting room. The children make lists of materials to be ordered and sometimes work out schedules of duties. It is extremely important that the feeling of responsibility should be spontaneous and proceed from an increasing maturity and a sense of belonging and not imposed as a routine. Growing maturity is illustrated by several examples taken from group records.

Teddy's problem seemed to be more with his mother's reaction than with anything in his own personality. She overprotected him, and now sets very high standards for him. She wants him to be a model boy, and grow up to be a perfect gentleman. The chief problem Teddy presented when he came to the group was that, although bright, he was totally uninterested in school and did very poor work. During the first twenty meetings of the group, Teddy's attendance was irregular and he displayed little interest. He would come, stay about half an hour, make demands for the worker's attention, and then leave. At the twenty-first meeting Teddy remarked it might be lonesome there if the other boys did not come. He is now very much a part of the group. The mother reports that Teddy's work has improved in school and that she feels it is due to the stimulus he gets in the "club." She is very much pleased with the boy's membership in the group and feels it is a great help to him. She said that he was never interested in anything before and was very much surprised to discover his loyalty to this group. In the beginning he did not like it, but he recently told her, enthusiastically, that he liked it very much.

Netta, a girl of nine, infantilized at home, whining, helpless, making a constant bid for and monopolizing the worker's attention, wanted help at every step on her projects, was jealous of other children, and was generally annoying. Alice, a domineering, rough child of about the same age, was rejected in favor of an older brother. The home was surcharged with conflict and Alice was constantly at loggerheads with her brother, who was also under treatment and a member of another therapy group. He was so destructive in a group of children of his own age that we reassigned him to a group of older boys, where he finally controlled his aggressiveness. Alice dominated and frequently made fun of Netta. The latter usually did not seem to notice this attitude on the part of Alice, but occasionally she would complain to the group therapist. The two girls lived in the same neighborhood and usually rode home together. After nine weeks Netta's growth is illustrated by the following incident:

The girls got dressed and Netta said to Alice, "I'm going home on the bus, because last time we went on the trolley." This is the first time Netta was so positive about her plans. Alice first insisted, then begged her: "Oh, Netta, come on the trolley." But Netta was firm, and Alice capitulated to Netta's insistence. Then Theresa said, "Miss Bailey, are you going to go home with me?" To prevent the other girls' jealousy, worker said that she was going in the opposite direction. (See also pages 141 ff.)

Worker at this meeting completed a linoleum block he had started last week, and took the impression from it. The boys were excited with the result, and each asked for prints; the worker made one or two, and then put the block down. The boys made prints for themselves. Particularly pleasing was this to Harold. His twin brother James, however, decided to make his own linoleum block, which he did and from which he later printed as well. (Note: James had been greatly dependent upon Harold. He hardly had an existence of his own. This was fostered by the home. The following year the two boys were placed in separate groups.)

Joseph and the worker played the second game. Joseph noticed that the worker had eleven checkers to his twelve and immediately removed one of his own. The worker offered to play eleven against twelve, but Joseph refused. He wanted to play even sides. The worker won this game, too. It was a very absorbing game as far as Joseph was concerned. He said he liked the game very much.

During the meeting Richard made up a list of materials for the worker to bring in. This he said he had to do because he missed the leather lacing which had been promised to him. The list read as follows: staples; linoleum blocks; lacing, dark brown and red; leather; wood; lock and key; steel wool; balsa wood; cord. To this list Benjamin later added sand paper. At the close of the meeting Richard asked worker if he still had the list, and worker took it out, showed it to him, and told him what Benjamin had added.

Gladys went over to the cabinet and began looking around for something rather haphazardly. "Where is the drawing book?" she asked the worker, referring to the book of outlines that she had used on previous occasions. "I don't seem to be able to find it," the worker answered. "Here is some drawing paper. Why don't you use this instead?" Gladys protested that she liked the book. After some more vain searching Gladys took the drawing paper, asked for a ruler and pencil, and sat down at the table. Worker brought out the water colors, and Gladys began to draw her own design, which she later painted black.

Harvey who came by himself told worker he had never traveled alone before.

Harold told worker he had to return milk bottles to the store in order to get money for carfare because his mother had again used his money sent by the agency. But he got here; "So it's all right," he said.

(Trip without worker.) The boys told worker that they had all met in front of the building and went together. They had no difficulty getting to the circus and back.

Developing a Group Super-Ego

The doctrine that the super-ego is solely an outcome of the infant's relation to his parents must be extended, for in the later stages of growth, it is modified and shaped through the interaction with the outer world. By accepting the restraints of the world as well as those of one's parents, the personality moves toward maturity. Because, in the past, development has been viewed in individual terms, extra-familial experiences and cultural forces in shaping character have been largely overlooked. Adequate attention has not been given to the constraints and controls exercised by groups outside the family as factors in the genesis of the super-ego.

The new awareness of the function of group relations in individual growth has brought to light the fact that the super-ego is determined by the total culture as well as by specific individual experiences. Variations in mores and values, as we find them in different nations and cultural groups and in different circles of the same society, produce distinct character and ego structures. Observation leads one to assume that character is formed and personality is evolved throughout life, even though early relations and hereditary and organic factors determine and shape the nature and complexion of later development. A striking illustration of this is the phenomenon of acclimatization to a foreign country by immigrants and the way they adopt values and patterns at variance with those of their former homes and of their parents. We also find confirmation of this point of view in what is known as the "cultural conflict" between immigrants and their native children. In this case, accommodation to extra-familial values operates so strongly that a break with the parents often occurs as a result.

If the home and the nursery were the sole and final determinants of character, no psychotherapy would be possible. Psychotherapy is based upon the empirically valid thesis that early experiences can in varying degrees be neutralized and counteracted. If this were not the case, psychological growth would not be possible. In almost every individual, personality *does* change and values *are* altered. For what does experience mean if not inner readjustment in conformity with outer necessity? These readjustments contribute to the final formation of the ego.

Thus character is derived from social demands as well as from parental disciplines and sibling rivalries, and the adult super-ego must be viewed as a result of one's total experience. We internalize the demands and inhibitions of the group as well as those of our parents. Other persons, adults and children, affect the child's psychological complex. Even during his very early life, the child does not internalize the restrictive attitudes of the father or the mother, but absorbs influences from both. He is affected, in addition, by their attitudes *toward each other* in which he, too, is a factor. When there are other siblings, relatives, or parent-substitutes, the group complex is enlarged and the child's ego is formed through these many interactions.

Psychological traumata may originate in parental and family relations in childhood, but many interpersonal and situational disturbances arise from cultural and group conflicts as well. Most frequently the determining group is the family, but in many instances the problem-producing situation is another group or circumstance. We refer again to immigrants to illustrate our point. Individuals well adjusted in their native surroundings frequently develop functional neuroses and neurotic symptoms when they are transplanted to an alien environment and must make new adjustments. We also find confirmation of this principle in the adjustment of minority groups, particularly persecuted minorities, in a hostile environment. Studies show that the incidence of functional neuroses in such groups is greater than in a native population and in dominant groups. We see here that the development of the ego and of the super-ego is affected by conditions other than parent-child relations.

That part of the super-ego acquired from the parent is derived largely through fear, while the super-ego derived from group life is of a more socializing nature. The group-generated super-ego is an outcome not of the direct fear of being unwanted, punished, or abandoned by the adult, but is in large measure the result of a willing accommodation to environment.[20] This is not to be taken to mean that society does not employ force and fear to bring the individual to conformity. On the contrary, these are the most universal tools of "socialization."

The super-ego is a by-product of natural accommodative tendencies and results from the desire for acceptance. That is, the child is *willing* to curb his impulses and actions for the returns he earns. These returns, acceptance and recognition, are immediate and direct, which is another characteristic that favors the establishment of the group super-ego. Restraint for the sake of parent or siblings does not always bring such immediate and telling rewards. The various accommodations to groups become absorbed into the personality as permanent mechanisms which make up the *group super-ego* as differentiated from the *infantile super-ego*. By accepting the restraints of groups and through finding attachments in them, the child dissolves or lessens the ties to members of his family. As is well known, maturity consists in this very process of dissolving early ties and becoming independent of them. We have also had occasion to indicate that the excessive severity of the super-ego creates tensions that lead to neuroses and dissocial behavior.

Since the infantile super-ego proceeds from fear of punishment, abandonment, or rejection, it is essential that the indi-

[20] Accommodation to environment is universal in nature in the fields of chemism (the physical and plant worlds) and zooism (animal world). The equalization of the temperature of a body with that of the environment and the balance of strain and stresses are among the most common of these accommodative phenomena in the inanimate world. Protective coloration of insects and other animals as well as numerous other organic changes to meet climatic conditions can be pointed out in biological phenomena. The accommodative responses in the world of psychism (emotion and intellect) are even more numerous and occur with greater facility and speed. The need for adjustment is infinitely more frequent here, for the demands upon a person are constantly changing and varying. The complexity and frequency of renewed demands for adjustment increase proportionately to the complexity of society. Thus the range and quality of adjustability must be greater among civilized persons than in primitive societies.

vidual divest himself of these early anxieties as he grows older. Impulses and attitudes must be reconditioned through identifications with others and behavior must be socially motivated. In persons where this does not happen and the adult retains the anxiety-producing infantile suger-ego, he stands little chance of attaining inner peace and will quite likely join the ever increasing ranks of neurotics. A balanced adult has overcome, to a large degree at least, the tensions due to the infantile super-ego.

The child constantly reevaluates his early impressions and experiences for, in his growing efforts at autonomy, he tests out reality in both his physical and human environments. He also tests behavior prohibited by parents and teachers. If checked or frustrated, he may withdraw or become destructive; if successful, his powers are released for constructive pursuits. It is essential for healthy development that there be consistency in the parental and cultural reactions. An overindulged child is in anguish when individuals and groups outside the family deny or control him and his fears and feelings of rejection are greatly sharpened. Such inconsistency begets insecurity and makes adaptation difficult. Similarly, when an overinhibited child is permitted to act as he wishes, his covert hostilities and destructiveness are intensified with a resultant increase in anxiety.

It is necessary for healthy growth that the infantile super-ego (in response to the family group) and the group super-ego (in response to the play, classroom, business, social, professional, or political group) have some continuum. Family and society must be at one in the molding of personality so that the individual can free himself of some of the reactions of childhood. Conformity to the demands of the adult world in which one lives is quite different from the obedience of the child, but is directly derived from it. They must, therefore, have many characteristics in common. Where there is no consistency in these two sources of the super-ego or where the infantile super-ego does not make adequate transition to the group super-ego, pathological reactions are inevitable.

To effect the transition from the infantile to the group super-ego is one of the objectives of Group Therapy. By helping to incorporate in the structure of the super-ego the controls and values of the group, social maladjustments are prevented and corrected. The maladjusted child who has failed, for reasons already indicated, to evolve the social side of his ego can correct it through Group Therapy. The child's anxiety (set up by the infantile super-ego) is lessened because he discharges hostile and aggressive feelings in the presence of an adult and other children, and thus becomes receptive to experiences that foster maturation.

The outcome of the total experience of a therapy group is therefore the change in the ego structure of the client. Through the relations he establishes in the group with children and an adult, he makes the transition toward a more balanced and realistic perception of adults, the world, and its demands. All intimate relations have a socializing influence. This is due chiefly, though not solely, to the fact that our need to be accepted by individuals and groups is a major motive in our lives. We curb and modify our egocentric preoccupations so as to be more acceptable. Because of the craving to be accepted, the individual in turn accepts traditions and mores and adjusts his behavior in accordance with group values. Every group, whether family, professional, or social, creates an atmosphere peculiar to itself to which the individual adapts himself. When one's pattern of behavior does not accord with that of the group, one must change it if one wishes to remain a part of it. Otherwise, the impelling need to be accepted (social hunger) is unmet. When an individual has a constant need to antagonize groups, there is a serious personality malformation, for one of the marks of wholesomeness is the ability to work with groups without excessive conflict. Groups "socialize" personality and thus contribute to the formation of the ego and the super-ego.

The following are a few examples of the growth of a group super-ego culled from a large number that illustrate this process:

Several of the boys ran in to tell worker that Teddy had turned the Western Union call switch. Ted said the others did, too. The boys asked if a messenger would come and if he did what would happen. Worker said he didn't know as yet. Worker was in another room when messenger arrived. He was small but bristled fiercely when he saw the boys. The boys ran around as if trying to hide. Only those who were not involved stood their ground. Worker came out and messenger said, "Someone rang Western Union." Worker told him the boys turned the switch, but they did not know it would call a messenger. He asked messenger to excuse it and if there was any charge to get in touch with the office. The messenger left and the boys reprimanded Teddy. . . . Going home, the worker left the group for several minutes to sign the building's time book. When he returned he found Benjamin taking a vote of the boys agreeing to "kick out" any boy who caused trouble hereafter. This was the immediate result of summoning the Western Union messenger. Only James hesitated, but finally the vote was unanimous including Teddy, against whom the vote was directed as a warning.[21]

"Are we going to cook today?" Ann asked. "If you want to, we will," worker replied. "Cook what?" Gladys asked. "Cocoa," Ann answered. "I don't like cocoa," Gladys said. "It's too sweet. I know what's good. Chocolate milk heated. That's delicious." Everyone thought that that sounded good. "Will you go with me?" Ann asked Gladys. "All right," Gladys agreed. . . . Gladys and Ann returned shortly. "We spent 44 cents," said Ann, "and we didn't get chocolate milk because it was too expensive."

It appeared that the boys had spoken during their little walk

[21] This incident occurred in the very destructive group described on page 226. The behavior of this group also illustrates the effect of unsuitable quarters.

about the incident of Ikar's refusal to cooperate in cleaning up last week, because Salo said, "Lou [group worker], we took a vote and we decided, if a guy don't wash and help, no eats." Then he added, "On the way home last week, we also decided that we take a vote on the kind of cookies we buy. You vote too." [This was in reference to the incident last week when Ikar ran back to the store to change the cookies Salo had bought.] As Salo spoke, Galen stood silently by and nodded in agreement.

Sometimes group pressure is more violent and more overt, as related in a report of an outing arranged by two groups of twelve to fourteen-year-old boys from which the following is taken:

As on another joint trip of two groups before, Lanny (a new boy in the group) annoyed the boys by pushing and wrestling. The boys of the other group avoided him without argument and either moved away or pushed him away with a mild warning. It is significant that the boys of Group D offered Lanny only passive resistance. Finding no opposition in these quarters, Lanny turned to his own group, grabbing Harvey quite suddenly about the neck and shoulders from behind. Although Harvey was shorter by a head, he let fly with his fists above his head, striking Lanny twice in the jaw. This was so sudden and surprising that the latter, non-plussed, let go of Harvey quickly and moved away quietly holding his jaw as in pain. He made no outcry and tried hard to conceal his embarrassment from the others. For the remainder of the ride Lanny was quiet and well-behaved.

CHAPTER VIII

FIVE TYPICAL CASES

WE have selected five typical cases from our closed files that concretize some of the more or less theoretic principles presented in the preceding pages. In the case of Ray Rosen, Group Therapy was used exclusively. John Sloan is typical of the client for whom Group Therapy is supplementary to individual psychotherapy, especially as a "tapering-off" device. For Ivor Brown case work was of a supportive nature and supplementary to group treatment. The record of Harmon Mancher demonstrates the application of many principles of Group Therapy, especially the satisfaction of social hunger and the place of adult authority. Paul Schwartz's record is presented in a form to show the parallelism and interaction of case and group treatment. Each case is discussed briefly.

It will be noted that all the five cases presented are rejected children. Rejected children are in the overwhelming majority among our clients, but a numerically large group have different histories. The choice of cases for this volume was made with a view to illustrating the process of Group Therapy, rather than the variety of clients.

THE CASE OF RAY ROSEN: *Exclusive group treatment of a rejected girl with delinquent trends*

Problem. Ray, aged fourteen years, was referred to the agency by her mother. Ray, a Jewish girl, was disagreeable and sullen, was going out with the neighborhood Puerto Rican and colored men and boys older than herself, and doing poorly at school.

Ray's family history was one of extreme poverty, neglect,

and rejection. Mrs. Rosen was deserted for the first time by her common-law husband when Ray was a little more than two years old. A number of reunions and desertions followed. The father had sent occasional remittances to help maintain the family, but these had stopped completely some time before the case was referred. Mrs. Rosen worked as a scrubwoman despite a serious physical handicap. In addition she had been ill for the past six or seven years.

Ray was the third in a group of four sisters, all illegitimate. The two older girls, May and Sophie, were four and five years older than she. May tried hard to obtain jobs. Sophie made no effort to get work. Ray's younger sister was brighter than she and well liked at school. She presented no problem at home. Ray, on the other hand, had difficulties at school. She was mediocre as a student and had no friends.

The mother freely admitted that she never wanted Ray and considered her a burden. At one time Mrs. Rosen, with the aid of a social service agency, tried to place the two younger children in foster homes, but she did not go through with the plans. For many years, Mrs. Rosen had been so harassed by the financial difficulties of the family and the pressure of her work that she had no time to give to her children. The family was always in a desperate financial condition. Mrs. Rosen constantly worried that she might become too ill to work and that the family would then lose its home. She was bitter and demanding, and had the parasitical feeling that she ought to be helped by people. The family was known to a number of social and relief agencies. The sisters did not get on with each other. The two older girls formed a clique and harassed the younger. Ray was enthusiastic about her younger sister's intelligence, but it was evident that she was extremely jealous of her. She was attractive and was "babied" by the two older girls, and Mrs. Rosen openly praised her for her high marks at school. Ray showered her affection upon a puppy the family had acquired which was her constant companion. She constantly talked about this pet.

As described by the Big Sister to whom she was first referred, Ray was a pale, slight girl of average height with a heavy-lidded, rather inscrutable face. Everything about her personality seemed lacking in color: she had pale-brown hair, palish eyes, pale, clear skin. She used no cosmetics and wore an ensemble of pale-brown clothing, worn but neat. She expressed "longing for her father." It must be noted that neither the neighborhood nor the family set-up provided a substitute. Her main difficulty, she told the Big Sister, was that she had no friends either in the neighborhood or at school. She felt lonely and too frightened to join a club. She was ashamed to bring friends, if she had any, into her home because of its shabbiness and poverty-stricken atmosphere. She had a great fear of being snubbed by girls. When several contacts were made for her with groups in recreational agencies, Ray refused to join. She tried one meeting of a club, but did not return.

Individual treatment. Several Big Sisters assigned to the case were not successful. In between the succession of Big Sisters the girl was seen occasionally by a case worker, but interviews were on a superficial level. The mother came to the office frequently, as did her two older daughters, to ask for direct financial aid or jobs. All complained of Ray's attitude at home, but Ray did not respond to treatment by the Big Sisters or the case worker. She seemed to identify them with the members of her family, did not trust them, and resisted all their efforts.

The case was carried with only occasional interviews. Ray came in during the summers to obtain free camp placement, which was given her. The transfer entry reads in part:

Ray and her mother were primarily interested in using the services of the agency for financial aid. It was impossible to reach

Ray on any but a superficial level since she had apparently decided that all she wanted from us was such aid. The case is transferred to Group Therapy, the needs of the family having been met so far as it was possible to meet them.

Group treatment. On the suggestion of the Big Sister Department Ray was invited by the group therapist, six months after her referral, to an outing of a "girls' club." Ray came but seemed very disturbed throughout the afternoon. She was withdrawn, kept to herself, and made no effort to be friendly with the other girls or the therapist. After this meeting letters were sent to Ray repeatedly, asking her to attend meetings, but she did not respond.

In December the group therapist arranged with Ray's Big Sister to meet the girl personally again. During the brief conversation the therapist asked Ray to come to the group meetings. Ray came to the following meeting which was a trip to Radio City. The girls, who had been meeting throughout the summer and fall, were very friendly toward her. She came again to an indoor meeting and acted confused and lost. In a gruff voice and petulantly, she inquired, "What do I do?" and later, "May I paint something?" Jane offered to help Ray with her painting. She gave her brushes and paper and showed her where the sink was. She also displayed a bird that she had painted and suggested that Ray could choose any colors and materials.

Ray hardly ever missed a meeting during that winter. She was especially friendly with Tess, who had definite neurotic homosexual tendencies. Her attitude toward Ray was that of a boy. The two girls quarreled and fought and then made up. Tess was hostile to everyone in the group. She had phantasies that boys were following her in the street. She planned to run away from home. Ray and Tess would sit together during the greater part of the evenings whispering to one another, excluding everyone else from their conversations. Ray's other friend was Jane, whom she had also met at the first meeting. Unlike Tess, Jane was a more normal, healthy girl, younger than the others, who clung to Ray for protection.

During the second month of Ray's membership the group discussed its affairs and the therapist suggested that someone should keep the books on the club's finances in order to budget for parties and trips. (This was considered advisable in view of the age of the girls.) Ray volunteered to do this. During her two years of membership Ray kept the books accurately, entered all items, and budgeted the money. Ray was thus for the first time made to feel a part of a group and given responsibility.

At a later meeting the group therapist brought a play to the meeting. When Ray read the part of a boy, the girls told her she wasn't suited for it. She at once became abusive and insisted she wanted that part. When the girls stuck to their point, Ray refused to participate in the play altogether. At an opportune moment, the therapist took Ray aside and suggested that she read a girl's part to her; if it did not suit her they would make other arrangements. Ray read the part to the therapist a few times and discovered that she liked it. She then read it to the girls. All agreed that she did it very well and that she should have the part.[1] The tension between Ray and the other girls diminished after this episode. It also created a closer bond between her and the group therapist, for Ray was still distrustful of her.

The play was rewritten and revised by three of the girls and Ray was one of the three. The project continued almost till the end of the season, and though the play was not produced, it yielded Ray a great deal of satisfaction. She was never practical in her suggestions. The few suggestions she did make were unplausible fairy tales about talking horses and the like. She did, however, work easily with the other members of the

[1] This was the critical event in the treatment of this girl.

group and now readily acquiesced in the ideas the others brought forth.

The members of the group accepted Ray from the very start, but they did not get close to her because of her sharp manner and hostile attitude. For a long time, therefore, Ray's chief contact with the group was through Tess and Jane. When there was a general discussion of such topics as school or boys, Ray sat quietly without making any contribution. Three months after she had joined the group, the girls talked informally of their plans after high-school graduation. On this occasion Ray participated in the group's conversation for the first time. When one of the girls announced her plan to run away from home and the group discussed with her the inadvisability of such a step, Ray took part in the general and heated conversation. Up to this point, Ray had not made much progress with regard to integrating with the group. However, in the report of the meeting at which the discussion of running away occurred, we read: "This is the first time Ray has entered into free and prolonged conversation with the girls. For the first time Ray has displayed some awareness of the girls' presence and their problems." At one point in the conversation one of the more mature girls disagreed with Ray. She accepted the criticism calmly enough to be able to continue with the talk, which was a considerable change in her previous quarrelsome and stubborn attitude.

Her changed attitude helped her to become more and more a part of the group. The girls began to like her and on Ray's birthday, of their own accord, they arranged a party for her. Ray, very happy, sat at the head of the table. The group sang songs to her and insisted that she make a speech. Ray stood up and said, "Thank you, my friends. I don't know what else to say except to tell you what a nice party this is." This was undoubtedly the first birthday party Ray ever had, and it was the first overt indication of her being accepted by the girls. From then on Ray became fully a part of the group.

In discussing their plans for the play the girls discovered that they had to have a name for the club to use on the announcements. A number of names were suggested and there seemed to be no agreement among the group. The group therapist said: "You've all been coming here for some time now, and you know what we do here. What do you think we ought to call ourselves?" One of the girls said, " 'Happy Girls.' That's what we are here: happy." Ray added, "That's true. Let's call ourselves that."

On her own initiative, Ray started a library with the magazines and books that the girls and the therapist had brought. She made a file with an index card for each book and magazine and took great pride in it. At one meeting Ray was absent and a new girl substituted. When Ray returned, one of the girls asked for a magazine. Both Ray and Josette (the new girl) walked over to get it. Ray: "Who is librarian here?" Josette: "I am." Ray: "I thought I was." Josette: "That's all right. You can be it." Ray: "No, if you want to be librarian I don't care. I'm the bookkeeper and that's enough for me." On the way to the subway that evening, she explained to the group therapist that she understood what it meant for a new girl to have something to do. She, too, had felt shy and uncomfortable when she first came to the club, she said, and she could appreciate how Josette felt on joining. She was glad to have Josette take on the job of librarian for that reason. Josette, who was infantile in appearance and manner, was never accepted by the girls, but during the two years the group met, Ray always displayed a protective attitude toward her, though they never became intimate.

Ray very rarely worked with the arts and crafts materials. She sang or danced, helped the group therapist with tea or clearing up. However, as she became more a part of the group, she took an interest in what the other girls were doing, but without distracting or dominating the group. At one time she started to play the victrola while everyone else was working.

One of the girls told her to stop; it annoyed them. She laughed good-naturedly and said, "All right, I'll wait till later."

Her friendship with Tess lasted through the greater part of the first season. They were frequently arguing and making up. During the summer when the group was at camp, Ray and Tess had a serious fight. From then on, while the two girls remained friends, they were not intimate. Ray turned to the other more mature and socialized girls for friendship. She had now lost her resentment and her fear of the girls who were more mature and socially superior. She saw them outside the group, attended parties with them, and entertained them at her home, the family having moved to a better neighborhood and a better flat. It would seem that Ray no longer needed to cling to immature and socially inferior girls like Tess and Josette to bolster up her own ego. She felt more secure now.

In the second and final year of the group's existence Ray presented no problem. Her attendance continued to be perfect; she missed meetings only when ill. She seemed to be better accepted at home and got on at school much better, graduating before the age of eighteen.

In March of this year it was decided that the group had reached a point where they could expand their social contacts. It was, therefore, arranged that the group should meet at a "Y," as one of its own clubs, with a regular club leader attached to that agency. Other girls from the "Y" membership were added to the group.

The report of the leader of the "Y" club at the end of the season reads:

Ray is less dependent on leader than others and seems to have definite ideas on what she wants to do. She shows particular interest in music and boys. She is constantly seeking excitement and romance but, despite this romanticizing, seems to have a good grasp of reality.

In the camp reports we find that the summer following her first season at the therapy group there was a vast improvement in her conduct. Though she excelled at no particular sport, she was friendly to the counselors and all the girls. She presented no problem and accepted criticism.

Ray graduated from school and from a stenography course. She obtained a job the following fall in an office.

Evidence of improvement. After the first few months of Ray's membership in the group, the Big Sister reports "a vast difference" in Ray's reactions. Where she had been hard to talk to and sullen, she was now appreciative of what the Big Sister did for her and her family. An example of this we find in the following: "When the Big Sister arranged for some dental work to be done for Ray free, Ray sent a letter to the dentist, thanking him for all his kindness and interest. She would not have done this before."

In Ray's case we see a continuous progressive growth from a shy, resentful, and maladjusted youngster to a more mature and positive personality. She ceases to be the petulant, sad, and lonesome individual with strong masochistic trends and a need for self-abasement. She now is outgoing and comparatively happy, chooses friends in some respects superior to herself, no longer draws solely upon a puppy for her love needs, and is able to accept and give affection without fear or apprehension. She is able to submit to the will of the group and adults and therefore does not create as many problems for herself as she did in the past. She graduated from school about nine months before the usual age of eighteen, although she was considered a dull and troublesome pupil before. She seems to be accepted at home, for she is permitted to bring her friends and entertain them there.

In every area of her life this girl feels more secure and more certain of herself and takes her place in society with comparative ease. Her romanticism must be viewed as a deep-seated longing structuralized in her character through extreme emotional, physical, and social privations, or an innate characteristic of her personality. We note, however, that it is not so intense as to interfere with wholesome functioning in reality.[2]

Interpretation. The record material brings out the fact that Ray was rejected even before she was born. She was deprived of love and affection, and had less physical and financial security than is common even to people of her social and economic group. This led to a deep feeling of insecurity and a sense of worthlessness. She therefore sought friends among groups that were considered by her family as "inferior" as a form of self-abasement. Ray became a Cinderella type of person, daydreaming to compensate for the unpleasant actualities of her life. This resulted in a defective ego structure. The group gave her a reality situation during the most critical years of her development, namely, adolescence. There was no adequate or consistent control in her life such as would come from a father, an emotionally wholesome mother, and an integrated family group. Among many of the undesirable traits that Ray developed as a result were impulsiveness and lack of self-discipline. At the time of intake Ray's chief problems were overintense phantasy, a lack of reality sense, and the absence of an integrating force within herself.

Ray was a sad girl needing security, acceptance, and love. The treatment program required the building up in her of a sense of self-worth and self-respect. It was also necessary to establish some inner reference datum for her behavior (superego). She was entirely at loose ends. This was accomplished through relating herself to members of the group and to the group therapist.

The adult was a very important factor in Ray's life. She was Ray's first supportive ego. Though Ray did not cling to

[2] Five years later it was reported that this client was married, had a child, and had made a satisfactory adjustment in the community. She insisted on paying a fee to the same dentist from whom she had accepted free service while a client in the agency.

her, the girl was among the first in the group to do things for the therapist. This child needed the support of an adult to make the transition to the group, and she got that support. Without such help, Ray would probably have dropped out of the group as she had from other clubs in the past. On many occasions Ray naturally turned to the adult. In the latter's praise of her work on the play and of her few attempts at drawing and linoleum cutting, Ray found the sympathy and support that she needed in such critical situations.

The other important factor in Ray's therapy was the group. The group accepted her. She was hostile and aggressive; in the group she was able to express her feelings without increase of anxiety. She was unloved; the group therapist and later the other members gave her adequate compensation. She was insecure and frightened; the adult at first, and later the entire group, provided an environment and relationships that gave her assurance with other people.

Ray's friendship with Tess and Jane gave her an opportunity to pass wholesomely through the homosexual phase in her development and the group helped her to pass on to the heterosexual stage through periodic parties with a boys' club and later at the "Y." Tess helped Ray in her reorientation to people, by virtue of the fact that she accepted Ray's irritability and her irascible behavior, and also because the relation satisfied deeper adolescent homosexual needs. Tess accepted Ray on her own terms. She did not reject her because Ray was unfriendly; rather, she accepted all this. In fact she liked her for it, and treated her patronizingly. This decreased Ray's anxiety concerning her behavior. But when she was able to act more constructively and positively toward people, she no longer needed Tess's support and turned to Jane, a more wholesome girl than Tess. To Josette, Ray gave a motherly love which she herself had missed in life, and thus received compensatory gratification through her love of the other girl, whom she took under her wing. In this development we see Ray overcoming her inner need to be in an inferior position and be debased. She had now chosen a friendship in which she was the superior.

The group removed Ray, sporadically at least, from the social pathology in her home, giving her a glimpse of a way of living different from what she was accustomed to. Faith in herself was built up through her activities and through her social success as a member of a group. The therapist saw to it that she never failed in her work or socially. Although she was not creative with materials, Ray participated in the group life: she was bookkeeper and librarian, and took part in writing a play. The group therapist gave her consistent security in contrast to the instability of her family. She had the feeling of being wanted as demonstrated by the birthday party given by the girls and in a number of other ways. All these experiences have counteracted the girl's feeling of loneliness and the need for self-abasement, the two pivotal destructive trends of her character.

THE CASE OF JOHN SLOAN: *Complementary individual and group treatment of a hyperactive, daydreaming boy who stole*

Problem. John was referred to the agency by the Crime Prevention Bureau of the Police Department. With several older boys he had broken the seal on a freight car and removed a case of canned food. John was eight and a half years old at the time, the youngest member of a gang consistently engaged in stealing from the local market.

John was the fifth of six children ranging in age from four to twenty-three years. In accordance with the wishes of the mother, the father was not contacted. The father was described as "irresponsible and callous with his family, self-centered, authoritative with the children, a strict disciplinarian, and hard and abusive to his wife." Although at times his business was profitable, he spent most of his money on lavish entertainment for his men and women friends and provided little food and clothing for his family. He had affairs with the neighbors' wives and his women customers, and furthermore became involved in some shady business deals which resulted in his imprisonment. All this time he accepted his wife's sacrifices, expecting her to overlook his various misdemeanors, unfaithfulness, and thoughtlessness. With the depression, his business went so badly that he attempted suicide and later took to drink. With the loss of money and prestige, he became even more irritable and difficult at home.

Mrs. Sloan was a pale, blonde woman who always looked disturbed and visibly suffering from emotional stress. She actually played the martyr. She was the abused and forgiving one in contrast to her husband's lording ways. Although she secured a certain amount of masochistic pleasure from her hard lot, life for her was a great strain. She had not the money to pay for her many confinements and several abortions. The latter were necessary because, as Mrs. Sloan explained, she could not afford more children, and because of physical weakness. Mr. Sloan, however, would not give her the wherewithal even for the abortions. In addition he transmitted a venereal disease to his wife soon after a serious illness and in spite of the fact that the doctor had warned him about it. Her martyr role made it easy for Mrs. Sloan to alienate the children's affections from the father and fix them upon herself.

The children were typical products of such a family set-up. They were deprived not only of parental love but also of physical needs. They disliked their father and turned to their mother for affection. The older children resented the fact that they had not had opportunities to learn a trade or to branch out and marry because they had to carry the burden of this large family.

At time of referral to the agency, John appeared a sweet-looking, small, anemic boy with large, blue eyes, slightly freckled face, and light-brown hair. The mother complained that he was wild and uncontrollable, extremely active and disobedient, and that whippings and beatings by various members of the family, especially by the father, did not help. Mrs. Sloan further narrated that as a baby, John always placed himself in danger. He was almost run over by a trolley. People often pulled him out from the gutter and brought him home. The mother said that although the three younger children fought, John's temper was the worst. "He climbs and jumps like a wild one, answers back, is always out of the house, and usually has to be called to bed." In addition he would hitch on the back of trolley cars and was twice brought home by a policeman.

John was in severe rivalry with his brother James, three years older, who was bright in school and therefore held up as an example to John. He used to hit Barbara, the youngest sibling, who was described by the case worker as "cute" and ingratiating—another strong competitor for Mrs. Sloan's attention and affection.

John was disliked and labeled "stupid" in school. Due to a reading disability, he was "left back" a number of times. His I.Q. was 86, Stanford Binet. When referred to the agency he was in Grade 2A, having repeated 1A and 1B. His conduct varied from B plus to C and his work from C plus to D. His teacher stated that he was a "daydreamer, stupid, doing poor work, somewhat unruly but usually not outstanding in any way." At the time the case was contacted, another teacher said that John was so meek that "one would at first never suspect him of anything." "He did not say boo," she added. She also said that he did not exhibit any antisocial traits but daydreamed most of the time. At the time John associated with Alfred, a recent arrival at the school. The two would go to the wardrobe and search the pockets of the children's coats. "John picks out associates similar to himself. However, the other boy is much brighter," said the teacher. Alfred was also a problem at home. The case worker, having had a chance to observe Alfred's conduct, described him as "bold and smart-alecky." On one occasion John was caught during lunch hour taking a pencil from the wardrobe of another classroom.

The school career of this boy presented a confused picture, if we are to judge by the reports of the different teachers. His social adjustment seemed equally pathological. Because of his small size and stealing activities, he was rejected by the children on the street and in school who refused to play with him. He was regarded as a subversive influence and felt bitter about this rejection. As a result, he became an easy tool in the hands of the so-called bad boys of the neighborhood, much older than he. Here his puny size was an asset as he was able to crawl through openings that the others could not negotiate.

Individual treatment. A case worker assigned to this case saw John and his family for two months. Then another worker continued with the case for three years.

During the early stages of treatment, John was meek, sitting with lowered eyes, hardly able to speak. He finally said, "I have nothing to say about myself." His fear of the worker was alleviated, however, when he was encouraged to make all the decisions concerning the interviews and no allusion was made to his home and gang activities. Play technique was used exclusively. Although various materials were employed, the boy seemed most interested in clay modeling. Finding confidence and freedom in this activity, he began to relate his own problems to his play. He usually destroyed the figures he made.[3] John hated his father and evidenced this on several occasions. During an interview he made a figure of his father from clay and repeatedly jabbed at it as if desiring to kill it.

---

[3] There is an interesting connection between this and his evident efforts to get himself killed. See discussion, Chapter VII, pages 195 ff.

He played the role of an all-powerful person meting out punishment and apparently gained great satisfaction from this.

It was quite evident from the objects he modeled and the accompanying play and phantasy that this boy identified himself with powerful forces. On a number of occasions John modeled all-powerful characters such as King Kong, the Shadow, or a magician. The boy definitely identified himself with them, creating havoc, establishing law and order, punishing people. At one interview he made a figure of Popeye, who is small, thin, and oppressed. "Popeye ate spinach and then hit everybody," he said. John acted this out and then intimated that he was Popeye. Furthermore, John once related to case worker a dream he had had. In the dream he possessed a "blue ray" which, when directed at persons, rendered them cringing and powerless.

As all this behavior was unconditionally accepted by the worker, John indicated that his destructiveness was directed toward his father and older brother. Case worker reported:

His conflicts about honesty and dishonesty find expression in his gang battles staged before worker. As time goes on, he assumes the role of the law-enforcing authority. He strikes down gangsters by joining forces with the Shadow. In his struggles with gangdom during this period, John exclaimed to worker, "I don't want to be a thief. I'm not going to be a thief!" He once made a picture in which the devil was fighting with the Shadow. The devil was repeatedly beaten and John finally presented the devil to worker saying, "I'm giving it to you."

About a year after individual treatment began, John's play began to assume reality and he was able to discuss school, home, street gangs, and actually began to assume new attitudes.

Through the efforts of the case worker, a program for remedial reading was introduced at school. The school was made more aware of his problem and greater interest was shown in him there. A year later the case worker reported that John's general school work had improved to the extent that he was counted among the best in his class and regularly promoted. The teacher likewise told the worker that John was good and that she had no complaint whatsoever. John began to attend a parochial school. His success and pleasure there had definite reverberations in the family. Mrs. Sloan was pleased and John taught the other children in the family the things he learned, which helped increase his prestige in the family group. John was referred to Group Therapy after two years of individual treatment.

An important angle of the treatment process was the periodic interviews between the case worker and Mrs. Sloan. It was felt that she needed attention since she influenced the family set-up considerably and evidenced many conflicts in giving information concerning the family.

As already stated, Mrs. Sloan labored under a burden of abuse, neglect, shame, and poverty. Her husband's drinking and affairs with women only added to a life that was already sad. Her martyr-like attitude enlisted the children's sympathy on her side and with them she tried to fight her husband. It took a long time before she trusted the worker with her difficulties; but once she did, she made a long detailed story of it, as if to convince him of her sad lot. She fought treatment of herself, but also resisted giving up the interviews with the case worker. As her difficulties were discussed, she gradually adopted new attitudes toward her family. She was able to recognize her husband's limitations and to understand his frustrations. She spoke of her children's having a right to their own life away from the parents and, furthermore, began to perceive her martyrdom as an excuse for exercising excessive power over the family.

The financial pressure was relieved by arrangements with Mr. Sloan so that he contributed to the family allowance a sum commensurate with his earnings, which resulted in his participating more in the family decisions and thereby in checking his wife's absolute power.

Group treatment. In referring this client to the Group Therapy Department, the case worker wrote:

We do not have a full picture of John's adjustment to other children. He is an active boy who mingles freely with boys but does not get along well with them. . . . He is very active and pugnacious when he is not apprehensive. He does not make new contacts readily but enters upon social relationships wholeheartedly once made. . . . He is to be encouraged and praised, as he is easily discouraged by adults, becoming taciturn and withdrawn.

John was invited to a meeting on December 1. Because he was so aggressive, he was assigned to a group of boys older and larger than he. He attended the first meeting December 13. Out of a total of thirty-four meetings he missed six, and out of thirty-seven in the next season, he missed seven.

His behavior was very disturbing to the group. He talked a great deal, created a commotion, screamed, ran around, or played by himself in a very infantile manner, always attempting to attract attention. Being the smallest in the group, he was seldom called to account by the others. The report reads:

He chased around the room, through the halls and into various offices on the floor, fighting with the other boys, wrestling, screaming, and using six-foot window poles for spears. Frequently he would rifle desks in the offices.

He was always ready to fight with the older boys at the slightest provocation in spite of the fact that he was younger and smaller than they.

At the second meeting he found a box of building blocks, emptied it on the floor, and built the blocks to a precarious height. He always built his structures top-heavy so that they would collapse.[4] He repeated this stunt numerous times.

---

[4] This may be another manifestation of a suicidal trend.

When they fell, he would let out a yell with a maniacal expression on his face, his eyes wide and glaring. At times he would throw himself on the floor and would repeat this as long as the other boys laughed at him. One month later John became interested in an electric jig-saw that was introduced as a part of the group's equipment. The effect on him was rather significant. He at once became interested and worked with it. The group therapist reported several months later:

John no longer acts like a little maniac as he did at previous meetings. He is calmer, gentler, and not so impulsive. Whereas before he used to throw things down on the floor or cast things from him, he now just places them down gently. He is always smiling now. . . . He has ceased his running around when there isn't anything at hand to do and now keeps himself busy. He prides himself on his work. Moreover, he displays his work very anxiously to the other boys whose compliments seem very gratifying to John.

In a summary report for the period from February to March, five months after his admission to the group, an interesting contrast was noted. One day John decided to work with building blocks again, though he had not played with them for a long time. The group therapist wrote:

He sat on the floor, quiet and peaceful, and began building tall structures. He called the worker's attention to the structures he made and said, "Want to see it fall?" With perfect calm and quiet he toppled the blocks over and then looked up at the worker smiling. He seemed so at ease that the worker could not help being impressed with the remarkable change and recalling his former behavior. John has been consistently improving. His childish interest in working with the electric jig-saw has extended. He now works with wood and leather in a mature, purposeful manner. His wallet drew complimentary remarks from the other boys. This had an astonishing effect upon John.

At a Hallowe'en party in the following October, he entered into all the games freely and participated in the entertainment and competitive sports.

In January of the second season, the group therapist reported that John was quiet and well behaved at meetings. He seldom quarreled with anyone and never entered into a fight or brawl of any kind. He was, furthermore, very sociable and accepted all the other members of the group equally, though "when he entered the group he was overactive and pugnacious. The materials seemed to have a quieting effect upon him."

John became very interested and adept in working with craft materials. Recognizing his interest in this direction, the group therapist worked more closely with him and helped develop his skill and interest in leather work, intricate leather braiding, wood work, clay, marionettes, and so forth. The boy was quite original in his work and frequently what he made looked like an expensive artistic product.

Once John made a copper plaque and a wooden background for it, stained the wood to match the copper, and attached the plaque to it with little brass escutcheon nails. The plaque, when polished down with steel wool, was exceedingly attractive and later John told the group therapist that his father gave him fifty cents for it quite voluntarily. There was an excited happy look in his eyes as he related the incident to the worker. In view of our knowledge of the character of Mr. Sloan and of the strained relations between John and his father, this bit of information was important. At this particular time, too, John told the therapist that his brother, who had recently married, had seen the plaque and had asked for one as a wedding gift. John seemed thrilled at the recognition he was receiving at home.

In June, it was felt that Group Therapy could do no more for John. He was adjusted, happy, and productive and was transferred to a neighborhood club. For about eighteen months, the boy had been treated by a case worker exclusively. For the following fifteen months the case was carried cooperatively by the Case Work and Group Therapy Divisions of the agency. It was then transferred to Group Therapy where the boy had been treated exclusively for a year.

Evidence of improvement. John became more careful about the way he dressed and his general appearance was considerably improved. He was quiet now, did not engage in any of the horseplay, and was rather amazed at the tumult raised by some of the new members of the group, of which he had been an instigator not so very long before. Twice he was accidentally struck or pushed by other boys at play, but he merely said, "Ouch," and accepted the excuse of "I didn't mean it," instead of starting a fight. He became cooperative and felt responsible for the maintenance of the room equipment and materials.

Since John was referred to the agency because of a reported delinquency and since he was known to be a member of a gang, it is interesting to note the following. The group therapist reports:

John never asked the group worker to lend him money either for carfare or for personal use although he knew that some of the other boys received carfare. At one time John needed carfare and hesitated to ask for it. It was only because the worker overheard another boy urging John to ask for the money, that it was offered to him. John still hesitated, but when pressed finally accepted it. As soon as he came in at the following meeting, he returned the five cents to the worker. When the latter asked whether he needed it and told him he could keep it longer, John insisted upon returning it immediately.

The camp reports for three consecutive summers record consistent improvement in adjustment. A passage in the report for the last summer states that he is "one of the nicest boys in the bunk. He doesn't fight, but isn't a sissy."

Eight months after the case was closed, a follow-up interview was held with the assistant principal of the school John attended. She stated: "The boy is a model child. I don't know what you have done with him, but it seems like a miracle to me."

There was also a marked improvement at home. In February of the last year of Group Therapy, Nat, one of John's older brothers, wrote in a letter to the case worker on another matter: "John was promoted and is behaving very well. He is not as wild as he was before. He is much more settled and takes an interest in everything around him."

Interpretation. The boy's need for self-maximation and extravagant behavior was an outcome of his feeling of inferiority because of his size and the rejection by his siblings. The emotional chaos in the family atmosphere engendered in him very intense anxiety which expressed itself in hyperactivity. His stealing propensities seemed to be activated also by a need for punishment. The neurotic conflict of this boy (in relation to his behavior) is evidenced by his struggle with the devil and his exclamations about not wanting to be a thief, and by the practice of placing himself in danger of being maimed or killed. The need for punishment seems to be tied up with his hostility toward his father and older brother. This is a classical case of delinquency resulting from an overstrict super-ego, which he undoubtedly derived from his martyr-like mother and is expressed in his seeking to be killed and hurt.

Stealing, however, served other purposes as well in the psychological cravings of this boy. Being an act of grandeur it compensated for his puny size. It served as a means of being accepted by older and bigger boys, which increased his sense of importance. John further used stealing as a tool of revenge against his family for rejecting him and against the community for stigmatizing him in school and in the neighborhood.

In the first stages of therapy, it was necessary to release the boy's emotional pressure without arousing guilt. This was done by the case worker in his early interviews and by the group. He was permitted to set the stage in the interviews and was not restrained in any way at the group meetings. The next step in releasing emotional pressure took place when he gained enough security with the case worker to talk about his hostility to his father and brother and vicariously to kill and destroy them in the worker's presence. The third stage in treatment occurred when John was helped to be accepted by the world. Remedial reading was one step in this direction; another was relieving the mother's emotional tensions and getting her to accept John. Still another was placement in the group where he was unconditionally accepted. As a result of all these changes in his life, the boy discovered that it was possible to get satisfactions without indulging in destructive behavior. Positive attitudes and constructive effort were now evoking recognition and affection. Status in a group came through his manual skill rather than through infantile exaggerated acts. The family also became friendly. The need for delinquencies was, therefore, eliminated, and with them guilt feelings that led to further punishment-provoking destructive acts. Anxiety was then reduced, the character of the boy became more balanced, and his personality socialized.

THE CASE OF IVOR BROWN: *Supportive case work and group treatment of an effeminate, withdrawn boy*

Problem. Ivor Brown, ten years old, was referred for psychotherapy by a physician at a city hospital who recognized psychological factors in the boy's constant illnesses. The mother appeared for an interview a month later, but in line with her general resistance to treatment of her son, did not bring him to the office for six months.

Ivor had been a sickly child since birth and had spent much time in hospitals, one such sojourn lasting seven months. At the age of two weeks he developed a chronic ear condition (otitis media) with an offensive discharge which persisted at the time of referral.

Ivor was the second oldest of five children: Harris, who was five years older, Mary, Thomas, and Celia, five, seven, and nine years younger. Mrs. Brown was an aggressive person who dominated the entire family. She was a woman of many interests outside the home, neglecting her family for these. At first she appeared cheerful, but later revealed herself as a hostile, hateful, and destructive person who managed all the affairs of the family. She dominated her husband as well as the children. It was very clear that Mrs. Brown had very little love for Ivor. He had given her so much trouble and, she said, she did not bring Ivor to the office at first because he was so unpleasant. All she desired of the agency was placement for the boy in an institution. She complained of his personality and behavior. It was evident that she was much more concerned over the boy's behavior as it affected her standing in the community than as indicating a serious problem in need of treatment.

Mr. Brown also was active in many organizations and spent little time at home. He earned hardly enough to support the family. Ivor mentioned his father briefly on only two occasions during the entire period of treatment. Once he related how brutally and cruelly he was treated by his father; on the other occasion he said resentfully, "My father gives more attention to Harris [the oldest child] than to me." There was serious conflict between Harris and Ivor. One day the older brother taunted him so severely that Ivor chased Harris with two carving knives and almost slashed him. The three younger siblings, on the other hand, were the recipients of Ivor's great tenderness and motherly care.

At the time of referral Ivor was enuretic as well as given to encopresis. Added to this was a habit of smearing the discharge from his ear on his clothing so that there was always a very offensive odor about the boy. He was known at school and in his neighborhood as "Stinky." He ran away from home on occasion and frequently stole from neighbors and neighborhood stores. His reputation as a thief was such that thefts in the neighborhood were almost always attributed to Ivor. Although very effeminate and withdrawn, he managed to get into fights with neighbors and children in the street and was known to play sexually with girls five years of age and younger. He had no friends. Ivor frequently truanted from school where he was treated as a special problem. Because of his unpleasant physical appearance and odor, he was isolated from everyone. He was forced to eat away from everybody else in the school dining room from special dishes reserved only for his use. The school psychologist described him as having "a mean and nasty disposition without a lovable trait in him." In addition, frequent illnesses caused his retardation in school by two grades. His marks were erratic, ranging from C to A in work, and from C to B in conduct.

Ivor spent a good deal of time picking up things on a dump near his home which he would offer to children as bribes for playing and being friends with him. He had only one friend, a boy much younger than he and, according to Ivor's own statement, very stupid. Ivor avoided competition with boys, preferring to play with girls. He did a great deal of drawing, always pictures of women, repeating the same faces and shapes. His drawings were described as phallic in outline. He made paper flowers which his father sold occasionally to friends, and offered himself as a housemaid to do cleaning for neighbors and mind the babies at stipulated rates. He wore girls' clothes and did much of the housework in his home in addition to caring for his younger siblings. He sewed his own clothes and when hurt cried like a little girl.

Individual treatment. Ivor became very much attached to his case worker. His mother tried in every way possible to prevent the boy's going to see her. She refused to give him carfare or left home forgetting to give him the money. During interviews, Ivor complained bitterly of his lack of friends. He found himself isolated and did not know what to do. "You see

my ear runs and makes me smell. Then the boys don't like me,"
Ivor said one day. The boys, he complained, called him
"Smelly" and "Stinky." Ivor spoke of his very unhappy home
life saying, "You don't know what a hard life I have." He was
often left at home alone to mind the younger ones while they
slept, and he was so scared, he would sit in a chair motionless,
too frightened even to think. "You know," he said one day,
"I'm just like Cinderella." He resented the fact that he was
used by the family as a drudge, washing dishes, sweeping the
floors, and doing everyone's errands. He demurred bitterly because his older brother got all the attention and new clothes
for the holidays, while he got none.

Ivor accepted the case worker as a "real friend," and spoke
with her freely. He seemed to feel secure in her presence since
she let him do whatever he wished: sing, dance, draw, or talk.
Because of the boy's insecurity, little direction was exerted
during the early interviews. He kept his weekly appointments,
despite the struggle with his mother over carfare. Treatment
was entirely on a supportive basis. No effort was made to discuss his problems on a deeper level. In March, after five
months of treatment, the case worker attempted to bring out
material relating to the boy's more basic problems. Little unconscious material came through, however.

Once in October of the same year, Ivor said that he had
come to the office because he didn't play games, didn't look or
talk right. When asked to explain, he said the boys thought he
was a girl. He himself didn't know what he was. Upon the suggestion from the case worker, he listed the characteristics of
the sexes. For boys he listed: "They are noisy and athletic and
play rough games." "Girls," he said, "are very quiet. I'm very
quiet. Girls sew dresses. I can sew dresses. Girls like to draw,
dance, and give entertainments. I, too, like to do these things."
In a very decisive tone, he added, "Girls have nothing to do
with boys. They play with each other, and I play with girls,
too. I have a girl's nature." He did not amplify on this or on the

following: "I'm just born to loneliness." He said he was con-
demned to play with himself and dream the rest of his life. Although he never again referred directly to his femininity during the treatment, he gave the indication of such identification
on a number of occasions. He once described a play which he
had written and which ended by his marrying his sister.

Ivor's home situation did not improve. He was still soiling
his clothing and doubtful of his sex. About a year after treatment had begun, Mrs. Brown came to the office to complain of
her son's running away from home in the early hours of the
morning to go to an aunt's. He was returned by a policeman.
He later told the worker that he hoped some kind lady who
could love him would pick him up on the street and adopt
him. The mother also accused Ivor of stealing twenty-five
cents from his older brother.

Ivor had become more and more attached to the case
worker and sought solace in her company. He wanted to go to
her home and see her twice a week. This plan was not carried
out since Ivor was attending a drawing class and could not arrange it. In school, however, Ivor had a little more acceptance
now because of a more considerate teacher.

Group treatment. A year after individual treatment, Ivor
was referred to a therapy group. When he received the invitation, he came to the case worker and very suspiciously asked
how the person who had invited him knew that he wanted to
join a club, where he had gotten his address, and how he knew
him. It was pointed out that the invitation stated that the case
worker referred him. Ivor was not satisfied, however. He felt
someone was playing a trick on him: "There is possibly no
building by that number." He offered all sorts of reasons for
not going to the group meetings. Even after verification in his
presence by telephone of the meeting place, Ivor remained
very tense and undecided. However, after considerable encouragement by the case worker, the boy came to the meeting.

Ivor was extremely withdrawn and secluded. His manners

were dainty and effeminate. He sat in the corner by himself, not saying a word during the entire meeting except to show the group worker his drawings. He did nothing but paint women, but his ability evoked occasional remarks and recognition from the other members of the group. Several months later, Ivor sketched the group worker and called the picture to his attention. When the latter held up the drawing saying, "Look what Ivor did! Isn't it nice?" the boys agreed that it was very good. Ivor was proud and said, "I'm glad you recognized who it was meant to be." *This was the first time the boy drew a man.* Thereafter Ivor's work was always praised and brought to the group's attention. It was felt that at this point praise and attention would not be threatening to the boy.

Once Ivor attempted to make what the others in the group were making, an aeroplane. For the first time Ivor participated in what is considered a masculine activity, sawing wood. He was extremely clumsy and uncoordinated and appeared under a great strain. He became upset if anyone watched this work, although he did not mind being watched when doing art work. Ivor's failure with tools brought about a regression in his social responses. He again completely withdrew from the group and seldom conversed with the others, except with one, a retarded boy. At this point, however, Ivor had made enough progress to help the worker with cleaning up and washing dishes. Because he did not challenge them, the other boys did not annoy him and left him to his own devices.

Despite the fact that Ivor had to walk a great distance from his home to the meeting place of the group, his attendance was perfect and he was always the first to arrive. He told his case worker how fond he was of the "club" and how he liked particularly the trips to places of interest. He criticized the boys' "rudeness and inconsiderateness." "They always demand things and fight when they can't have what they want." For these reasons, he had little to do with them, he said. The drawings he made during this period began to take on new form. They were "life-like sketches, and exaggerated fashion-plate poses."

His difficulty with his older brother persisted. Once Harris refused to accompany Ivor to the circus for which the agency had given him two tickets. Ivor was now able to discuss the soiling of his clothes. This he could not do before, but he blamed it on the food he ate. In March during the first year of Group Therapy, he spoke for the first time with violence about his mother's blocking his coming to the office. In May Mrs. Brown reported that the soiling had practically ceased during the previous three months. She expressed further gratification at having placed the boy in a club (therapy group) because of the deep interest her son evinced in it. Ivor was doing better in school. His grades improved and he enjoyed his school work. The ear discharge was no longer a handicap, for Ivor treated and washed the ear regularly and the odor was eliminated. This routine was worked out by the case worker and he carried it out in a mature, responsible manner. Gradually the discharge stopped altogether.

In July, Mrs. Brown again saw the case worker. She expressed amazement at the change in the boy in the past few months. She described him as being "so much more manly," more outgoing. The soiling occurred very infrequently. He had made friends with whom he now played easily. That summer Ivor did not hesitate to go to camp, although he had refused to do so the summer before. In fact Mrs. Brown, who had held up the oldest boy as the ideal after whom Ivor should pattern himself, spoke of her misgivings concerning Harris and asked for help with him.

In December the family moved to a better neighborhood a considerable distance away and though Ivor was willing to travel to attend a "club," no suitable group was available. However, the boys in the new neighborhood were of a higher caliber and more suitable for a boy of Ivor's sensitive temperament. He had no difficulty in making friends. He attended a progressive public school where pupil activity was encouraged, and he was happy there.

During this period Ivor continued to see his case worker. He began to relate instances and stories calling for aggressiveness on his part. In school he had written four short stories for which he received the grade of A and special commendation. Ivor now drew pictures of men. They were imaginative types and of a more masculine nature.

In February the family was forced to return to the old neighborhood due to financial reverses. Ivor was definitely conscious of the progress he had made. He now found himself again in a repressive school with an impatient teacher who no longer was his "friend." His only friend, he felt, was the case worker. Immediately upon return he asked to be placed in the "club." He was also referred to an art school which required an hour's ride on the subway each way, and although he did not like this mode of travel, he was happy at the opportunity to learn art.

Until June, when Ivor again went to camp, he attended the therapy group regularly. He made several leather key cases for members of his family, but continued with his painting in which he felt secure. In May, at the ninth meeting after his return to the group, the group therapist asked Ivor whether he would like to buy the refreshments. He eagerly accepted, but as a result found himself, unwillingly, in the midst of a brief tussle between two other boys who wished to go with him. When it was over, Ivor walked to one side and began to examine his limbs and neck as though to ascertain whether he was still intact. His face expressed utter consternation and fear. Ivor was definitely shocked by this experience. It would appear that he had never been in physical contact with boys before.[5] From this date on, Ivor became definitely outgoing.

[5] Although we can recognize a number of critical events in the treatment of the boy, developments later indicate that this was the major event.

He would volunteer to buy the refreshments, worked with leather, joined group singing, played ball, and seemed to enjoy the other games with the boys. At an outing a month later, he rowed a boat and joined the others in calling one of the boys "fat."

He appeared to have developed a feeling of security and self-confidence in the group setting. On a trip to a beach the following September, Ivor yielded to group pressure to participate in a ball game. Ivor was startled when he hit the ball. The cheering of the boys was encouraging and he subsequently joined the various athletic activities of the group. Ivor developed to the point where he would assert himself and actually argue with the other members. He told a boy irritatedly, "Well, if you know how to do this, why don't you show me instead of wasting my time?" Ivor continued to progress. He became more assertive and developed normal aggressiveness in relations with others. "I feel," reported the group therapist, "Ivor is now working with the boys as one of the group, rather than as an isolated individual."

Evidence of improvement. Mrs. Brown continued to report extreme satisfaction with Ivor's adjustment. In his case work relationship, he was most vehement when the question of his being a "sissy" was brought up. He discussed even more freely his home relationships. The case worker was now able to point out the reality of his mother's personality and his need for accepting her as she was. But Ivor felt that he was accepted at home now as well. When Ivor received tickets for the circus and planned to take a friend, he agreed to take his brother along instead, after prolonged entreaty by the latter. It must be remembered in this connection that Harris had refused to go with Ivor two years before.

The boy had given up his infantile ways of revenge such as wetting and soiling himself and stealing. He had accepted and adjusted to a masculine role in life and had become less dependent and love-hungry. He no longer felt that the world was hostile and persecuting and that his destiny was loneliness and tragedy. His total outlook on life had become a more hopeful one.

By April of his third year in the group, Ivor's behavior in the group was that of a typical boy. On trips he played, shouted, and displayed physical prowess on an almost equal plane with others. When conflicts arose he did not withdraw but offered resistance. He volunteered information and opinions, he teased his playmates and worked harmoniously with them. He now had his own football, baseball, and bat and played with boys of his own age on the streets. His attendance at the group dropped off considerably. At this time, the group worker received the following letter from Ivor:

> Dear Mr. Kent,
>   I'm sorry to inform you that I wish to discontinue my membership in the club. You might as well know the facts, and here they are: I found since I am getting older I haven't the time. Please try to understand the situation.
>
> Very truly yours,
IVOR BROWN
>
>   P.S. Please say good-bye to the boys for me.

The case worker continued to see him until July.

Interpretation. When this boy was referred for treatment his ego structure was seriously malformed. The rejecting and emasculating (castrating) treatment he had received at the hands of his mother and his older brother caused him to doubt his own sexuality. To ingratiate himself with his mother, the boy helped her with the housework, which caused him to assume a feminine role. Further fixation in this tendency grew out of his mothering his younger siblings. His own infancy and childhood having been tragic, he sought to supply love and care to them so that they would be happier than he was. He was giving them what he desired for himself and thus received vicarious love satisfactions.

Because the boy received some attention, even though of a

negative nature, and got even with his persecutors by being annoying, he practiced annoying behavior not only in the home but outside as well, stealing, quarreling, smearing pus on his clothes, soiling and wetting himself. It is inevitable that a child so thoroughly rejected as Ivor should be addicted to such infantile behavior. He used enuresis and encopresis also as means of retaliation. But the fact that he used such weapons indicates that anal eroticism was an important factor in his character structure. The boy's social disorientation was a direct result of his history. He was sexually disorientated, he had a fear of growing up, he used extreme behavior for getting attention, he stole, and at the same time he had a perception of danger and felt threatened by the world. This symptom picture was further complicated by his strong "moralistic" standards. He was disgusted with the other boys' aggressive and demanding attitudes because of his phantasy as to the destructive and undesirable character of masculinity. Ivor, however, was fundamentally a very hostile boy. This fact did not come out in treatment, because he would not permit the case worker to go below superficial levels. He probably withdrew from the group before he was activated in this direction, but it must be noted that he discussed his mother and family more freely after the release he gained through the group.

Treatment goals in the case were threefold: 1) correct orientation toward sex and its concomitants; 2) discharge of repressed hostility toward members of the family, especially the boy's mother; and 3) acceptance of a masculine role.

The non-threatening relation that the case worker succeeded in establishing was the first major step. Without the security of such a relation no treatment of any kind would have been possible. If the case worker had attempted in her interviews to go beyond the limits set by the boy, either he would have withdrawn or therapy would have been stopped or retarded. This type of supportive treatment requires great skill and subtlety, especially when it extends over three years.

The case worker served as a substitute mother, but the boy also reacted to her as a woman. As one reads the original record, one is impressed with the fact that the boy strove to impress her with his masculinity. He was very resentful of any suggestion that he might be considered a "sissy" or unmanly. The striving to be a man in the eyes of a woman undoubtedly aided greatly in his acquiring more masculine attitudes.

Without the support of the case worker, Ivor could not have faced joining a group. By joining it, he realized the dream of his life: to be with other boys, not to be lonesome and neglected. The permissive atmosphere of the group proved entirely non-threatening, which was contrary to his expectation. He was accepted, praised, and eventually successful. The group supplied him with a masculine environment which he did not find to be at all dangerous. He found that physical contact, even of a violent nature, did not destroy him and that it was possible to work at his own pace without failing or being ridiculed or unfavorably compared with others. These and similar experiences changed the boy's perception both of himself and of masculinity. As he grew more secure and his personality more balanced, he was able not only to accept the members of his family as they actually were, but also to talk more freely about them. This discharge of hostility took the place of his substitutive infantile attacks on them through enuresis, encopresis, and smearing himself with pus. It must be noted in this connection that the ear discharge diminished and presently disappeared completely. This gives rise to speculation whether the causes of this condition were physical or psychological.

The group served as therapy here in a number of ways. The major service seems to be the fact that Ivor was supplied with a masculine environment through which he overcame his fear of his own masculinity. This is confirmed in many ways in the record. Perhaps one instance would be of interest here. After the jostling episode and Ivor's ball playing in the park, he climbed a Jungle Jim, which is intended for small children. (Ivor was twelve years old at the time.) He stopped only a short distance from the ground. Another boy, following Ivor's example, also took to climbing, but reached a point a rung or two above Ivor's. Ivor tried to climb up to the same height, but as he moved the other boy climbed higher still. Two or three times Ivor attempted to climb up, but in each case the other boy climbed higher. Ivor finally settled down on a level lower than his rival, apparently fearing the challenge. His fear of getting the best of a boy asserted itself again. We see, however, that later he quarreled and fought with the boys.

The second important service was that the group gave him a field for relating himself to others on the level of his own psycho-social development rather than to girls half his age. As he gained security there was a testing ground close at hand. With each successful try he grew more certain of himself and less fearful of his masculinity. Ivor's developing security began when the group therapist recognized himself in the picture Ivor drew. It could be seen also in such acts as Ivor's going out for food and his response to being inadvertently pushed by the two boys engaged in a tussle.

A third service of the group was that it supplied him with an identification object and an ego ideal in the person of the male group therapist. One of the outstanding features of Ivor's group experience is that he had not cultivated a supportive ego among the boys, which is unusual in our groups. Although Ivor did not express it in so many words, the group therapist was a major factor in his life. When by an error the group meeting and the interview with the case worker fell at the same hour, Ivor came to see the worker, but he was "on pins and needles" and left in a few minutes to go back to his own neighborhood where the group met. The trip took over an hour each way, and he stayed with the case worker only long enough to make his excuses. He could not miss the meeting. He needed both the woman (case worker) and the man (group

therapist) in his life and was afraid to lose them if he neglected either.[6] The image of a man who was kind and calm
counteracted his phantasy that masculinity was evil, destructive, and something to fear and reject. *Seeing* boys act out
their aggressions without calamitous results also helped correct his ego structure in this respect.

We cannot, however, overlook the value of the group itself
in this case. Ivor verbalized his feelings of loneliness, his need
for other boys. The social hunger, which in this case derived
from his ego needs as well as from affect hunger, was met.
("I was born to loneliness.") There is little doubt that his rush-
ing away from the case worker to the group was determined
by this need. He treated the group more impersonally, however, than is common. His supportive ego did not come from
the group, probably because of his sensitivity. The other boys
were really too rough for him. His close friends were chosen
from those in his neighborhood who were possibly more suitable to his temperament.

This client's problem is a clear case of disorientation complicated by other factors. Disorientation here is in the area of
sex, but social and personality maladjustments may come
from disorientation in various other areas such as the vocational and relational. Individual treatment in Ivor's case could
not and did not proceed profitably until he had the experience
of reality situations. This boy would not have corrected his
sexual disorientation except in a male environment and he
would not have responded to a male case worker because of
his distrust and fear of men. Hence the group was the pivot
of treatment. The case worker supported him when he ven-
tured out into the new world (the group) and supplied him
with an opportunity to discharge hostility (verbally) toward
his family.

---

[6] In a similar case, a rejected boy brought his woman case worker and the
group therapist together and suggested that they get married, this despite
the fact that the woman was probably twenty-five years older than the intended groom.

An important aspect of Ivor's case is that, probably because of his age, he had no distinct neurotic characteristics. This was rather a case of behavior disorder of both conduct and habit types. What facilitated the treatment is that he was able so easily to establish relations with kind adults. When anxieties in a neurotic patient are allayed through individual treatment, he naturally gives up the neurotic behavior. A behavior disorder does not yield as easily to such treatment. It would seem, therefore, that *situational therapy* is indicated in such cases.

THE CASE OF HARMON MANCHER: *The utilization of social hunger in the treatment of an overaggressive, neurotic boy*[7]

Problem. Harmon Mancher, ten years old, was referred to the agency by his mother, who complained of his being "wild and unmanageable." In school, the teachers described him as "fresh and absent-minded."

Harmon, the youngest of three children, the others being a brother eight years older and a sister six years older, was unwanted and was "an accident baby." Mrs. Mancher described Harmon at birth as "the funniest-looking baby I ever saw." He had the "biggest knuckles," and his skin seemed to hang from him. However, as he grew older, he seemed to improve. He was breast-fed for eight or nine months and was not given the bottle during this period. He did not cry when he was weaned and was described by the mother as "a very good baby." Harmon began to teethe at seven or eight months, walked at fourteen months, and talked at about eighteen months. *Training in excretory habits was achieved at four months.* This was done by placing him on a receptacle and

---

[7] We are indebted to Miss Dorothy Dunaeff, senior psychiatric case worker, and Mr. George Holland, senior group therapist, for gathering the original material in this study during a series of discussions between them. The interpretation is the author's.

spanking him gently. However, up to the age of thirteen, he suffered from occasional enuresis. He had many illnesses throughout childhood: abscesses in the ears at the age of two, an operation for rupture at the age of five, chicken-pox, measles, and double mastoiditis.

Harmon's home environment was a disturbed one from the time he was an infant. There was a long history of marital disharmony pre-dating his birth. The father seemed to be an immature, narcissistic person, intellectually inferior to his wife, and irresponsible. At times he would enter into rivalry with his son for the attention of Mrs. Mancher. Characteristically, he deprived his wife of the large part of his earnings and otherwise frustrated her. Mrs. Mancher, though chronically ill, helped in the support of the family. Her husband criticized his wife for attending classes in English. To the case worker, Mrs. Mancher spoke of her hatred for her husband. Although she claimed to desire a separation, she could not go through with it when financial help to make it possible was offered her.

In spite of not having wanted him, Mrs. Mancher did not seem to reject Harmon. In fact, there was some evidence that she gave the child warmth and acceptance. However, she did use him as an object on whom to redirect much of the irritation and hostility she felt as a result of her unhappy marital life.

Much of Harmon's difficulty in the home was with his older brother and sister. The brother attended college in the evening and earned a meager living from a part-time job. Harmon was irritable, impatient, and hated his father. Despite the intense antagonism between them, the two brothers slept together in the living room. The older brother would study late into the night, play the radio, and in general disturb Harmon's sleep. He was inconsiderate, rejecting, rigid, and demanding with Harmon. The sister was a selfish, neurotic, disturbed person; she was demanding, completely absorbed in herself, and openly cruel and abusive toward Harmon. The latter had little privacy of any kind in his home. He was driven from one room to another by the siblings and the parents. As already stated, Mrs. Mancher rejected him less than the others did and, as a result, he felt some acceptance of himself by his mother.

Mrs. Mancher related that Harmon was a very stubborn boy, always wanted his own way, was disobedient and extremely restless, and reacted violently to discipline. One of the worst punishments was to forbid him to go to the library or to play the radio. He would constantly argue with his siblings and would throw at them whatever he found nearest at hand. He read seven books a week and was very irregular in his reading habits, reading at his meals and during the bedtime hours (which was not entirely his fault). He did not keep himself clean.

In school, he exhibited the same restlessness and attention-getting qualities. Although his I.Q. was 135, Harmon was doing very poorly at school. The case worker was told by his teachers that the boy was the most unpopular child in the school. He sometimes fell asleep in classrooms and was considered "a dull and difficult boy." All efforts failed with him, they said. Outside of school, also, Harmon had never had friends. When he was younger, he did play a little with children, but as soon as he learned to read, he spent most of his time reading and going to the library.

Individual and group treatment. In June, immediately on being referred, Harmon was assigned to a case worker, whom he saw once a week. He came regularly. Mrs. Mancher was seen only occasionally, when there was a pressing problem or anxiety that needed immediate attention.

During the early interviews, Harmon was glib, verbose, intellectual, superficial, and self-protective. He used every provocative trick he could invent to incite the case worker to anger. He was ingenious in his avoidance of discussing his problems, and exceedingly restless, constantly toying with something on the case worker's desk as he spoke. Underneath his restlessness and hyperactivity, evasiveness, and intellectualization, there was felt to be an underlying tension and anxiety, insecurity and uncertainty. It was almost as though he could not permit himself to be accepted by anyone, but had to force the individual into rejecting him by extreme means.

A varied play technique was used with Harmon in the attempt to tie up some of his reactions and difficulties to the play situation. This approach met with no success. He merely came to the office to play. Interviews with the boy were constant battles. He refused to acknowledge problems, always talked away from the subject, and, whenever pressed, intellectualized and challenged the worker. When confronted with the fact that the reason he was coming to the agency was to secure help with his difficulties, he simply replied, "I don't ask you about your private, personal affairs and I see no reason why you should ask me." Although Harmon did make some reference to the conflicts with his siblings, these statements lacked depth. At no time during the first year and a half of case work treatment was the worker able to get him to discuss his disturbed relationship with his parents and his feelings about it, nor was she able to secure from him any expression of hostility toward his parents. He was completely protective in this area. An attempt to relate some of the boy's school difficulties to his general problems or to discuss with him his feeling that he was not liked did not meet with success. When the case worker touched on an area that was painful to him, Harmon told her that what she had just mentioned was private and he preferred not to discuss it. He was evidently in conflict about his sexual phantasies. However, he would resist talking about them and became upset when they were touched upon.

The boy was sent to camp for the second summer after individual treatment began. His adjustment there was very poor.

During this year and a half of treatment, it was reported

that the boy did not change in any respect; he was unable to make or hold friends or to play with children. The case worker felt that, while a strong relationship had been established with the boy, she had reacted to him in many situations in much the same manner that his mother had, falling into his neurotic pattern. The boy was getting the same satisfaction from annoying her as from annoying his mother. He was aware of the reaction he was getting from the case worker. In February, after twenty months of case work treatment, the boy was transferred to another woman worker.

With the new worker as well, Harmon employed his intellectualization, glibness, restlessness, and provocative behavior. But by now he had acquired some psychiatric knowledge by reading books, and would refer to his behavior as "my attention-getting mechanism" and use other technical terminology. Playing with the telephone, he disconnected it. He was firmly told that there were certain things he could play with, others he could not, and unless he abstained, he would have to leave. There was a noticeable decrease in the boy's destructiveness. It was difficult to tie him down to any subject of discussion, but the case worker continued to be firm with him.

Play technique (largely with clay) was used at first. The case worker initiated the play and, to a certain extent, Harmon's conflict and phantasies about sex came through in the play situations. He continued to be resistive to revealing these phantasies, however, and it was constantly necessary to bring him back to the subject. In one interview, when he was playing with clay, the case worker suggested making a family. Upon his suggestion, the case worker made the woman, while he made the man. As the worker put breasts on the woman, Harmon became very disturbed and found it difficult to finish the male figure. It was with great difficulty that he brought himself to place the penis on it. His disturbance about masturbation and his phantasies about intercourse were touched upon. He was also greatly disturbed about the possibility of contracting a venereal disease. Whatever information he had on these subjects was confused. He admitted that he was puzzled and wanted information about sex matters, but felt it was difficult to discuss such matters, especially with a woman. Harmon felt that it was a father's duty to take up these problems with him, but said that his father was "just no good." For the most part, however, the boy persisted in his evasiveness in all discussions, including those concerning his behavior at school.

In October, after two years and a half of individual treatment, Harmon was referred to Group Therapy. He responded to the very first invitation, and of the sixty-five sessions that his group held, Harmon was absent from only five and then because of illness. The group to which Harmon was assigned was composed of boys all approximately of his age, but none of his intellectual caliber.

The first meeting that Harmon attended, he devoted to questioning the group therapist as to the why and wherefore of the invitation to attend this "club." At later meetings he wanted to know why he had been invited, what the therapist thought of him: "Don't I talk too much?" "Don't I annoy you? I do everyone else." "You don't want me to come any more." "Do you enjoy having me around or do you consider me a pest?" The therapist quietly explained that he thought Harmon was like any of the other boys, that he was not annoying him, that he enjoyed having him come to the group, and that he would like to have him come every week just as the others did.

During the meetings that followed, Harmon rapidly became part of the group, but a very undesirable member. He did not relate himself to activities and chores, but rather tried in every conceivable manner to be as troublesome and obnoxious as he could possibly be. Harmon knew some of the boys, having been at camp with them. The boys referred to him as "the pest," but this did not embarrass him. He seemed to revel in the notoriety. He was quarrelsome and noisy, constantly at odds with one or another of the boys, managing to get into one fight at each meeting and sometimes three.

Week after week he was beaten by one or another of the boys. At times the cruelties inflicted upon him became serious. At first Harmon was hesitant about fighting back, preferring to wrestle. He soon found, however, that if he wished to remain intact, he had to learn to use his fists, and this he did. As he actually began to fight back, the fights became more intense and the punishment to himself more severe. He appealed to the adult to step in, but the latter refused, explaining to him repeatedly, "This is your club. If that is what you want to do, it's O.K. with me." Although Harmon threatened to leave meetings in a huff, he never did.

One evening, when he had suffered an especially severe thrashing, he frantically exclaimed, "I am going home. I can't stand this any more. Where shall I put this?" (referring to a leather wallet he was making). When the group therapist calmly directed him to put it into the cabinet, Harmon did so, then walked around the room once or twice, made his usual appeal for justice, but remained for the balance of the evening. His usual reaction to a fight was to straighten his clothes, go out to the anteroom, compose himself, and return to the meeting room. He would remain quietly seated for a few minutes until he had fully collected himself and then proceed with his annoying behavior.

These regular fistic encounters left him little time for any constructive or creative work with materials. He started a few pieces of work, but never finished them because he lacked sufficient composure to concentrate.

Harmon's obnoxiousness during these months grew very disruptive and disturbing and caused a few of the older members of the group to stay away. On the rare occasions when Harmon was late in coming to a meeting, the comment of the boys before his arrival was, "It'll be quiet if Harmon doesn't come tonight." Upon arrival he was greeted with "That nut is here again." Harmon brought further resentment upon himself by his constant bragging: "I'm a genius. Everybody tells me so." From his brother, he learned that he had a superior I.Q. rating and never hesitated to flaunt this fact before his companions. He frequently told the boys in the group, "I'm considered a genius by everybody" and "I'm smarter than anyone in the club."

On trips he proved to be the most annoying and quarrelsome member. He delayed the group by his idling and quarreled at the slightest provocation. He would refuse to travel with the group, preferring to go by himself to the destination and wait there for the others.

The boy's evasiveness with his case worker continued. He seemed to place the responsibility of treatment on her. Characteristic remarks were, "What problems shall we discuss today?" and "Well, let's list my problems," and he would then jump from subject to subject. It was almost impossible to confine him to the discussion of any one subject. He was very much disturbed over the plans his parents were making to separate, but could not discuss this subject freely, either. He felt it was all his father's fault, and at home sided with his mother in arguments. His intense quarreling with his older brother continued, and he placed all the blame for the quarrels entirely on the latter.

During this time the case worker managed to discuss masturbation with Harmon and dispelled some of his fears about it. He admitted thoughts of his parents having intercourse, but added that he had perceived his mother did not enjoy it because his father was not nice to her in any other way. One of Harmon's principal objections to the separation of his parents was that this would make him "feel different" from other boys. When this led to a discussion of why he had no friends, he tried to dismiss the question by saying that it made no difference to him. He did not care. However, when poor adjustment in the therapy group was mentioned and he was told that it might result in his being dropped from the group,[8] his attitude changed. At first, he tried dispelling the danger with the explanation that he was "just having fun." When the question was pressed as to whether or not he enjoyed being disliked by the other boys in the "club," Harmon became more serious and replied that he did not. He said that he would really like other boys to like him, but somehow they did not, attributing this to the fact that he did things which seemed to be objectionable. This was the first time that Harmon had actually made such an admission.

In February, after more than thirty-two months of case work treatment and twenty-one weekly therapy group meetings, an Integration Conference attended by the case worker, the group therapist, and the director of Group Therapy was held to evaluate Harmon's adjustment and to plan treatment. It was evident that, despite the beatings and abuse from the other boys, a social hunger in this boy brought him back to the group week after week. The decision was that treatment, both in the group and in case work, should be altered. The group therapist was to deviate from the usual procedure of not restricting the behavior of members. He was to discuss Harmon's behavior with him after meetings. This was possible since the therapist and the boy traveled home on the same subway train for several stations. The case work treatment was to be on a more direct and authoritative basis.

At subsequent interviews, the case worker questioned Harmon on his reason for coming to see her and what he felt he was deriving from these interviews, pointing out that his behavior at school was still very unsatisfactory and that his attitude at home was no better, since he still quarreled a good deal. He was told that there was no point in his coming any

---

[8] This is an unusual procedure, but in this instance we agreed that the case worker should use this information. The matter was thoroughly discussed in an Integration Conference before the step was taken.

longer, since the case worker did not see boys for social reasons but rather to help them. The prospect of terminating the relationship aroused a great deal of anxiety in the boy, and he said he could improve if he made the effort.

At the same time, the group therapist had been using slightly restraining measures during meetings and was discussing the boy's behavior with him during the short train rides. At first, Harmon tried to justify whatever he did and, in his characteristic manner, attempted to talk his way out. The group therapist, however, persisted. Gradually Harmon began to give way. There resulted from these weekly discussions an "agreement" which the boy himself suggested. He said, "You remind me whenever I do something wrong." When the therapist said that he did not see why it should be necessary to do this each week, Harmon insisted, replying, "You don't have to say anything to me. Just look at me hard and I'll know what you mean." The week following the "agreement," Harmon asked the group therapist, as soon as they were alone, "Well, how was I tonight?" "Much better," was the reply. The second week Harmon volunteered with lowered head, "I wasn't very good tonight." When the group therapist agreed, he replied, "Well, I'll have to try next week."

Evidence of improvement. Two months later, the group therapist reported improvement in Harmon's behavior. He worked at more frequent intervals, although he still found it difficult to remain at the same task all evening. When he tired of his work, instead of annoying others, he would go out to the adjoining anteroom, where he would make himself comfortable in a soft chair and read. He often reverted to mischief. However, in place of the very real fistic encounters in which he had previously always managed to become entangled, he now substituted games, such as fencing with dowel sticks, wrestled for fun, or attempted to play some practical joke on one of the boys.

Both case worker and group therapist were careful not to

nag the boy. By actual count, the latter had eight talks with Harmon. Much of the restraint was exercised by the method Harmon had suggested: by simply looking at him hard. In the last talk, the adult took occasion to compliment Harmon on the calm manner in which he had taken, at the last meeting, the rejection of his suggestions by one of the boys.

In June, six months later, Harmon was described as being able to control himself and to continue a job for a considerable length of time. He participated in group activities and in the chores of the group. He was considerably less disturbing and gradually was accepted by the others. He no longer teased or criticized the other boys in the group or argued with them; he moved about more quietly, occasionally sitting down to read or to talk with one or with a number of the boys. He conceived the idea of making several hand projects—among other things, a bird house which took several weeks to complete. At the refreshment table, he was more mature. He was no longer restless or boisterous, nor did he monopolize the conversation as he had formerly.

During the same period Harmon began to discuss freely with his case worker his relationships at home, admitting that he started some of the quarrels with his brother. He was led to understand that the home situation would not change appreciably and to realize the source of the difficulties. He recognized a need for developing interests outside the home and not reading so much. He once said to the case worker, "I don't read seven books a week any more. I play with the fellows on the street more and read only three books a week, but I have a much better time. I fight, all right. But I don't run away as I used to. I take a beating sometimes, but I stick it out." He admitted that he wanted friends, wanted to be liked, but he had got into the habit of being a pest, which hindered him from cultivating friendships. He was proud of his adjustment in the "club" and reported that he was having much more fun there because he did not fight with the boys as much as he used to.

The mother reported that Harmon was greatly improved and now played with boys in the street instead of spending all his time reading.

During the summer Harmon made a good adjustment in the same camp where he had failed previously. He participated in activities freely and got along well with campers and counselors. When the case worker visited him at camp, he said, "I never knew I could have such a wonderful time." The report from the camp indicated that his behavior had shown a marked improvement in all areas over the previous years. He responded very well to the routine activities and would often volunteer for duties even when they were not part of his job. He had made a "tremendous improvement in the area of friendship, in ability to enter a well-rounded program of activities, in leadership, and in overcoming his physical cowardice."

When he returned in September, the boy showed he had retained over the summer the progress he had made in his adjustment to the group. He worked throughout the meetings, helped others with their projects, took responsibility for group chores, and purchased food for refreshments. He was well behaved and well mannered during trips as well. A new member was no longer the signal for attention-getting and extravagant behavior. Rather, when a new boy came, Harmon would help him become acclimatized by explaining the use of the tools and materials and in other ways.

He continued to discuss his family problems with the case worker with a great deal of frankness and maturity, accepting his disturbed home situation as unalterable. He no longer became involved in the quarrels between his parents, explaining that his intervention merely prolonged the hateful scenes and so he left the house when they quarreled. His school work had shown improvement and he admitted that if he tried a little harder, he could do even better. Harmon spoke of the good times he had at the therapy group and the satisfaction he was getting from the social contacts he was beginning to form in school. Discussing a routine for study, he said, "It used to be that I didn't have time to study because I was always reading, and now it is because of playing." He talked more freely with the group therapist as well. Without any encouragement, Harmon told him of the family's economic plight, of his father's inadequacy, his mother's superiority, and similar personal matters.

At this time, the case worker decided definitely to terminate the contact. At first, Harmon was frightened by the prospect, but accepted it after a few talks with her, saying, "I am sure I can get along now. If ever I need help I'll come to see you." The case worker agreed to this, and the case was closed in January. At the last Integration Conference where plans of treatment were outlined, it was decided to continue the boy in the therapy group, with a view to transferring him to a settlement house club in the near future. The group therapist reported that he continued to function well in the group, and in March of the same year he became a member of a neighborhood settlement. There Harmon made a number of friends who visited his home and to whose homes he was invited. The settlement house staff report that he is taking a prominent part in activities there, having been elected representative to one of the governing councils. He attends the science laboratory and is a member of a science club. He has also joined a "Psychology Project" and takes part in social activities.[9]

Interpretation. We have here a boy acting out a neurotic conflict produced by a pathogenic home situation. The extreme restrictions and rejections suffered by the client fixated

[9] About one and one-half years after the closing of the case, Harmon returned on his own initiative for help. He felt that he was not getting along as well as he might. The pressure at home had not abated and he was aware of anxieties that disturbed him and he felt uneasy generally. He was assigned to a male psychiatric case worker.

him at a level of infantile behavior. The defensive aggressive pattern that he adopted was a means of satisfying emotional cravings for love and status. This mechanism was carried over to school, social life, and case work relation, and into the therapy group. The chief characteristics of this pattern were 1) attention-getting hyperactivity that served to relieve his anxieties, and 2) inability to submit to authority. The nuclear neurotic conflict here was the boy's craving to be accepted and loved, on the one hand, and on the other, a compelling need to activate rejection and hostility on the part of those with whom he came in contact. The inner turmoil that resulted from this and the setbacks to his ego from the series of debasing experiences in the home and at school served only to intensify his anxieties and drive him on into hyperactivity.

The boy refused to accept the case work situation because to do this meant to submit to another's will. We see that he could not submit even though he constantly met with the natural consequences of his acts, counter-aggression in the home and school and from other boys. To allow the case worker to set the stage would be an act of submission which he could not bear. He, therefore, determined the content and the nature of the interviews.

The difficulty here lay in the fact that the boy could not perceive the possibility of gaining his ends—namely, love, acceptance, and status—through the case worker. He had to be convinced, somehow, that more acceptable behavior could bring him the satisfactions he desired. From the discussions with the case worker and from the material in the Group Therapy records, it is evident that the boy had a strong need to be accepted by others his own age. This social hunger was utilized successfully in this case. When he was placed in a group with other boys, Harmon saw value in curbing his behavior. When the case worker suggested that he might be dismissed from the group, he was almost thrown into a panic. He decided to do better in the future, and he did. Previous to this, he had accepted severe punishment as a price for being part of the group. He was now ready to submit to restrictions from the case worker and group therapist for the same reason.

The important therapeutic situations in this were three. 1) The case worker changed her method of treatment by applying restrictions to the boy's behavior. He needed authority in his life, which he did not have in any of his relationships at home or in school. Familial authority had failed with him because of his father's immaturity, the inconsistent treatment by his mother, and his hatred of his brother and sister. His teachers, largely because they were women, also failed to establish a relation of authority with him. The boy continued his pattern of teasing and irritating. 2) The group therapist did not reject or hate the boy despite his disturbing behavior. Instead, he was tolerant without showing approval. 3) Neither in case work nor in group treatment were reasoning and discussion used to control him. The boy met with physical, direct impeding of his aggression. This prevented him from evading or allaying his feelings of guilt by means of explanations and arguments.

The point must be made here again that this boy would not have submitted to these restrictions without a substitute satisfaction. This satisfaction was belonging to a group of boys. In addition, he accepted the group therapist as his supportive ego. Security and membership in a group not only impressed him with the need for maturing, but also gave him courage to break through the self-protective mantle of resistance which he assumed during the case work interviews.

Both case workers in this instance were women, but the fact that the boy talked to the group therapist about his problems after a short period of acquaintance indicates that he should have had a male worker. This seems plausible since his identifications with his father and brother were negative. The critical event in the treatment of Harmon was the case worker's threat of dismissal from the group if he persisted in his behavior. All improvement dates from that incident.

The Case of Paul Schwartz: *Integration of individual and group treatment of a hostile and aggressive boy*

Problem. Paul Schwartz was referred to the agency at the age of thirteen by a neighborhood center, where his behavior was described as "intolerable." Previous to that time he had been treated in the mental hygiene clinic of a hospital where his younger sister was a patient in the cardiac clinic. He was brought to the agency by his mother, who stated that he was a behavior problem at home and in school, was disobedient, inclined to be nagging, and finicky with regard to food. Paul refused to take plain milk, cooked vegetables, or cereals. His mother claimed that he was "too lazy" to chew. He was a shut-in child, who showed definite signs of infantile behavior. He scored an I.Q. of 107 on the Stanford-Binet test. Later, he obtained a score of 91 on the Kuhlmann-Anderson test, and 95 (Binet) at another hospital. The tests showed that he had superior mechanical ability.

Paul lived with his family, which consisted of his father, mother, a sister six years older, and a sister four years younger. The family was known to seven social service agencies, and Paul was also known to the police.

Paul was irascible, had a very intense temper, beat his younger sibling, quarreled with his older sister, and threw a knife at his father on at least two occasions. He was brought into court twice during treatment: once for truancy and once for commitment because of beating his father.

Developmental history indicates that Paul had a normal delivery and weighed ten pounds at birth. He was breast-fed up to fourteen months, never bottle-fed. He had his first tooth at eight months, walked at ten months, talked at fourteen months. He had whooping cough at three months, measles at one year, and mumps and chicken-pox at the age of four. The boy slept with his mother until he was seven and occasionally even at the time of referral.

In the neighborhood center his behavior was described as being exceedingly disturbing and that he was "very difficult . . . he would enter a room in the middle of a meeting and shout at the top of his voice so that everyone would turn around and look at him and could not continue with their business. He has been put out of many groups in the settlement house." He was also suspected of stealing tools and other objects.

Adjustment in school was equally bad. He took no interest whatever in his work and the teachers were at their wits' end what to do with him. Paul did not like school and openly expressed his dislike. He wished to leave school and get a job, his preference being to work on a farm. (The first six years of Paul's life before coming to New York had been spent in the country.) Various plans had been worked out for Paul in school, where wood work was substituted for academic subjects, but with little avail. Several hearings were held during treatment by the School Attendance Bureau, and the officer declared himself "helpless in this situation."

Paul was particularly contemptuous of his father because he was inadequate, helpless, and incapable of meeting his responsibilities to his family. Paul was afraid that he would be like his father and, being ashamed of him, did not want to be like him. He referred to him and his mother as "Mockies." (This is a term of derision applied to foreign, that is, un-Americanized Jews.) However, the father was described as being a nice person—well dressed, quiet, and dignified, though not an educated man.

Paul's feelings toward his mother were ambivalent. At times he was very affectionate and attempted to please her.

At other times he was very destructive and disobedient—screamed at her, called her names, and annoyed her in every way possible. The mother is described as being superior to her husband, a responsible and intelligent woman who carried the burden of the family, which lived on relief because Mr. Schwartz was out of work nearly all of the time. The mother did not reject Paul. Although at times she became strongly provoked at him and wanted him removed from the house, she did not carry out these plans.

The object of Paul's most intense hostility, however, was the younger sister, who, having been a cardiac case since infancy, received special attention from the mother. This, to Paul, constituted a rejection of himself. However, as the treatment proceeded, other psychological drives became apparent which complicated the picture. He beat his young sister frequently and annoyed her in every way he could think of. A few times, when the father interceded for his daughter, Paul beat him too. This hostility was not confined to the family, however, for he once attacked with a hammer a boy in the neighborhood center which he attended. He annoyed girls and sent "dirty" notes around in school and elsewhere.

The object of Paul's greatest affection was a dog which he continuously talked about to the case workers and other people, and one summer when he was in camp, he became so homesick for his dog that he wanted to leave camp in the middle of the season. Paul had no other friends.

Individual treatment. In the discussion of the case, the psychiatrist suggested that Paul be assigned to a male worker because of the lack of father identification. Whether it was because Paul's needs were not met by a man or whether the personality of the worker was not suitable for him, we cannot say, but for seven months no progress whatever was made in individual treatment. Paul was hostile, "determined and contemptuous" toward the worker and seldom came to see him. It was, therefore, decided to transfer the case to a woman worker. Although resistive to her also at first, Paul gradually thawed and became communicative. He stopped hanging his head and refusing to talk, and confided to her many of his problems, some of a very deep nature. This did not take place until some time after treatment was begun, however.

He confided that he felt that the previous male worker did not like him, and that he in turn did not like the worker, but he liked her. Paul alternated between savage hostility, and resistance and friendliness. At times he was affable, communicative, and cooperative. At other times he refused to talk, teased the worker, and called her vile names. He did, however, reveal the fact that he felt different from other people; also that people did not like him and so he never faced them. (One of Paul's characteristics was that he did not look directly at people.)

At this period he began to talk about his home situation, indicating again resentment and hostility toward his mother. He felt she did not like him; she had always threatened that she would either give him away or leave him. He said that he had never felt secure with her. The worker pointed out that he carried this feeling over to other people, and that if it were true that his mother didn't really love him, he must find enough satisfaction in other people and in other things to feel secure within himself. He grinned and said he guessed he was a baby. He said that he hung around like a dog looking for a word of affection from his master.

At another time, when he talked about an accident he had seen in the street, he revealed that whenever he saw anybody killed or hurt he thought of his mother. He sees her dead and feels guilty about his thoughts. At the same interview he talked about running away from home, which he did on at least three occasions. Once he stayed out all night. When his mother was upset and ran around to all their friends and relatives looking for him, he was pleased by the fact that she had been discomfited.

His father was a coward, he said. If he were worth while, he would not allow himself to be bossed by his wife. He was afraid that he would be like his father, and he did not want to be like him. He spoke of his desire to kill him, and was afraid of his impulses. He often phantasied about destroying his father and taking his place. (In a way, he did this by shining shoes and turning all his earnings over to his mother. Thus, he vicariously displaced his father.)

Similarly, when he talked of his younger sister and was questioned by the case worker, he revealed that he was afraid he might kill her. This homicidal drive expressed itself in other ways as well. He talked many times to his worker about train wrecks. When he played with a toy train in the worker's office, he talked of enemies in those trains and the need to kill them. His drawings often consisted of dismembered bodies. One of the drawings in the therapy group showed a man, a dagger in his hand from which blood dripped, poised on his toes over the prostrate body of a dead man. He also talked about killing people with knives. His play included soldiers and guns.

After five or six months of treatment, he was able to discuss sex with the new worker. He was constantly preoccupied with sex, having phantasies about sexual intercourse between his parents, and later on he became aware of his incestuous drive toward his younger sister. This was later tied up with an early experience he had had at the age of seven. It seems that he was induced, by a ten-year-old girl, to take part in sexual play. He told the case worker that he had a terrific fear at the time, and this fear seemed to persist. There seems to be a very definite tie-up between this experience and the boy's incestuous drive toward his sister, which proved to be the center of his problem. He also talked about the fact that he was sometimes called "sissy," which made him very mad.

At the same period in treatment, he began to dress much better, combed his hair, and became aware of the case worker as a woman, addressing her as "Hey, Toots!" However, his total behavior was very irrational and confused. He frequently ran away from home, truanted from school, insisted on leaving school, and wanted to get a job—he wanted to work on a farm. He also wanted to go away and live in another city with his aunt. The psychiatrist thought his special attachment to this family was due to the fact that his aunt was married to her own cousin—a relation which to Paul constituted a tolerated and accepted form of incest. It was also thought that the boy was definitely taking a homosexual trend.

At one time he dictated into the dictaphone which was in the worker's office. The confusion in the boy's mind is revealed in this monologue and is quoted below:

I hate school. I hate school. I like Angelica [a girl at school whom he admired] very much—do you hear me?—I like Angelica very much. I always think of her when I go to bed. That's what takes me so long to go to bed, I always think of Angelica. My little sister likes to get me in trouble. I never liked school, and I'd like to run away from school and I'd like to run away from home. You people have the wrong system here, if you know what I mean. You should see the mother and the child because then you could hear both sides of the story and you might be able to figure something out, or you might be able to help the child more. Do you know what I mean? I wish I could go to Hawthorne [school for problem boys] to get away from home. I hate home. You know, I never liked to stay there. I wish I could go to Willimantic. I could live there with my aunt, work there in the meantime and could go to some professional school there. I wish I could go to Ramapo [summer camp] next year, too, for the whole summer, or maybe I'd rather go to my aunt's and work there and make money, or I'd like to work on a farm. I thought of you lots of times, it's quite true, if you know what I mean. I wish I had a lot of dough and a bike too. If I had a bike I could go to Willimantic, ride around, and have fun. You know what a bike is, fifteen dollars. Brand new parts, except the body. Well, I see our time is nearly up, so this is Paul signing off. Now let me see, we have a quarter of a minute to go yet. It is very rapidly nearing.

Frequent conferences were held between the Case Work and Group Therapy Departments on this case. One of these was called to discuss committing Paul to the agency's school for delinquent boys. Because progress in case treatment was so unsatisfactory, the case worker thought that he should be removed from his present environment. However, the boy showed definite improvement in his group adjustment, and the psychiatrist felt that he should be continued in treatment rather than helped to escape from a difficult situation.

Because of Paul's persistent truancy from school, he was, at the insistence of the School Attendance Bureau and with the consent of the agency, committed for observation to the psychiatric ward of a hospital. The report from the hospital ruled out psychosis. Paul was described as a boy who "cooperated actively in diverse group activities including dramatics, gymnastics, school work, and so on. He showed no evidence of emotional instability and admits that he quarrels only with his family." It was recommended that treatment in the agency be continued.

Both case worker and group therapist reported considerable improvement in Paul after he returned from the psychiatric hospital. He said he liked it there. He looked better, healthier, more mature, more outgoing, and generally happier. He told worker that he had witnessed homosexual practices and considerable masturbation. He now masturbated also, but had no guilt about it. Previous to this, he had read about the ill effects of masturbation in some pamphlets; as a result, he had had great conflicts, feelings of guilt and fear, tied up with it. He did not have these any longer.

He began to express doubts about his masculinity, to talk about feeling weak and being like his father. But despite this he displayed considerable maturity. He talked of himself as being good-looking and said that the boys in the neighborhood center called him "Handsome."

Treatment moved rapidly from this point on. Paul was now able to accept the worker's interpretation of his negative identifications, his attitudes toward his sister, his mixed feelings toward his mother, his destructive drives toward his father, and his attitude toward himself. He now came out with his sexual drives toward the case worker also, and was shocked to learn that she had a son. Paul ridiculed her husband (whom he had never seen), and made fun of him both verbally and in his drawings. All this was discussed with him. In evaluating the material at a psychiatric conference, it was felt that the boy had worked out his basic problem, his incestuous drive, through the worker, for now he accepted her as a woman and discussed freely with her his interest in girls.

Camp also reported considerable improvement. He was described as "an ideal camper."

Group treatment. Paul was referred to the Group Therapy Department three months after individual treatment had begun. At first, he was inordinately withdrawn. For months he made no contact with the other boys, working by himself in a corner, and at the refreshment periods he sat apart. He spent much time lying on the floor on his stomach reading "funnies" and playing with toys like a baby. He later became noisy and troublesome at meetings and was usually the one to cause all the disturbance. Feeling incapable of bringing himself before the group in any ordinary manner or through his special talents, he would run through the hallways, yelling and screaming and uttering all sorts of peculiar sounds to attract attention. He allowed himself to be closed up in one of the glass-partitioned offices and, while there, pretended he was a monkey. On another occasion, he had himself locked up in the bathroom and then banged on the door and howled like a maniac. However, he did not miss a meeting in a year.

This manic behavior was directed toward the other members of the group as well. He interrupted their work, annoyed them, took away their tools and materials, and fought with them continually. For months he was not able to settle down to any job of his own.

In a report of February of the following year, eleven months after the beginning of treatment and four months after membership in a group, we read that he had attached himself to twin brothers, members of the same group, who had an interest in science and who were very skilful at it. He participated with them in many of their experiments and identified with their achievements, which were of a high order. The twin brothers often demonstrated their experiments to the rest of the group, and at one time Paul said to them during such a demonstration, "Come on, give it to me, and let me show off for a while." For a long time, the two boys treated Paul as an inferior, called him "baby," and made fun of him. However, Paul, who lived in the same neighborhood as the twins, seemed willing to accept their derogatory remarks in exchange for being accepted by them. In March of the same year a statement in the record reads:

Paul seems to have made the greatest progress of any member of the group. He seems almost like a normal and well-adjusted boy in spite of the many handicaps and personal inadequacies from which he suffers. His facial expression has greatly improved. He no longer looks hostile and resentful, nor does he mope. The color of his cheeks is better, and the expression of his eyes is healthier. His vision is no longer directed inward. His social manner also is greatly improved, and he is now interested in definite activities of his own.

This improvement puzzled the director of Group Therapy, and an inquiry was sent to the case worker as to whether the change was noticeable in his other relations. In response, the case worker replied that there was still considerable inconsistency in the boy's behavior. However, he no longer threw things around at home, as he used to, and he seemed somewhat quieter, although at home he still got into temper tantrums and quarreled "for no apparent reason." The worker reported that the boy was less obstreperous in the neighborhood and in the center, and that he had become more acceptable.

Paul came to group meetings ragged and unkempt; his clothes, besides being dirty and worn, were always badly in need of mending. In a Progress Report written about a year and a half after group treatment and eight months after the case was transferred to the woman worker, we read the following:

When worker told group that something will have to be done about cleaning up after meetings, Paul suggested and drew up a schedule chart for the group. Still another time, when he couldn't attend a meeting because of illness, he sent worker a letter telling about some plans he had for the club, of which he had been thinking a lot. On a number of occasions, Paul referred to his sister whom he had never mentioned in the early part of the year. He has, on occasion, sat around with other members of the group to discuss radio and other interests of his. He has also helped others with work they were doing. During conversations at the table, Paul was quiet and attentive and told stories himself, asked riddles, and participated in solving puzzles. He has, on occasion, told other members of the group to clean up the dirt they had made when he saw worker doing it. After the refreshments, he has been cooperative in cleaning up the room.

Six months later, the group therapist reported that Paul had developed interests of his own, had become more independent and more self-critical, and had challenged one of the twins who mistreated him. Paul would not have been able to do this before. When Paul made a plaque and worker praised him for it, he said, "But I copied the picture; it isn't original." The group therapist said that while the actual drawing was not original, the transfer to copper and the workmanship on it were original. Paul said with justifiable pride, "Yep, I think it really is good."

At about the same period of group membership, Paul is reported as enjoying his work with materials and tools and "deriving a good deal of satisfaction from what he is doing." When he returned from the hospital in which he had been confined for four weeks, he freely related his experiences to the boys in the group and expressed delight at being back, saying, "Boy, it feels good to hear that jig-saw again." In his conversation with the other members of the group, he continued to express the hope that he would have a home in the country and a farm of his own. His ease in relationship with the boys kept increasing. The same progress was noted in camp as well, as is indicated by the abstract quoted below:

Paul's relationship to both the staff and co-campers this year was excellent. He was well accepted by his immediate group and became the leader of the bunk. He showed a deep sense of loyalty and cooperation and asked to be appointed a junior counselor. Although this request was not granted, he was made an unofficial junior counselor within the bunk group, and reacted splendidly without resorting to domination of his mates. On several occasions he defended younger boys against the onslaughts of bullies. No negative opinion was to be had on him from any member of the staff. All found him to be respectful, friendly, and warm.

If we are to judge by last year's report, Paul's improvement in his ability to make friendships was indeed remarkable. He seemed free and at ease in the group. In general, this boy seemed to have made a phenomenal adjustment.

In the closing summary, approximately two years after his admission to the group, we read as follows:

Paul continued to improve each year he spent in the group. The last report notes that he displayed more self-confidence, assurance, and independence in his work during the meetings. When he ran into difficulty with his work, he did not run immediately to worker for help but managed to work out his own problems. Paul was enjoying his work and deriving satisfaction from what he was doing. He refused to permit himself to be bullied by the twins and his resistance to their efforts at abuse brought the relationship to an end. Paul has become assertive and no longer submits to abuse or debasement.

He is at ease, converses freely, and participates in all activities. He helps with group chores. His conversation indicates an interest in girls.

At no time during the last year did he give any evidence of the infantile behavior he had previously exhibited. Paul's whole appearance and attitudes have undergone a complete change. He functions as a boy who has been released, associates freely with boys, and appears to feel that he is actually the equal of any other boy.

Four months later his case was closed out from individual treatment as well.

Evidence of improvement. The irrational and disturbing behavior in the school and at home has decreased, according to the studies made of this client. We also see considerable improvement in his adjustment to boys, and his preoccupation with girls and sex has declined. In a follow-up inquiry, six months after closing the case, at the settlement house where Paul had given so much trouble a few years before, the report is favorable. The Activities Director stated that Paul is "all that one could expect from a boy his age." The improvement also continued in camp and was sustained by Paul when he returned from camp to the group. In addition, a year after the case was closed, Paul came in to see the group therapist who was in a room at the settlement. He was very friendly, optimistic, and hopeful. He said that everything was going along swell. He was in a vocational school, belonged to a regular club, and played basketball three times a week. He told the worker that he had been asked to play on the team. He had also broken away from the twins, who were superior to him and who mistreated him. He now has friends more on his own level and feels happy about it. He also reported that he had a girl friend.

The favorable impression produced by Paul on the group

therapist was sustained again a year and a half later when he came across him at the settlement in the company of boys and girls of his own age. Paul seemed pleased, and seemed to be enjoying himself.

Interpretation. This boy was described as "psychopathic, with manic incestuous trends." He was also diagnosed as having "an incipient psychosis," as being "schizophrenic," and finally as having "a primary behavior disorder, conduct type." It is rather difficult to arrive at a definite diagnosis of a child with a character as complex as Paul's. It would seem that at different stages of treatment, these various diagnoses were justifiable. There has been no consistency in this boy's behavior. He has run the gamut of personality disturbances and behavior deviations. There is very little doubt that what seemed to be neurotic pressure in the boy originated from his incestuous drive toward his sister, which he repressed very strongly and turned into a homicidal drive toward her. He was also made very dependent upon the mother; at the same time, he wished to destroy her. Because of the father's weakness, there was no adequate masculine identification. The case worker had worked through these deep-rooted problems with the boy quite successfully.

In the group he was also able to discharge through increased manic behavior much of the emotional pressure caused by his wish to take the place of his sister in his mother's affection. He wanted to continue being a baby and helpless. He therefore acted like a baby, as demonstrated by the fact that he pretended to be a monkey and ran around the room, screaming at the top of his voice. He also played with toys at the meetings, like a baby, lying on his stomach. The group helped him by accepting all this behavior. Because he was not blocked by the group therapist, he had no cause to continue it. At the same time, his guilt and his doubts concerning himself as a boy and as an adolescent were not increased.

His close friendship with the twins, his ability to take his place with boys, and his growing affection for the group therapist, which has not been described here because of necessary brevity, helped Paul become more secure in his masculinity.

His attachment to the twins, who were quite mature and purposeful in their work, gave him an incentive for acting like a more mature person. They were his supportive egos. He was willing to accept their derogatory remarks for the opportunity to identify with superior boys. Paul's native mechanical ability was utilized constructively through the opportunity to work with tools and apparatus. This developed his interests and won him recognition, which in turn helped the maturing process.

However, one must be cautious as to the prognosis in such a case. One is impressed with the intense neuroticism of this boy's character and the deep-rooted sexual content. Whether a child like this can retain improvement through the treatment he has received must be left for the future to determine.

Integration of case work and Group Therapy. Myra Shallit parallels in tabulated form the process of the two types of treatment in this case, as follows:[10]

Case record	Group record
5-20-34 (3rd interview). Paul would like to join the Boy Scouts or some group, but didn't know what group to join. He wants one that will make him feel at home. He has but one boy friend. Worker (woman) mentioned a club connected with the Jewish Board of Guardians (Group Therapy). Paul seemed eager to join.	(This group of 8 boys had been functioning for 20 weeks when Paul joined.)
6-17-34 (7th interview). Paul happily told worker he received a letter from the "club," inviting him to join.	6-18-34. Paul attended his first Group Therapy meeting. He gave the impression of a quiet, serious boy. He

[10] Unpublished thesis for the New York School of Social Work, entitled Group Therapy as an Adjunct to Individual Therapy, June, 1938, pages 18–27. The material quoted here covers only a part of the treatment period.

Case record (cont.)

Group record (cont.)

neither talked nor mingled with the others but regarded with disapproval the mischievous behavior of the boys.

6-21-34. Paul is friendly with the twins who are fairly well adjusted boys and keenly interested in mechanical things.

6-24-34. Broken appointment.

7-9-34. Paul spoke praisingly about the "club." He likes the leader and is making friends with some of the boys. Went swimming.

August. Sent to camp.

9-23-34 (new case worker; man). Seen in camp for first time by new worker. Talked about his "club" leader to new worker. Was anxious to know when the club would begin again. He and another fellow had written to inquire. Spoke of desire to belong to Group Therapy rather than to settlement house club.

10-12-34. Continued to discuss interest in therapy group. Seemed to indicate distrust of case worker.

10-19-34. Although he is apparently friendly, worker has the feeling that Paul is still distrustful. Mentioned that his mother has not improved. She still blames him and there are many quarrels at home.

10-26-34. Paul discussed sex and his fears about it.

11-9-34. Paul was restless. He complained about his teacher and mother. He projected blame on everyone and refused to acknowledge any responsibility.

11-23-34. Restless, not talkative. He requested to come every two weeks

6-25-34 to 11-17-34. Paul attended the meetings regularly. The group did not meet during July and August as most of the boys were in camp. During the above-mentioned period of attendance, Paul became more friendly with the twins who live near him, but had little to do with the other boys in the group. He exhibited noisy, disturbing behavior in the group. He was troublesome, disrupted many meetings, and would attempt to attract the attention of the group by running down the halls, screaming and yelling.

11-17-34. The boys locked Paul in one of the glass-partitioned rooms.

Case record (cont.)

instead of weekly. Reported he joined the Boy Scouts.

Group record (cont.)

Paul made a great deal of noise and pretended he was a monkey. The boys accused Paul of ringing the elevator bell and rousing the wrath of the elevator man. Paul retaliated that they were "full of ——." One of the twins told him to "cut out the dirty words." When the boys seated themselves to eat, Paul took the head of the table and broke out in a prayer and blessing. The boys were annoyed and called him a dope. Paul continued to make queer sounds until one of the twins took him by the throat, threw him on the floor, and kicked him. Paul continued with his noises. The other boy unintentionally squirted milk on the floor. The boys became hilarious. Paul began to drink milk from the paper container and when it spilled all over, the boys called him "stupid," "slob," and "dope." Paul seemed to delight in so much attention. When worker started to clean up Paul's mess, one of the boys made a caustic retort, whereupon Paul grabbed the rag and wiped it over the floor.

11-25-34. Paul continued to annoy and fight with the boys who persisted in reprimanding him with physical punishment.

12-2-34. One of the boys locked Paul in the toilet; he banged on the door and howled like a maniac. The boys called him "dopey" and "stupid." Paul's behavior continues to be infantile. He frequently resorts to temper tantrums.

12-7-34. Broken appointment.

12-21-34. Showed much anger at worker. Belligerent. Said he wanted to discontinue coming as he has other

12-9-34. Paul's wild behavior has calmed down considerably.

Case record (cont.)

things to do. Doesn't feel that worker helps him. Expressed anger at women. Said he was going to stop attending both Group Therapy and individual treatment meetings.

1-6-35. Paul's mother complained of boy's belligerent behavior and incessant quarreling. For a while he showed improvement, but he has become extremely difficult recently.

1-11-35. Discussed family difficulties and sex. Boy tried to avoid both subjects which were too painful to face.

1-25-35. Broken appointment.

2-10-35. Joint conference with Group Therapy Department. During this period Paul has been aggressive, difficult, and defiant with case worker. In the group during this same period he has been quiet, gets along well with others, and seems interested in his work.

2-15-35. Still belligerent. Expressed much hatred toward girls in general and his sister in particular.

3-8-35. School visit. School complained boy dirty, uncooperative. Worker assisted in school adjustment of program.

Group record (cont.)

1-13-35 to 2-3-35. Paul's behavior is undergoing a marked change. He is now a close friend of the twins who dominate the group. Through association with them, Paul seems to find them a medium for attracting attention and therefore tries to identify himself with them. The twins are aware of his dependency on them and call him "baby" and "kid." For the past four or five weeks, Paul's clowning has subsided. He is no longer as disturbing, and frequently goes off from the group to work by himself.

2-10-35. In this meeting (38th of the group and 18th for Paul), the worker commented that he had been doing all the cleaning up and wondered if the boys would care to pitch in. Paul immediately took the initiative and made out a systematic chart which indicated the duties of each boy.

2-17-35. When outsiders visited the group, Paul, who is usually so careless about his appearance, washed up and combed his hair.

3-3-35. Had a fight with the boys.

Case record (cont.)

3-10-35. Broken appointment.

Group record (cont.)

3-10-35. Paul came in washed and with his hair combed. The boys commented on his appearance. When the boys related stories, Paul, who at one time would have been the chief annoyance, was quiet and attentive and made favorable comments about the story.

Because of Paul's radically changed behavior, the Group Therapy director requested a report from the case worker. It was learned that Paul's behavior with the case worker was the reverse of his behavior in the group. He was hostile and defiant, and was getting into difficulty both at home and in school. The case worker commented, however, that Paul's group experience has enabled him to get along better with his companions. He is less obstreperous and more readily accepted by others.

Paul continues to attend regularly and to date has not missed a meeting.

3-22-35. Boy restless and defiant.

3-23-35. Request from Group Therapy for a report on Paul's adjustment in school, home, etc. as "boy's adjustment in group is perfect and group therapist wonders if it may be symptomatic of some other problem."

3-24-35. Paul seems to have made the greatest progress in the group. He seems to be almost like a normal, well-adjusted boy. . . . His facial expression has improved and no longer expresses constant hostility and resentment. He no longer mopes, and his color has improved. . . . He has now become part of the group, although he still concentrates most of his attention on the twins.

3-31-35. Paul came to the meeting without the twins. This was unusual because in the past he never came alone. He talked about his interest in farming. Also discussed his case worker and disclosed much hostility toward him. Hostility toward the

Case record (cont.)

Group record (cont.)

Jewish Board of Guardians was also revealed. However, he remarked that the "club" is O.K. because he met the twins there and likes the other boys.

4-9-35. Because of boy's increasingly hostile attitude and failure to keep appointments, it was felt that a woman worker might be assigned on an experimental basis.

4-23-35 (woman worker). Paul said he had disliked to talk about sex with former worker. Said he has few friends. Has none in school but some in the therapy group. The boys deride him and say he is different. It was worker's opinion that boy's anger toward both his family and school is out of proportion to cause. Seemed withdrawn and phantasies he is a superior being.

4-21-35. Paul was dressed very shabbily as usual. The group was preparing to attend the circus. Paul protested against going with the group and became upset when he learned that another leader was going to take the group. He gave vent to his anger by throwing clay against the wall.

4-26-35. Broken appointment.

4-28-35. First absence in almost a year of regular attendance. He wrote to worker saying he was ill.

5-3-35. Paul brings out hostility toward mother; jealous of attention sister gets. Says he likes father best. Evident that a good relationship with worker is being established.

5-5-35. Paul disclosed to group that he has a new worker—a woman, and that he likes her. He talked about his sister for the first time and made derogatory comments about her. Paul agreed to make up a play for the puppet show.

5-10-35. Extremely untidy; clothes torn. Friendly and talkative. Expressed liking to come and see worker. Talked about fear of meeting people. He daydreams that he is popular and well liked. Talked about dislike of girls and hatred of sister.

5-12-35. Paul looked rather neat. He was wearing a clean pair of knickers and a freshly laundered shirt. He talked enthusiastically about the farm he someday hoped to buy.

5-17-35. Broken appointment.

5-24-35. Neater than before. Wearing clean shirt and pressed pants in contrast to usual tattered ones. Discussed

5-26-35. Paul again mentioned his new case worker and how much he liked her.

Case record (cont.)

sex and curiosity about girls. Expressed strong positive feelings for worker and jealousy of her husband.

6-7-35. Expressed inability to "look people in the eye." Fears people don't like him. Expressed hatred toward sister and jealousy of mother.

6-15-35. Broken appointment.

6-21-35. Talked about vocational ambitions, desire to be a farmer. Did not want to discuss sex.

6-28-35. Neatly dressed. Likes worker. Talked about fear of being unaccepted by people. Wants to be like other boys and be well liked.

7-6-35. Restless. Complained of lack of respect shown him by mother and sister. Turned hostility toward worker. Called her names. Rushed from the office in anger.

7-13-35. Broken appointment.

August. Sent to camp.

Camp Report

Seemed lonely at camp. Participated in activities, but spent much time alone. Had no special friends. Later became homesick, especially for his dog.

9-8-35. Neatly dressed. Hostile toward mother. Called her a "dope." Then called worker a "dope." All women are "dopes." Discussed sex. Projected anger on worker by calling her names.

9-13-35. Quiet and calm. Wants to get a job. Revealed anxiety about parents. Unhappy because they quarrel constantly. Says he will never marry.

Group record (cont.)

5-29-35. Paul objected to going with younger boys, when the group joined another group for a swimming party.

6-2-35 to 6-23-35. Paul has shown great improvement. However, he is still too much under the influence of the twins who take advantage of his dependence on them. They make him run errands and call him belittling names when his conduct does not meet with their approval. The twins have influenced Paul to enroll in their school.

Group did not meet during summer months.

Case record (cont.)   *Group record (cont.)*

9-22-35. Broken appointment.

9-28-35. Restless. Projected all blame
for quarrels on mother and sister.
Feels hurt and unimportant at home.
Parents beat him. Wants to leave
home. Hates school. Would like to
live in Willimantic with his aunt.
Talked about girls. Wondered how
he could get acquainted.

10-5-35. Psychiatric Conference with   10-6-35 to 10-13-35. The group was
case worker and Group Therapy di-   reorganized on the basis of emotional
rector. Psychiatrist reported that   maturity, and Paul was transferred
much improvement had taken place,   to another group.
substantiated by Group Therapy re-
ports. In the earlier stages of both individual and group contacts boy
seemed uncontrolled, wild, almost
maniac. Now he gets along well in a
controlled group and is being placed
in a semi-formal therapy group to
see his adjustment there.

10-5-35. Quieter than ever before.
Didn't become angry when discussing sex. Talked his girl friend.

10-11-35. Ill at ease. Appearance improved. Released anger toward
worker. Revealed sexual phantasies
about her.

10-15-35. Mother reported his recent
outbreak as the first in several months.
Has had a long period of healthy behavior. Is truanting from school.

10-19-35. Whining and childish.   10-20-35. Absent.
Tried to arouse worker's anger.
Talked about incestuous impulses.
Because guilty, said he hated worker.

10-21-35. Broken appointment.

10-26-35. Mother upset; reported boy   10-27-35. Absent.
had left home after a fight with his
father. Psychiatrist requested suspen-
sion from school for a period of time.

Case record (cont.)

11-1-35. Paul returned from Willimantic where he had visited with relatives. Was tense; doesn't want to return to school.

11-2-35. Broken appointment.

11-5-35. Paul phoned. Doesn't want to see worker again. Angry at her. Wants to live with relatives in Willimantic.

11-8-35. Excited. Wanted to go to Willimantic immediately. Refused to return to school.

11-12-35. Constant truancy. Case taken over by the Attendance Bureau, with hearing scheduled for 16th.

Later. Paul phoned. Said he was going to run away. Called worker names.

11-18-35. Neatly dressed, calm. Paul discussed his conduct, his hatred for his sister, and his sexual impulses. He talked quietly in contrast to his usual hyperexcitable state.

11-24-35. Downcast and blue. Expressed feelings of shame about father's business failure. Indicated his depression.

11-26-35. Secured a job in a radio store. Was fairly calm.

11-29-35. Broken appointment. Remanded to mental hospital.

Group record (cont.)

11-3-35. Present.

11-10-35 to 12-15-35. Absent for six consecutive meetings.

12-22-35. Paul greeted worker enthusiastically, said he had missed him and was glad to be back. He had been busy with a new job in a radio store. Cooperated in sweeping the floor.

12-27-35. Absent.

12-29-35. Absent.

Case record (cont.) 　　　　　　*Group record (cont.)*

1-4-36. Paul was transferred to a group of older boys. When he entered the meeting room he was shy as if he were a new referral. He remained quiet and industrious throughout the meeting. He later told the leader that he hasn't seen his case worker in over a month.

Paul missed the following five meetings. It was learned from his case worker that he has been going through a very disturbed period during which he neither attended school nor saw his case worker. He was later brought before the Attendance Bureau for repeated truancy. On the petition of his father he was brought before Children's Court and subsequently remanded to mental hospital for observation on the recommendation of his case worker. It was recommended that Paul remain on the active list.

Hospital Report

Paul without a psychosis. He was friendly, alert, and cooperative. It was felt that the problem is centered in the home, as boy adjusts adequately on the outside. Since he requested to be returned home, it was deemed advisable to give him another chance. The hospital advised a transfer to another high school.

2-7-36. In a conference with the Group Therapy Department it was noted that Paul did not attend meetings during the period when he was so disturbed and was not coming for individual interviews: "There seemed to be a correlation between his coming for treatment and his attendance in the group." It was felt that prior to his present disturbance Paul had made progress in the advanced group.

2-7-36. Case worker reported that Paul is home and requested that group communicate with him relative to his return.

2-14-36 to 4-1-36. Paul was seen six times. Since his return from hospital he has calmed down, and discusses problems with less show of anger. Paul has developed into an attractive masculine person. An increasingly good relationship continues with worker.

3-29-36. Psychiatrist made the diagnosis of a "primary behavior disorder,

2-15-36. Paul attended group for first time since return from hospital. He had a broad grin on his face as he greeted the worker. He was cheerful, addressed the worker by his first name, for the first time, and said he was glad to be back. Without reservation he discussed his hospital experience with both the worker and the boys. Paul remained near the worker and was very talkative. As he

Case record (cont.)

conduct type." He felt the boy was making progress in that he was able to work out his incest phantasies with worker.

Group record (cont.)

was working on a leather wallet, he heard the jig-saw being set in operation. He stopped for a moment, smiled as he leaned back in his chair in a relaxed manner, then pointed to the saw, and said, "Boy, it feels good to hear that saw again."

Miss Shallit concludes:

It is evident, in analyzing the interplay of the case and group work process, that many intangible psychological factors derived from the interaction of the two types of experiences greatly affected Paul's personality. His earlier rejection of the male case worker was possibly bound up with his hostility to all men as representing the father person. In the group situation, contacts with the male worker were less threatening because they were less direct and not of such an intensive nature. The transfer to a woman worker was essential in helping Paul work through his hostility and ambivalent feelings toward women, before he could be rendered capable of accepting them. The group gave the boy a much needed outlet for his pent-up hostilities which, when permitted expression, gradually subsided and gave way to group acceptance.

CHAPTER IX

VARIATIONS IN GROUP TREATMENT

THERAPY in groups is a method of treatment that has been introduced in comparatively recent years. Among the leading workers in this field are Dr. Alfred Adler, Dr. Trigant Burrow, Dr. Paul Schilder, Dr. Louis Wender, Dr. James Sonnett Greene, and others. These psychiatrists have carried on treatment with groups of adults who are led to discuss problems, reactions, and ideologies under their guidance and direction. Patients ventilate problems, discharge emotional pressure accumulated in the course of traumatic experiences, clarify reactions, and receive guidance toward reinterpreting their feelings and behavior in a more mature and more normal manner. It was found that some patients gain greater release and deeper insight when others with similar difficulties are present and are involved in the treatment. The presence of persons in addition to the therapist has the effect of stimulating the formation of problems and thoughts that can be used profitably in the treatment situation.

In some instances patients distrust the therapist and refuse to communicate their conflicts to him, and the presence of a nurse, a case worker, or another psychiatrist counteracts this fear. This method has been put into practice by Dr. Hyman S. Lippman. Interpersonal therapy is being employed also by Dr. Lauretta Bender in the children's ward of the psychiatric division of Bellevue Hospital in New York, and by Dr. Frank Curran in his work with adolescents in the same institution. During the observation period of one or two months the patients in wards are provided with possibilities for manual, group, and recreational activities. One of the devices used by Dr. Bender in cooperation with Adolph G. Woltmann is the puppet show in which the children's unconscious motivations are released through suggestions that they make to the puppets during the performance.

Interpersonal therapy in groups is being increasingly recognized as a possibility in institutions for the mentally ill and delinquent children and youth. Cottage life has been found to be of great value in the treatment process, provided the grouping of the residents is made with a view to therapy. In order to create a therapeutic atmosphere in the cottage, it is necessary to assign cottage parents and supervisors who fit the particular group and have the personal and training qualifications for this job.

It was found also by psychiatrists in small sanitariums for mental patients that interpersonal relations in the institution supply effective treatment possibilities. Schizophrenics and other types of psychotics, even catatonics, often become aware of other patients, physicians and their assistants, and other members of the staff, if they are permitted to come in direct contact with them long and frequently enough. Patients develop intense likes and dislikes for others in the institution. The practice of eating together in one dining room is now being extended with salutary effect both for diagnostic and therapeutic reasons. Attractions and antipathies activated by these contacts are utilized by the psychiatrists in the interviews and serve as a key for grouping patients for treatment purposes during meals, recreation, and occupations.

There is a trend also in larger institutions to use group relations as a part of treatment. In discussing the value of recreation for psychotics and psychoneurotics, Dr. John Eussele Davis and Dr. William Rush Dunton, Jr., state:

In inducting the patient into applicable exercise, it is necessary to consider (a) Individual treatment; (b) Group treatment. One notes two lines of thought expressed by (1) the believers in severe individualism and (2) those who perceive practical and distinctive therapeutic practice through group psychology. The former declares that the patient representing a most distinct and unusual character formation, should be studied and treated from his highly individualized clinical picture; the latter viewpoint does not deny this basic position but holds that as a matter of practical administration, the patient must be subjected to numerous group relationships, that the conventional social status upon which level we are attempting to elevate the patient contains numerous group contacts and that there is much to be found which is provocative of sound and healthful conduct through group psychology. While the physician individualizes the patient to ascertain his therapeutic picture, this does not, as some believe, indicate a prescription of essential and exclusive individual treatment. He soon learns to follow an eclectic method of individualization coupled with the many effective elements of group treatment. . . .

We must come back to some attempted evaluation of the individual's personality as indicated in his social reactions. With the present stage of direct and related knowledge, the therapist may well follow the empiric and pragmatic approach.[1]

In the psycho-drama employed by Dr. J. L. Moreno, treatment is predominantly centered around the interpersonal reactions of the actors as expressed spontaneously in the impromptu dialogue formulated by the actors themselves. One can readily discern attitudes toward parents, siblings, and others in the life of the patient as he responds to his fellow actors. Different participants in the play activate different responses from the same patient toward the same situation. The presence of other patients, visitors, and staff in the audience also has its influence upon the actors, who in turn affect the patients in the audience.

Occupational therapists as well have found that the manual activities alone do not constitute the total value of treatment. In many instances the growing awareness in patients of the presence of others in the room and the occasional help that they give one another have definite effect upon the mentally

[1] *Principles and Practice of Recreational Therapy for the Mentally Ill,* New York, A. S. Barnes, 1936, pages 31–32, 33.

ill. When attachments grow out of the casual contacts during the occupational periods, they serve as beginnings in developing relationships with others. The relations that originate in the occupational therapy work room lead to better adjustment on the part of the patient to people within and outside the institution. This improvement has been noted in outpatients as well as in inmates. In some hospitals group recreation is included as a part of the occupational therapy program. "In addition to the individual type of activity," say Drs. Davis and Dunton, "there are many forms of mass occupational therapy in which the individual is given opportunity to associate himself with group enterprise and this type of therapy has definite socializing tendencies. The patient thus identifies himself with strong stabilizing forces and, in many cases, is able to enhance his feeling of self-respect in the recognition and growing understanding of the group accomplishment."[2]

Dr. James Sonnett Greene has employed the group in treating speech disorders. In an article dealing with this part of his work he says:

. . . our group approach is of paramount importance. This group approach was developed because it was found that individual therapy proved ineffective in the stutterer's case. The stutterer suffers from a social neurosis, and the narcissistic barrier that he has built up between himself and others makes it impossible in most cases for him to cooperate with the therapist under orthodox psychiatric procedures. However, when the stutterer is part of a group, all of whom have the same problem, this barrier is soon broken down. Having thus established a more or less "neutral" atmosphere, we can force him to act against his symptom and his anxiety. In this way the stutterer in time acquires an emotional stability that enables him psychologically to bridge the gap between our special environment and the regulation environment of the outside world.[3]

[2] *Op. cit.*, page 160.
[3] Speech and Voice Disorders, *The Medical World*, 57: 719–722, November 1939. Dr. Greene is Medical Director of the National Hospital of Speech Disorders.

In an unpublished statement, Dr. Greene says further:

The new patient is placed in what might be termed the "low-pressure" group. As he learns to adjust to the group milieu, he "graduates" to other groups. Therapy has been devised to submit the stutterer to a gradual increase of environmental pressure in proportion to his growing ability to withstand it. . . . During the last stage of treatment, the patient participates in round table discussions with other senior patients, no longer as a speech sufferer but as a normal person ready to face the realities of the outside world. The object is to accustom him to think and react as a normal individual.

Interpersonal therapy for adults is carried on by means of the interview or discussion directed or set by the therapist. This is the major difference between this type of therapy and the activity Group Therapy described in the preceding pages.

ACTIVITY-INTERVIEW GROUP THERAPY

To meet individual needs it is necessary to modify any given method of treatment. This is equally true of Group Therapy, and we have changed procedures accordingly. The major variations will be outlined in the following pages.

In a group of children nine to ten years of age, it was found advisable by one of our workers, Mrs. Betty Gabriel, to combine interview with Activity Group Therapy. Mrs. Gabriel carried on regular interviews with most of the seven clients in the group and used group play and discussion at the same time. Under her leadership the children discussed many of their traumatic problems such as birth, sex, masturbation, defecation, and attitudes toward parents, siblings, teachers, and other persons in their environment. The children were given freedom of action and speech and were able to discharge their aggressions, but the worker imposed definite limitations. When the members of the group became excessively aggressive to the point of hurting other children or damaging the room and furniture, the worker stopped them. This group was provided with arts and crafts materials, they ate together, and generally resembled as nearly as possible a substitute family. In discussing the experiment with this activity-interview group, Mrs. Gabriel concludes:

My part as leader was to stimulate the production of material by interpreting to the individuals in the group and jointly, their play activity whenever it seemed that the material they were bringing forth was meaningful to them. The outstanding gains to the children in group treatment is that feelings and inhibitions were released and the children realize they were not different from other children. They were able to reactivate the family set-up and to relive their sibling rivalries in the group situation, satisfying and constructive compensatory behavior resulting.

Simultaneously with the group meetings, contacts were had with the schools and with the parents to remove stresses and strains and to effect change in attitudes of parents and teachers wherever this seemed indicated.

It must not be overlooked that group treatment was supplemented by individual treatment, and treatment of the home and school was carried on at the same time. One child's problem might require only individual treatment . . . another child might require group treatment, but there were many who need the combination of these treatment methods by one worker and such differential treatment must be diagnostically determined.[4]

Describing the value of the activity-interview therapy to this group, Mrs. Gabriel gives the following summaries of two members which are taken from the same report:

Hilton

Hilton, aged 10, IQ 87, was referred to us by the school. He was reported to be disorderly, disobedient, and a stealing problem. He is the fifth child in a family of six children. Shortly after his birth his mother became insane and was committed. The child was placed in a shelter and later in a series of private boarding homes. However, his behavior was so uncontrollable that he

[4] Betty Gabriel, An Experiment in Group Treatment, *American Journal of Orthopsychiatry*, 9: 146–169, January 1939.

would rarely be kept for more than a week or two. He did adjust in one home but had to leave after a year because of the illness of the foster mother. Foster mothers would always complain about his excessive eating, his stealing, disorderly conduct, disobedience and destructiveness. On one occasion he attempted to set a house on fire.

The mother was returned to her home about five years ago. She became pregnant immediately and it was considered unwise to bring Hilton back into the home. Treatment revealed that for three years Hilton did not know he had parents, since they never visited him. When he was finally returned to his home in 1935 he became extremely destructive, hyperactive, fidgety, impertinent and disobedient, stealing from the home and from tradespeople. He was often discovered standing before a mirror making facial grimaces. Of the entire family group the only one exhibiting any positive feeling for Hilton is the older brother, but he is tubercular and unable to do very much.

The mother is a manic type, has a winning personality, and rules the family, the children being strongly attached to her. The family is devoted to the youngest boy who presents no problem and comparisons unfavorable to Hilton are constantly made. The father is a completely negative personality, very sickly.

PROBLEM

Disorderly child, disobedient, stealing problem, eats beyond all bounds, destructive, hyperactive, impertinent, facial grimaces, can't get along with children, sibling rivalry.

BACKGROUND

Mother has a dominant personality, rules the home as a matriarch.

Father, a weak, ineffectual person.

Mother is hyperactive, was at one time committed to Ward's Island. On her return two years later became pregnant immediately and it was therefore inadvisable to return Hilton to his home. He had been living in foster homes. For a period of three years he was never visited by his family and during this time was shifted from one home to another because he was difficult to cope with. On his return to his own home two years ago his behavior became extreme, as already described.

Extremely noisy and hyperactive. He used the playroom as though it were a playground. He struck at the children and me. Once kicked Mike severely in the jaw. Was frightened and asked, "What shall I do? Kill myself?"

Though Hilton's behavior was so asocial, he reached out for group play and generally introduced activity which included the others. He seemed the only one who wanted group play from the first. He was alert and generally ready with suggestions.

He never used bad language but frequently engaged the children in rough play. He insulted me when I did not give him all my attention.

Hilton freed himself of a feeling that his father broke up his home by beating, tearing, and biting the father doll. Through the play activity he disclosed feelings of rejection when he told that he had not been visited for three years by his parents or siblings.

PROGRESS

Frequent reminders by the children gradually had an effect on the boy. He definitely showed that he was eager to be liked, though he did little at first to gain this end.

As Hilton felt the friendly interest of the girls and boys and of myself, his behavior became considerably modified both in the group and at school.

Then there set in a period when he became ingratiating. From the first he carefully guarded our play material and enjoyed the responsibility and feeling of superiority which grew out of this.

As Hilton became more sure of himself he was able to play more quietly and with greater concentration, although he did at times lapse into his former behavior. Where at first Hilton was greedy when refreshments were served he later shared treats with the children and his entire behavior became more restrained.

An outstanding improvement is Hilton's restraint in eating. Where formerly he was wont to eat the meal prepared for the entire family, if he could get at it (and often did this), his food habits are now more normal.

Linda

Linda, aged 9, a bright, alert child, was referred to the agency in August of 1933, because of "nervous hysteria." She was frightened by any unusual sound. At an early age she began to suffer from vomiting spells and this became a problem when she entered school. She did not allow her mother out of her sight and refused to play with children.

Investigation disclosed that during the mother's pregnancy with Linda the father lost his job and they were forced to live with his mother. Conflict arose between the two women after the birth of the infant over its care, and the mother finally had to assume a dictatorial attitude toward her mother-in-law. The mother ascribed the child's nervousness to the worry and aggravation which she herself had endured during pregnancy. The mother blamed herself for the vomiting episodes, confessing that she neglected to consult the clinic for advice in working out a feeding formula because she was ashamed to admit that she had a baby who required so much medical attention.

The crisis in this child's development was due to a shock. Linda had been struck in the back by a truck, but she was not injured. Several other seemingly minor accidents then followed which served as traumatic experiences as evidenced by her apprehensive attitude, fears, insecurity and fantasies.

The parents are intelligent but emotionally unstable, middle-class, fairly young. Under favorable conditions their living standards would be good but, due to intermittent financial reverses and enlargement of the family by the birth of twin boys after our advent into the situation, the family of six moved into one room, renting out the remaining three rooms in the apartment in order to make ends meet. Both parents are interested in their children. The mother is inclined to gossip before them.

Linda's fantasy revealed an intense sibling rivalry, a running away from unpleasant situations, a feeling of rejection and insecurity.

PROBLEM

Nervous since birth, fears, anxieties, sibling rivalry, running away from unpleasant situations into illness. Feels unloved and insecure. Gets satisfaction from claiming mother's attention through her fears.

BACKGROUND

Mother apparently rejects this child who was born while family was under severe financial stress and they had to move in with father's mother. Struggle between grandmother and mother ensued over care of the child as mother felt she was spoiling her.

This mother seems unable to exert authority and recognizes that she is inclined to take the line of least resistance. She seems to prefer Emma because of no overt problems presented by her.

Linda seems to get positive satisfaction from father. Since the birth of twin brothers, feels rejected by father, too. Father leaves bringing up of children to mother.

EARLY BEHAVIOR IN GROUP

Petulant when doesn't get own way. Always wants to be first. Plays she is a baby and goes through all the motions. Fears the dark. Refuses to go to the washroom. Became hysterical when accidentally locked in a room with Jean. Quarrelsome with sister. Imitative. Jealous and feels that children talk about her.

PROGRESS

Suspicious at first. Soon established a friendly relationship. Group interaction stimulated in more grown-up response. No longer plays baby. (Mother helped here by playing Linda is a baby once again.)

In the group Linda learned to make the adjustment which helped her to accept a minor place, especially when the club was being organized.

She learned that I could like all the children equally well and therefore she did not need to stay at my side continually.

Her changed attitude carried over into the outside. She made and kept friends.

A free discussion of sex fantasy and the reality relieved her curiosity regarding birth, her fears, and helped her overcome most of her fears such as dark rooms and locked doors.

Gradually she became more aggressive in the group and at home. She has less need to claim attention on levels formerly utilized. Some recurrences might be interpreted as trying me out to see whether I can still love her and maintain an interest in her under any conditions she sets up.

GROUP INTERVIEW THERAPY

Another type of interpersonal therapy with which we experimented is the group discussion. This involved a group of six girls, fifteen to sixteen years old, of superior intelligence, with serious emotional disturbances. Two of them were parent beaters. One appeared to have conversion neuroses (although this was not established with any degree of certainty). One of the girls was comparatively well adjusted: she held a job as usher in a movie house continuously for a year or more. Another of the members was a typical "dead-end girl." Only one of the clients received consistent individual psychotherapy during the group treatment period; two of the others were seen occasionally by the case worker; the others were treated through the group exclusively.

These girls were not interested in arts and crafts or any other type of manual work. The wanted to "talk about anything at all; about ourselves," and insisted on meeting at the office of the case worker because they felt that it was cozier and homier there than in the special club room or the large conference room. Most of the conversation centered around their personal problems although some of it dealt with peripheral interests such as school, careers, clothes, boys. On a number of occasions the girls related their dreams to the group and the others discussed and interpreted them together. The following is taken from the record of such a discussion:

Betty said she liked to come here and she liked the group just as they now were. She wondered why the girls couldn't be happy to just do what they were doing—talk about all kinds of subjects. She added that she got a great deal out of talking about these things here. What does she get? "I'm getting very sophisticated." She added that she thought she was beginning to understand the psychology of boys, that is, she was understanding herself better in her relations with boys. Laughingly she told that formerly she had to be the domineering one: they always had to do just what she wanted. Now if a boy says "I like fish," she says "I like water." "In other words," said Sonya, "you play up to the boys." Betty said, "Of course I do. I remember well how I used to hate the boys. That's when I wanted to have the upper hand. Now I don't hate them any more. I have a good time when I'm with them.

Therefore I try to be nice and gracious to them. You see, girls, I'm talking straight from my heart."

She elaborated further, telling that when out with a certain boy he insisted that she should drink milk. She loathed milk and never drank it, but she suffered herself to drink the milk because her escort liked it. However, finally one day she got very tired of that escort, and she blurted out all the things she had done to please him and told him that none of the things he did pleased her; he was boring her and she was through with him.

Rita said that boys bore her. She was restless when with them. The only boys she ever had a good time with were the group she had been seeing this winter.

There was a general discussion then about kissing boys and all admitted that formerly they hated boys, but now when they were with them they did not mind except when they were kissed.

Rita went on then to say that she feared high places and boats. It was difficult for her to look out of the window of an upper floor. Betty said if there was one thing she feared it was a dead dog. Sonya, Ella, and Henrietta said that they feared nothing at all.

This stimulated Betty to tell of a dream which was still very vivid in her mind. She dreamed that she was walking with her friend Archie. They went to the park; they climbed many, many steps. . . . They thought it would be dark at the top and they wanted to spoon. (She told, incidentally, how she had the first petting of her lifetime with Archie. It only lasted ten minutes. She was surprised to find that she really enjoyed it.) When they got to the top of the hill they were climbing and were in the park, instead of finding a dark bench, they found many "lindy-hoppers" there. Betty did not want to stay. Archie then took her to a hotel. She did not want to go but they finally did go in and he registered them as "Mr. and Mrs." The clerk said, "You're not man and wife." He pulled out a match-cover and on it was Betty's baby picture. They went back then to the park, climbed all those stairs once again, and this time when they got to the top they found a nice, secluded bench. As they were about to seat themselves, they discovered Betty's mother seated on the bench.

The girls did not let Betty go on but told her that they could interpret her dream. Henrietta said that it indicated that Betty really was afraid to go through with the petting with Archie. Rita said that it indicated to her that Betty was insecure and therefore felt she needed to be saved. What surprised her was that Betty could sort of rely on her mother to save her. It seemed to the worker that what Rita was trying to say was that Betty had a good contact with her mother. Rita added that she herself would feel very self-conscious about telling any personal things to her mother. I (worker) wondered why. She said, "Because my mother gets a smirk on her face. I know what my mother is thinking. She is thinking, Mmmmmmm, so my girl is growing up."

Ella said her mother did not do these things but yet she would fear to tell her mother anything because her mother simply did not understand. "My mother forgets that she was a young girl once. My mother doesn't trust me. If I'm going out she wants to know all the places I'm going, and what I'm going to do, and asks a hundred questions." Betty said, "My mother trusts me. She never asks me where I'm going or anything. She always asks me what did I eat, did I have a good time." Worker turned to Sonya and asked her what she thought of Betty's dream. Sonya thought that Betty felt very secure with her mother and that she knew her mother would always be there for her to depend on.

At a later meeting we read the following:

Talking about the plays apparently stimulated Betty to think of marriage. She said that she could not think of herself as married "poor." Worker asked her what she meant. She always saw herself in furs and rich. She would not be self-conscious at all if her social status were to change suddenly and she were able to dress richly. She can picture herself having a beautiful home with beautiful furniture, and she would know how to furnish her home. She was already dreaming about all such things. She was hoping to get some kind of work and she would not give her mother any money toward the household expenses, but would save every dollar toward refurnishing the home so that they could move. She added that she would, of course, help her sister. Her sister said that she would never want to be conspicuous; she did not like having people stare at her.

In a later study of the adjustment of the girls it was shown that all six have made good adjustments: four of them made complete recoveries; the two others are making satisfactory social adaptations, though we doubt whether their nuclear problems were reached either by the group method or by individual psychotherapy.[5]

The therapist did not lead the discussions, suggest subjects, or attempt to direct conversations toward any conclusion. Only very occasionally she would ask a question of a speaker in the hope that the client would gain greater clarification through it. However, she did not pursue the topic. In this instance notes were kept of the conversations in the presence of the clients (which is not done in activity Group Therapy). The girls, all of whom were of superior intelligence, accepted this as a part of the situation and referred to previous discussions by consulting the notes. In evaluating this experience to the six girls, the following major points stand out:

1. There was evident improvement in the personalities in all the girls. The parent beaters stopped this practice completely and one of them, who occasionally beat her younger brother, stopped that also. Another in the group planned a career for herself requiring an extension of her education, which she was preparing to pursue. Another who was known as the "dead-end girl" corrected her behavior considerably.

2. All the girls became aware of their own mechanisms and impulses and brought themselves under control. The girl who used to beat her brother once said in exasperation, "If I had not learned self-control, I'd beat you up now." Another formulated her feelings about her family after discussion by saying, "I guess my ideas about parents and families are cock-eyed."

3. There developed a very close friendship among the girls.

[5] The group here and the activity-interview group described earlier were not entirely satisfactory. It was felt throughout that one of the girls in the interview group was greatly threatened by it because of her unresolved anxieties in relation to her mother. When relations to mothers were discussed she would become frightened and withdrawn. Concerning the younger group of boys and girls in the activity-interview group, Mrs. Gabriel states: " . . . it is doubtful whether Mike and Hilton should have been included. However, the other children may have been helped to attain some degree of tolerance by their presence. Individual values need further observation." *Op. cit.*, page 169.

They helped one another with make-up and dresses, saw each other outside of the meetings, and invited each other to their birthday and other parties.

4. They related themselves to an older woman as a substitute mother. This was important to all of these girls but one, whose relation to her mother was a satisfactory one. (This was Betty, who had the dream which we have already narrated.)

5. Most of the members of the group used it to clarify their vocational interests and made plans with the help of the others.

6. Their tolerance of defects in each other greatly increased.

Follow-up interviews with parents and schools confirmed the impressions in the group of the clients' general improvement.

TRANSITIONAL GROUPS

As the boys and girls of our therapy groups reach a level in their development when they can make an adjustment to a larger social setting, they may be transferred, as a group, to a neighborhood center with the group therapist as their leader. By gradual stages they are introduced to the activities in the center. By arrangement with the center, the groups are invited to visit there. This is done so as to provoke suggestions from the members themselves that they join. It is also hoped that the individual members will be attracted by the occupations and the clubs. When the transfer is made, usually at the suggestion of the boys and girls themselves, they are not provided with arts and crafts materials, food, trips, or any other advantages which they had enjoyed before. Among other things this denial serves as a test of their growing independence and maturity. Some of the children demur. The majority, however, accept it without complaint. Some of the groups set up officers and their own treasuries to defray expenses.

However, as we have already indicated, there are usually one or two of the children in a group who are not able to make an adjustment to a larger environment. The bevy of activities and numbers of people seem to constitute a threat and they either beg to return to the protected environment of the "old club" or drop out of the new group. These clients are continued in Group Therapy during the following year (but not during the same season).

The groups that are thus transferred are known as *transitional groups* during the period when they are directed by the group therapist. Members are placed in the larger environment about three months before the closing of the club season and are observed for that period. In the fall of the following year all but those who cannot make an adjustment are referred to the center as regular members of that institution.[6]

From the standpoint of social prophylaxis and prevention of personal maladjustments, groups of low pressure, such as transitional groups, should be of great value. There are numerous children and young people who, though not personally disturbed, are unable to belong to an ordinary club. They withdraw from hyperactivity and boisterousness and cannot take part in them, or are overboisterous themselves and are not accepted. Many of these children and young people do not need the degree of permissiveness of a therapy group, but at the same time they cannot function in the average club.

Staffs of neighborhood centers and "Y's" are very much aware of these maladjusted individuals. Many of them escape into hobbies or manual activities, but do not develop through these occupations the ability to communicate, make contact with people, and acquire friends. Their feeling of isolation is intensified, and as they grow older they become more and more lonely. Because they cannot find the friendships they crave, a large number of them drop out.

[6] Because of lack of space no records of this type of group are given here. Records have been kept of the discussions, activities, and relations in these groups, as well as of individual reactions and adjustments to the larger social environment of the center.

There are other children and young people who do not follow this pattern. They are rather mildly aggressive but, because of the high degree of extraversion in the average club, become overaggressive themselves. A group with a constructive atmosphere offers the restraint they need. (These are the mildly suggestible children and those with prolonged infancy whom we have already described.)

There is therefore a need for more transitional groups so that a larger number of children and adolescents may be helped to adapt to social living and all it implies. Organized clubs, with definite aims and objectives, proscriptions, rules, laws, and group pressures, present a higher form of group living than many can accept. They need, rather, a period of attenuated social atmosphere that would serve as substitutes or correctives. These groups may generally resemble activity therapy groups; there would be freedom of communication, libido-binding occupations in accordance with individual needs, fluidity, and variety. They would differ from therapy groups by the fact that the membership personnel need not be so carefully balanced; there can be a considerable degree of group planning; limitations can be set without injurious effects; and the leader can act as authority.

Therapeutic Play Groups

Another application of group therapy is the *play group.* Play therapy is an accepted technique in psychiatry and psychotherapy for young children. We are at present exploring the possibilities for organizing play groups for children under six years of age. The plan is to group children in accordance with their interpersonal therapy possibilities, provide them with a variety of appropriate play materials and group situations, such as eating together and sharing toys and apparatus, and place them under the supervision of a trained psychotherapist or nursery supervisor toward whom the children can develop constructive attitudes. Because of the age of the clients, the psychotherapist in charge of the group (which should be limited to four or five children) needs to use more restraint and authority than in any of the groups so far described.[7]

MOTHERS' GROUPS

Another project under discussion, and which should receive greater attention from psychiatric and child guidance clinics is the *mothers' group*. Clinics for mental patients that treat children are aware of the role of parents in creating the emotional problems in the latter. Because of the present-day home setting, the mother is the greatest single factor in the etiology of emotional maladjustments in the young. Some mothers are frustrated, often power-driven and destructive persons who reject their children. In others these frustrations express themselves in overindulgence of their children and overfixation upon them. With the latter the sole and only focus of interest in life is the child. If it were possible to give both types of mothers some satisfactions outside the home, their emotional pressure would be relieved and, as a result, the child would become more accessible to treatment.

At the present time, manipulation of the home environment consists of vocational guidance, financial relief, changes in the physical set-up, school and educational adjustment, and individual interviews with parents and siblings. However, most of the clients in social work agencies and public clinics come from underprivileged homes in which the social and the intellectual status are comparatively low. Interviews with such parents are frequently unproductive and unrealistic. Outside interests are of considerable value in releasing their emotions and normalizing their behavior.

In addition to this release, there are no doubt other thera-

[7] See Chapter VI, pages 160 ff., for discussion of the relation of age and authority.

peutic values in group treatment for adults. In one such group for adult women, the members brought along their knitting, crocheting, and sewing, and worked together. The agency provided the coffee and the ingredients for cakes and pastries. Members who were expert at any of the activities demonstrated to the others. Upon the request of some of the members, trips were arranged to various points of the city. This became a major and valuable self-motivated interest for the group.

At later meetings members helped each other with their knitting and other manual work, and learned to share things with one another. There were a number of quarrels and in one case a fist fight, which was resolved by the group itself. One of the members, a patient in a local clinic, was afraid to travel and whenever she left the house, walked holding on to walls. After a few months she traveled to and from the meetings by herself and even talked to some of the members of the group. Some of the patients brought their children to the meetings (but never their husbands). As the group progressed there was definite and observable improvement in the individuals composing it.

The program in this group consisted almost entirely of manual activities. It would be possible, however, to include discussions like those carried on by the group of adolescents described in this chapter, and thus to extend the possibilities of group therapy to adults as well as to children. Such an extension requires criteria for intake and grouping that are not so sharply defined at present as are those for children. Grouping, especially, presents more difficulties here than with the latter. Factors such as race, nationality, economic status, social background and amenities, and language are important considerations with adults, but do not affect the attitudes of children or do so very little. Social disparity, an unattractive personal appearance, and uncleanliness, for example, which are not as important for children or even adolescents, are great deterrents to the familiarity and friendliness necessary for free interchange of ideas and feelings among adults.

Another element that must be considered in group interview treatment of this kind is intellectual and language parity. Persons inferior to others in the group in either respect would only be further traumatized. Under such circumstances their feelings of inadequacy would be further emphasized with consequent withdrawal or compensatory aggressiveness. All members must be able to grasp meanings and communicate their thoughts with approximately equal facility; otherwise the situation may become pathogenic rather than therapeutic.

Another factor in grouping of even greater significance than the two already mentioned—social and intellectual parity—is the essential nature of the problems the adults face and their psychological syndromes. If a topic under discussion is the major and repressed unconscious fear or concern of a member, he may not be able to face a discussion of it. This we saw in our girls' group. One of the girls became panicky whenever mothers were the subject of conversation. Another was puzzled by sex discussions; she was not sufficiently aware of sex and not ready to grasp a discussion of it, and as a result withdrew from these conversations.

Matching the psychological syndromes of adult patients is both very important and very difficult, and requires considerable thought and experimentation. Equally important are the skill and alertness of the therapist to grasp the significance of any situation to every member of the group. However, a safety valve is provided here by individual interviews. When a group member is distressed as a result of a discussion, the psychotherapist in charge can provide release, clarification, or treatment in an individual interview which must follow immediately after the group meeting. This procedure was employed in the adolescent girls' group and to some extent (though for different reasons) in the activity-interview group of the nine and ten-year-old boys and girls.

An experiment with a group of mothers along the lines indicated here, conducted by Mrs. Fanny Amster, a psychiatric
case worker at the Jewish Board of Guardians, revealed some
significant sidelights. Though the experiment itself is in its
very beginning, some developments noted by her indicate
considerable possibilities. She says in part:

The group discussions, initiated by the mothers or myself,
cover many areas and all the mothers participate very freely.
They each present the problems of their sons as they see them,
their methods of handling these problems, and their feelings as
individuals. They openly criticize, elaborate, and suggest to each
other. They challenge freely, express their own convictions, and
ask for advice. The situation includes all that occurs in individual treatment plus the social components which a group offers.
The emphasis is on their everyday problems, their everyday
handling of these problems, and their feelings in these areas. Only
twice has it been necessary for me to ask for historical material.
After the first meeting, I discontinued taking notes during the
meeting as I felt I could not participate as fully as was necessary
and take minutes at the same time.

My own activity consists of using their specific material to
secure their elaboration, release feeling, point out similarity of
problems, and help the members to acquire lay understanding of
such concepts as aggression, compliance, love hunger, parental
expectations, what a child experiences in growing up, and so
forth. I also use their specific material to point out the confusion
in their feelings in their relationship to their sons. I find I can be
very direct in my questions, comments, suggestions, and discussions. The mothers seem able to accept the directness and have
verbalized their pleasure in the group. "We come, we ask questions, we get answers," one of them said.

As anticipated, they react strongly to group approval and disapproval and show resultant changes in their everyday handling
of their sons. Their relationships to each other and to me have
components similar to those in the interpersonal relationship in
individual treatment: sibling rivalry, hostility, efforts to please,
and similar mechanisms. They recognize each other's attitudes as
parents, and call forth defensiveness and aggressiveness readily.

On several occasions, I have found it necessary figuratively to "rescue" a mother from the attack of another. Frequently, I have to relieve the tension. I have candy and cookies available and I have found that eating is correlated with their tension, rivalry, and relaxation.

In the meetings to date, I have been impressed with their freedom in speaking, their lack of resistance to each other and to me, the amount of new historical and dynamic material which emerges, the removal of their feeling of isolation, their assimilation of concepts, and the way they take over group standards and pressures. Several mothers have already shown changes as individuals and as mothers. Our objective check on this is the information we get from the sons of these mothers and from their individual case workers.

APPENDIX I

OUTLINE FOR A REFERRAL SUMMARY

Date: Case worker:
Name of client: Office:
Address: Father's name and age:
Birth date: Mother's name and age:
I.Q.:   Siblings and ages:
Grade in school:

1. FAMILY BACKGROUND AND ECONOMIC SITUATION

   Describe the main points of the family maladjustment. What is the economic status of the family? Will the client be able to supply carfare, or shall the agency provide this?

2. PHYSICAL DESCRIPTION OF THE CLIENT

   Give as full a description of the client's physical appearance as possible. Is he oversized or underdeveloped for his age? Does he appear undernourished? Does he dress neatly or shabbily? Has he any visible physical defects? Any speech defects?

3. CLIENT'S PERSONALITY

   Describe as fully as practicable the problem for which the client is being referred. A description of his personality should give us an insight into his emotional difficulties and help us assign the client to an appropriate therapy group. We should like to know, for example, whether the child is aggressive or withdrawing; whether he is infantile or over-sophisticated; hostile or submissive; and how these characteristics exhibit themselves in his behavior.

4. SCHOOL ADJUSTMENT

5. ADJUSTMENT TO OTHER CHILDREN

   What recreational resources are being used by the client at present? Is he a member of a gang or other unorganized play groups in the neighborhood? Does he belong to a neighborhood center? What are his hobbies and leisure-time interests? How does he get along with other children?

6. ADJUSTMENT AT CAMP

Has the client attended camp? If possible, attach a copy of the camp report or give short description of this adjustment.

7. DIAGNOSTIC STATEMENT ON THE CLIENT

8. REASON FOR REFERRAL TO THE THERAPY GROUP

Please note that the foregoing outline is to be used by the referring worker as an aid in summarizing the history of the client, with a view to pointing up the particular problems and difficulties which may be treated in the group. It is not essential to follow the outline exactly as it stands, if the necessary information is given in the body of the summary.

Submit four copies of the Referral Summary. Instructions should be given the typist to allow 1½ inch margin on the left side for binding.

APPENDIX II

OUTLINE FOR A PROGRESS REPORT

1. CLIENT'S ATTENDANCE IN THE GROUP

   When he first came to the meetings; whether he came regularly or spasmodically since the last progress report. Does he come late or on time? Is he consistent in his habits of attendance? How many meetings has he missed since the last progress report, as compared with the total number of meetings attended?

2. PHYSICAL DESCRIPTION

   Does the child appear tall for his age, overweight, underweight? What is his general facial expression? Does he have any malformations which might cause him to withdraw from the other children? Give any other pertinent information.

3. PERSONAL APPEARANCE

   Does the client dress well, neatly? Is he clean about his person? Is he well mannered? Have there been changes in his personal appearance since he became a member of the group or since the last Progress Report?

4. USE OF LANGUAGE

   Record any language peculiarities such as stuttering, stammering, lisping, drawl, halt in speech, baby talk; whether he is sparse or effusive, calm or excitable while speaking. Record vulgarisms, curses, and stereotypes. Give actual quotations.

5. ATTITUDES

   a. *Cooperation.* Does he help others in working with materials? Does he help in cleaning up the room? Does he offer to assist in washing dishes, setting the table, preparing the refreshments? Does he abide by group decisions? Has there been any improvement in these respects? Give examples.

   b. *Economy in materials.* Is he economical in his use of materials? Does he request expensive tools and games? Does he exercise care in working with tools? Any improvement here?

    c. *New members.* What is his reaction toward new members in the group? Does he offer to show them what the group does during meetings and help them acclimate themselves to the new environment? Does he resent the new arrival?

    d. *Group therapist.* Is he dependent to a great extent upon the group therapist? Does he seek his attention unduly? Does he resent sharing him with the other boys? Has he become more or less self-reliant and reliable?

    e. *Fellow members.* Has he established friendships within the group? Do these continue outside the group? Is he accepted by the group? Does he try to "buy his way" into the group? Has there been any progress here?

    f. *Food.* Describe in detail manner of eating; preferences in food; peculiarities; behavior in club room and restaurants at mealtimes; gluttony, anxiety, or indifference.

6. MONEY

Does the client try to get money from therapist on false pretenses? Does he exploit, wheedle, take advantage of therapist? Does he try to steal rides? Does he talk about or refer to money frequently? Is he avaricious, parsimonious, economical, or too conscious of money? Give examples.

7. ADJUSTMENT AT SCHOOL

Does the client talk at all about school? Does he tie up his work at school with the work in the group? Has any change been noted in his attitudes toward school since he has been in the group?

8. ACTIVITIES

Does the client work steadily, sporadically, occasionally, or not at all? Is he calm, excited, or tense? Does he finish jobs or is he a floater? Does he prefer special materials? Does he work with others or entirely by himself? Describe the general nature of the client's work such as shape, color, etc. Does he plan work or is he impulsive? Give details.

9. INTEGRATION OF THE CLIENT'S PERSONALITY

Has the child grown? Has he become more mature during the period covered by the Progress Report? Is he part of the group or does he withdraw and have little to do with the other members?

10. GROUP THERAPIST'S COMMENTS AND INTERPRETATIONS

APPENDIX III

OUTLINE FOR INTEGRATION CONFERENCES

(Cooperative Cases)

FIRST INTEGRATION CONFERENCE

The intent of this conference is for the group therapist to gain insight into the general problem of the client and for the case worker to learn of the child's behavior in the group. It includes psychiatric material and clinical diagnosis. The home relationships and adjustment in school and out of school are further elaborated.

First step. The factors in the client's life that gave rise to his problems are explored in detail. This information helps the group therapist understand the dynamics of the client's behavior and treat it more intelligently. From this material we can also determine which members of the group are either helpful or detrimental to the given client.

The second step in the discussion should be a brief summary of the client's relation to the case worker and the plan of the case work treatment. The group therapist describes the child's behavior in the group and other observations that are important concerning his personality and reactions. His relation to specific children and the total group are outlined. The group therapist also describes his plan of treatment.

The third step is a brief discussion of this material.

Fourth step. A joint plan for treatment is evolved.

SUBSEQUENT INTEGRATION CONFERENCES

First step. The case worker outlines any changes in the home or school situation since the preceding Integration Conference that may affect the child's behavior positively or negatively.

Second and third steps are the same as in the outline of the first Integration Conference.

Fourth step. An evaluation is made by the case worker and group therapist of the progress of the boy in and outside of the group, his case work relationship, and his total adjustment.

Fifth step. An evaluation is made of the values of the group in the treatment process.

Sixth step. Recommendations for future plans for treatment or for discharge of the client from the group are made.

OUTLINE FOR FOLLOW-UP STUDY

(Exclusive Group Therapy)

Date of visit: Name of client:
Follow-up case worker: Group:

1. We should like to get a general picture of the adjustment of the client at home, with special reference to the original problem for which the client was referred.
2. His activities in his own community: whether he has friends, plays with children of his own age in a normal way, belongs to organized groups or other groups in his neighborhood, whether he attends a neighborhood center or is a member of groups of other agencies such as Boy Scouts, etc.
3. Adjustment at school, with special reference to the problem as stated in the original referral to the agency.
4. If possible, an interview with the client should be arranged, so that the follow-up case worker can form some judgment as to the client's personality as a whole.
5. An evaluation and recommendation as to the further need of treatment for this client are desirable.

GROUP THERAPY TERMS AND PHRASES

THE following terms and phrases are listed for the convenience of the reader. Some, though in common usage, have a special meaning as they relate to Group Therapy; others have been formulated especially for our purpose. Only the page on which definition or explanation first appears is given. For further references, see the General Index.

GENERAL INDEX